The Month of Mary According to the Spirit of St. Francis of Sales

D1521802

THE MONTH OF MARY.

JESUIT

THE

MONTH OF MARY,

ACCORDING TO THE SPIRIT OF

ST. FRANCIS OF SALES;

OR,

Thirty-one Considerations,

WITH

EXAMPLES, PRAYERS, Etc.

BY

DON GASPAR GILLI.

Translated and Abridged from the Italian by a
SISTER OF THE INSTITUTE OF CHARITY.

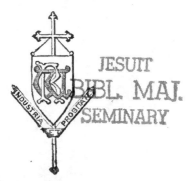

ROBERT WASHBOURNE,
18 PATERNOSTER ROW, LONDON.
1890.

𝔑𝔦𝔥𝔦𝔩 𝔒𝔟𝔰𝔱𝔞𝔱.

Fʀ. T. A. SMITH, O.P.
Censor deputatus.

𝔈𝔪𝔭𝔯𝔦𝔪𝔞𝔱𝔲𝔯.
✠ HENRICUS EDUARDUS,
Card. Archiep. Westmonast.
Die 14 Martii, 1890.

CONTENTS.

Contents.

PREFACE.

Of the many who by their writings have laboured to celebrate the sublime prerogatives and virtues of the Mother of God, there is not one whose language is more adapted to the devotions of the month of Mary than St. Francis of Sales. Everything, says a pious author, in this admirable Saint enchants and fascinates us; whoever reads his writings attentively, feels constrained, not only to honour and venerate him, but also to love him. With him there is a peculiar grace to console, as well as to perfect, the soul. He adapts himself to the capacities of humble minds, whilst no one has more knowledge than he of the most exalted perfection.

The sweet mildness of this Saint sprang from the meekness of which his soul was full. It is a difficult task to preserve peace in the soul, and well he knew it, declaring that he 'lived in a continual fear of losing, in one quarter of an hour, all that meekness which he had acquired by twenty years of combat.' St. Bonaventure learnt all his science at the foot of the Crucifix, and it was there, also, that

St. Francis acquired all his benignity, fighting for
it, we may say, hand-to-hand against his natural
impetuosity.   This virtue by degrees penetrated
the inmost parts of his soul, so that it was not only
manifested in all the actions of his life, but it
directed also his pen, and enabled him to make
use of the most delicate comparisons and ingenious images.   All that is sweet, and pure, and
amiable in Nature--doves, bees, flowers, all took
hold of his imagination.   From his lips, as well as
from his pen, issued loving invitations to perfection.
His singular privilege, however, is that this meekness and grace appear always fresh to the devout
reader, and are ever pleasing, even when he lays
open the festering wounds of the heart.   The great
Fénélon, whose spirit and heart so vividly retraced
the holy Bishop of Geneva, thus wrote to a lady:
'The books most useful for you are those of St.
Francis of Sales.   Everything in them is amiable
and consoling ; everything is solid experience,
simple practice, and the feeling and light of grace.
*To have become accustomed to this kind of food
is a mark of great perfection.'*   Bishop Parisis also
says : 'Everything that can contribute to make
this most amiable of Saints more known to the
world, is of the greatest utility to the cause of
religion.'

For this reason we have composed this little
work.   It is a sort of résumé of the doctrine of St.
Francis of Sales upon the prerogatives and virtues

of the august Queen of Heaven, and we may gather
a delicious bouquet for her month of May. Hence
the devout reader will always meet with the genuine
text of the Saint without any paraphrase, though
not always in consecutive order. In each of the
thirty-one considerations we have been obliged to
discard those matters which did not relate to our
subject. However, such suppressions only produce
greater clearness in the whole work. We must
say two words upon the manner in which this
exercise can be rendered fruitful:

1. If you are not able to assist at the public
services or devotions in honour of the Blessed
Virgin in your own church, erect a little altar to
Mary in your house, and adorn her picture, or
statue, with flowers, and there, every day, either
alone or with others of your household, meditate
upon her virtues, and implore her powerful intercession.

2. It will be an excellent preparation to spend
the last day of April in holy recollection, and to
examine what is the principal passion that you will
sacrifice to Mary during the course of the month,
and the grace or virtue that you propose to obtain
from God by recurring to her intercession. Do not
fear to ask too much, she is the Mother of God,
and our Mother also.

3. Read every day the appointed meditation,
with tranquillity and recollection, that your soul
may relish the subject, and apply what is read to

its own necessities. After your lecture, follow this advice of St. Francis of Sales : 'When you have concluded your prayer, take a little walk and gather a small nosegay of devotion from the considerations you have made, that you may inhale its spiritual odour throughout the day.'

4. You should consider it a duty to approach the holy Sacraments more frequently than usual during the month, and never leave the Altar of Mary without having made a spiritual communion.

5. Let no day pass, or, at least, no Saturday, without practising some mortification, sanctified and directed by obedience. 'Our devotion, however small,' said St. John Berchmans, 'is always pleasing to Mary, provided it be constant.' But let us not forget that interior mortifications are the most perfect ; such as to abstain from speaking or looking about without necessity, etc., because in such mortifications there is less danger of vainglory, and they attack our passions in the innermost depths of the heart.

6. Endeavour also to become familiar with ejaculatory prayers to Mary. 'This kind of prayer,' says St. Francis of Sales, 'may supply for every other kind, but no other kind of prayer can supply for this. Spiritual exercises without aspirations are like a firmament without stars, or a tree without leaves.'

7. The month should be concluded by an offering of the heart to Jesus and Mary, after Holy

Communion. And that you may more securely persevere in the service of the best of all Mothers, let it be your care to renew your resolutions every Saturday, to examine in what manner you have kept them, and by a protestation of sorrow for past omissions, and a determination of greater fidelity for the future, to repair the failings of the week.

The sovereign Pontiff Pius VII. has granted to all who shall say some public or private prayers in honour of the most holy Virgin Mary during the course of the month of May, three hundred days' Indulgence each day, and a Plenary Indulgence once in the month if, having confessed and Communicated, they pray for the holy Church.

The same sovereign Pontiff has granted to all the faithful who, with a contrite heart, shall recite the Litany of Loreto, three hundred days' Indulgence each time. All these Indulgences are applicable to the souls in Purgatory.

PROTESTATION.

In conformity with the decree of the sovereign Pontiff Urban VIII., I declare that I wish to give only a purely human authority to all the miraculous facts related in this work, excepting those that are confirmed by the decisions of the Holy, Catholic, Apostolic, and Roman Church, to whose infallible judgment I intend to submit my person and my writings; nor shall I cease to declare myself her respectful son, believing all that she proposes to my belief, because she is the sole depositary here on earth of sound doctrine, of faith, and of catholic unity.

PRELIMINARY INSTRUCTION.

Doctrine of St. Francis of Sales upon Devotion to Mary.

HOLY Church, speaking of the most Blessed Virgin, says that she went up from the desert of this world *flowing with delights, leaning upon her Beloved.* In fact, all the praises bestowed upon the Saints, and upon Mary in particular, terminate in Christ our Lord ; because all these praises should be directed to the glory of her Divine Son, Who led her by His grace to the most exalted degree of merit and happiness.

It is related in Scripture that the Queen of Saba, taking a multitude of gifts to Jerusalem, offered them *all* to Solomon. It is thus that all the Saints act—and the Mother of God especially. She is ever attentive to recognise that her virtues, her perfections, her merits, and her happiness proceed from the mercy of her Divine Son, Who is alone their source, their origin, and perfection : *Soli Deo honor et gloria.* All honour and glory to God alone ; all should return to Him, because *from Him alone is every perfect gift.*

If Mary be holy, who is it that sanctified her but her Divine Son? If she be saved, who was her Saviour but Jesus Christ?—*Innixa super dilectum suum.* Her whole happiness has its foundation in the mercy of her Divine Son. She may be called a lily of purity and innocence. This lily has acquired all its purity by being washed in the Blood of the Immaculate Lamb. She is a rose, on account of the ardour of her love, and her rich vermilion can be nought else than the Blood of her Son. If she is likened to fumes of odoriferous sweetness, the fire which produces them is the charity of her Divine Son and the wood of the Cross; in a word, everywhere and in everything, Mary is leaning upon her Beloved. Behold, devout souls, how we ought to be jealous of the honour of Jesus Christ. Do not imitate the enemies of holy Church, who think that they honour the Son more perfectly by refusing all honour to the Mother. On the contrary, the worship of the Mother is referred to the Son, and thus exalts His glory and mercy all the more.

In order to show more clearly the purity of the worship which holy Church pays to the most Blessed Virgin, I will mention two contrary heresies, both equally injurious to the veneration deservedly due to Our Lady. One of these heresies sinned by excess; calling Mary *the Goddess of Heaven,* and offering sacrifices to her as such; the other sinned by default, condemning all honour paid to

Our Lady. The Church, who walks in the royal road of moderation, in which virtue consists, condemned both these heresies, defining against the former that no sacrifice whatever could be offered to Mary, as she was a pure creature; and against the latter, that this holy Virgin, being Mother of God the Son, was worthy of special worship, infinitely less than that of her Son, but incomparably greater than that of all the other Saints. To the first, she says, that the Virgin is simply a creature, yet so holy, so perfect, so closely united to her Son, and so much loved by God, as to render it impossible to love the Son sincerely without loving and honouring the Mother. To the second, she says, sacrifice is the supreme worship of latria, due to the Creator alone, and the Blessed Virgin is simply a creature, although most excellent. Indeed, in speaking of Mary, I call her more the creature of God and of her Son than the rest of creation; because God created greater perfections in her than in all other creatures, and she had a greater share in the Redemption than all others, being rescued not only from sin but from the power and inclination to sin. And who does not know that it is a greater benefit to rescue a person from slavery before he is made a slave, than to deliver him after he has become captive! How far are we then from placing the Son and the Mother on an equality, as our adversaries falsely assert?

It is true that we call her beautiful, and the

most beautiful amongst creatures ; but she is beau-
ful *as the moon,* which receives its light from the
sun ; because all her glory is communicated to her
by her Son.   Pliny writes that the thorn, named
aspalathum, is not naturally odoriferous, but that
if the rainbow rests upon it, it quickly exhales a
rare and sweet odour.   The holy Virgin is a thorn
of that burning bush which Moses saw and which
was not consumed, as the Church says : ' *Rubum
quem viderat Moyses incombustum, conservatam
agnovimus tuam laudabilem virginitatem.'*   Of
herself alone, she is certainly unworthy of our
worship, for she is without odour.   But when the
great sign of reconciliation between God and men
came and rested upon this holy thorn—first, by
His grace in her Immaculate Conception, and afterwards at the Incarnation, when God became her
Son, and reposed in her immaculate bosom—
then, indeed, so great became the fragrance of this
thorn that no other plant ever could produce
before God so sweet and pleasing an odour.   Nor
will He ever reject the prayers that are perfumed
in this fragrance.   We repeat that all this perfume
came to her from her Divine Son.

Jesus Christ is our Advocate, and so is Mary;
but with what difference !   In right of justice, the
Saviour is alone our Advocate, because when He
pleads our cause He justifies His petition by showing His Blood and His Cross.   He does not hide
our debts from His Father; but at the same time

He urges the value of the price that He has laid down for our salvation. Mary and all the Saints exercise, also, the office of advocate in our favour; it is only by way of intercession. They entreat the Divine Justice to pardon our iniquities; but it is through the merits of the Passion of Jesus Christ In a word, they do not add their prayers to the prayers of the Saviour, but to ours; in order to help us to obtain the graces which are necessary for our eternal salvation.

THE MONTH OF MARY.

THE IMMACULATE CONCEPTION.

THE wonderful variety which is observable in the works of nature gives us a very high idea of the immeasurable riches of the Almighty Creator. And yet He manifests His power still more in the super-natural order, and the wonderful diversity of the works of grace preaches more loudly the munificence of His mercy. God, in the excess of His goodness, did not merely grant a general redemption to men, sufficient for the salvation of each one, but He diversified and multiplied the super-natural gifts which accompany this redemption with infinite liberality and wonderful variety. But His highest favours were lavished upon the most holy Virgin. From all eternity the Heavenly Father had ordained in His love to form her heart to the perfection of charity, that she might love His Divine Son with the most perfect maternal love—as He had loved Him from all eternity with the most perfect paternal love. The Son of God cast His eyes upon this Virgin, and chose her for His Mother, and co-operator in the great work of the world's redemption, a merciful Mother, a most powerful advocate of mankind—the most amiable, the most loving, and the most beloved of all creatures.

It is the opinion of many theologians that our Lord sanctified St. John the Baptist in the womb of St. Elizabeth, by a ray of His light and grace, and gave him the use of reason together with the gift of faith, so that he knew his God, hidden in the immaculate womb of Mary, adored Him, and consecrated himself to His service. If such a grace were granted by Our Lord to His precursor, who can doubt for a moment that He should have granted not only a similar, but a much greater privilege to her whom He Himself had chosen for His Mother, and that He should not only have sanctified her in the womb of her mother, St. Anne, but should have, moreover, raised her from the very first instant of her conception to a state of purity and sanctity?

The adorable Redeemer of the human race, the eternal object of the love of His Heavenly Father, considered His Mother from that first moment, as a delicious garden which was to produce the fruit of eternal life, and He cultivated this garden in order that every kind of perfection should flourish therein. He adorned her with the gold of charity and with a wondrous variety of virtues, that she might be able to sit at His side as a Queen—that is to say, occupy the first place amongst the elect, and, in this manner, enjoy the delights that are found at the right hand of the Eternal God.

This Divine Mother was redeemed, therefore, in a manner becoming the dignity of the Son, for Whom she was created.   Hence she was preserved from reprobation and from all danger of it, because she was enriched with the perfection of grace and with everything necessary for its preservation. Well is she compared to a beautiful aurora, or dawn, which, from its very beginning, went on increasing until it reached its perfect day.   O first-fruit of the Redemption ! O masterpiece of the Redeemer ! It is just, indeed, O my Divine Saviour, that as a Son full of love and devotion towards Thy Mother, in preventing her with the blessings of Heaven, Thou shouldest have preserved her, not only from sin like the Angels, but even from every danger of sinning, and shouldest, moreover, have removed from her path all that could hinder or even retard her in the exercise of Thy holy love.   It was written in Thy eternal decrees that Thou wouldest at one day prefer her to all rational creatures who were dear to Thy Divine Heart, and that Thou wouldest call her *the beloved object of Thy predilection, Thy dove, Thy spotless and beautiful one, perfect beyond compare.*

A special privilege was reserved for Mary,

worthy of a Son Who loved her with an infinite love, and Who, being infinitely good, wise and perfect, was to choose for Himself a Mother, and form her according to His own heart. He willed then that the grace of Redemption should be applied to her as a preservative remedy. Like the waters of the Jordan that, in the days of Josue, interrupted their course through respect for the Ark of the Covenant, so the stream of original corruption stayed its course at the feet of Mary, at the conception of this living tabernacle of the Eternal Covenant.

From the first instant of her conception, Mary knew her God, and loved Him sovereignly; from that moment she became impeccable, through the special assistance of the divine protection, and through the continual inflow of efficacious and preventing graces, to which she never offered the slightest resistance. God not only adorned her with the most abundant habitual grace, but He preserved it in her, keeping her always fiee from every evil inclination, every idle thought, and every feeling in the slightest degree contrary to the most perfect sanctity.

As to her body, we may believe it was endowed with singular perfections. St. Joachim and St. Anne received her from God through a particular, and we may say, even a miraculous grace, so that she was one of the most excellent works of the Holy Ghost, and breathed only sanctity and purity.

This Queen loved, then, her virginal body, not only because it was docile, humble, pure and obedient to Divine Love, but still more because from it was formed the Body of her Saviour.

Truly has this holy Virgin been called *elect as the sun*, because as the sun shines resplendent above all the stars, through the excellence of its prerogatives, so there is no one amongst all the Saints who has obtained, or can ever obtain, graces superior to those bestowed upon Mary. There are Saints who have received signal graces from our Lord, and these, compared with the rest of the world, are like queens crowned with charity, and occupy a distinguished position in the love of our Divine Saviour. But His most blessed Mother is the Queen of all Queens, for she is not only crowned with charity, but with the perfection of charity, and to use an expression of the Holy Spirit, Who says that *the Son is the crown of the Father*, her crown is in truth her Son ; that is to say, the sovereign object of charity, the Eternal Love, forms her crown.

Spiritual Flowers.

How lovely is the rose ! and yet it causes great sadness in my soul. It reminds me of my sin, on account of which the earth was condemned to produce thorns.—*St. Basil.*

Mary, conceived without sin, is compared to the incorruptible cedar, the scent of which puts serpents to flight.—*St. Alphonsus Liguori.*

How great will be our happiness in heaven, where we shall be able to contemplate Mary, to love her and be loved by her ; for she alone forms a paradise of delights.   Mary is truly, after God, all that is beautiful, sweet, glorious and amiable in that celestial realm ; all is in Mary, all through Mary, all, in fine, is hers. —*St. Bonaventure.*

Nothing is of greater service to our soul, nor more sustains and strengthens it, than the frequent thought of Mary.—*St. Teresa.*

EXAMPLE.

Devotion of St. Francis of Sales to the Blessed Virgin Mary.

Of all the festivals of the most holy Virgin there was none more dear to the tender piety of St. Francis of Sales than the Immaculate Conception.   When but a subdeacon he instituted a confraternity of penitents, under the title of the Immaculate Con-ception.   Every year he prepared for this feast by fasting and prayer, and his zeal induced him to proclaim this day a festival of obligation through-out his diocese.   In order to place his episcopate under the protection of the Immaculate Virgin, he chose this solemnity for the day of his consecration, and during the ceremony he was rapt in ecstasy, and saw the most Holy Trinity working in his heart all that the Bishops were doing exteriorly, and moreover, he saw the most holy Virgin take him under her protection.

Once, as he was making the visitation of his diocese, he arrived at the foot of a steep and rugged hill, upon the summit of which was the church of the most Blessed Virgin of Nancy-sur-Cluses. He climbed it with great difficulty, whilst blood streamed from his feet ; but in reply to those who would dissuade him from the attempt, he said : 'It is true that I am almost sinking from fatigue, but whilst I am ashamed to be so un-accustomed to labour for the service of God, I feel the greatest joy to shed my blood in honour of the Mother of God.'

Continuing his visitation he found three parish churches in succession which were dedicated to Mary. ' What a consolation I feel,' said he, ' to see so many churches in my diocese dedicated to the Mother of God ! Whenever I enter a place conse-crated to this august Queen, well do the beatings of my heart tell me that I am in the house of my Mother ; for I am the son of her who is the refuge of sinners.'

Prayer.—O Mary ! Immaculate Lily of Purity, I rejoice with you that you have been filled with grace, endowed with the use of reason, and have loved God more than the Seraphim from the first instant of your Immaculate Conception. May the most Holy Trinity be eternally thanked and adored for so many and such rare privileges bestowed upon you. I humble myself profoundly before you, seeing that I am so devoid of graces and poor in merits. O my most loving Mother, make me a partaker of the graces which you have received so abundantly, that I also may be able to love God ardently during life, and not be separated from Him in death. Amen.

Practice.—Recite three *Paters,* three *Aves,* and three *Glorias,* to thank the most Holy Trinity for the grace of the Immaculate Conception conferred upon Mary.

Aspiration.—O Mary, conceived without sin, pray for us who have recourse to you.

FIRST DAY.

MARY, A MODEL OF PERFECT SELF-DENIAL FROM HER BIRTH.

LET all who are devout to the most holy Virgin approach the cradle in which lies the royal infant, Mary. Consider attentively this sacred child, and you will see how perfectly she practises every virtue. Ask the Angels, the Cherubim and Seraphim, who surround her, if they equal this little creature in perfection, and they will all reply that they are immensely inferior to her in graces, in merits, and in virtue. Contemplate, Children of Mary, those heavenly spirits around her cradle, and you will hear them repeat in ecstasies of admiration of her beauty the words of the Canticle of Canticles : *Who is she that goeth up by the desert as a pillar of smoke of aromatical spices of myrrh, and frankin-*

cense . . . . Who is she that cometh forth as the morning rising, fair as the moon, bright as the sun, terrible as an army set in battle array?

This virgin child is not yet glorified, but glory is already promised her; she expects it, not like others, in hope, but with certainty. On this account the celestial spirits, enraptured by such incomparable perfection, cease not to celebrate her praises.

Meanwhile, this most perfect Virgin lies in her poor crib, and there practises, in a most special manner, the virtue of self-abnegation. Consider, I beseech you, how, amidst angelic praises, she wishes to appear like all other children of Adam. Who will not be filled with admiration and love, to behold Mary in her cradle, full of grace, endowed with the perfect use of reason from the first instant of her Immaculate Conception, able to meditate upon the perfections of God, filled with His love, and entirely resigned to His holy will; and yet, notwithstanding such privileges, wishing to be considered and treated as a poor little infant, without in any way manifesting the precious gifts she possessed? O my God! how attractive is such a spectacle; and not only attractive, but wonderful; and how clearly does it convince us of her perfect renunciation of all that savours of worldly pomp and glory and ambition!

The second kind of abnegation which this august Virgin teaches us to practise, is the renunciation of the flesh, of which in her nativity and infancy she offers us most moving examples.   Children are obliged to make many sacrifices, and the more they are attended to, the more are their affections and inclinations opposed.   These mortifications, nevertheless, are not occasions of merit to them, for they have not yet acquired the use of reason. But the most holy Virgin, being endowed from her infancy with the perfect use of reason, exercised the virtue of self-abnegation in a wonderful degree, enduring voluntarily all these contradictions and mortifications.

The third kind of renunciation is that of our own judgment and will, even in things which seem to us better than those that are commanded us. This includes what is most difficult and meritorious in the way of Christian perfection.   How excellently did the most holy Virgin practise this abnegation in her nativity !   Although possessed of the use of reason, she never made use of her liberty to manifest it.   We always see in her a constant state of dependence.   When she goes to the Temple she is led by her parents ; through obedience to them she gives her hand to a humble carpenter, although she had consecrated her virginity to God.   She leaves Nazareth for Bethlehem, flees into Egypt, and returns to Nazareth ; and in all these journeys, as well as in all the other vicissitudes of her life, she maintains perfect subjection and docility.   She even assists at the death of her

Son and her God, through submission to the decrees of Heaven, her will being perfectly united to that of the Eternal Father. It was not by constraint, but with the full concurrence of her will, that she assented to the death of this Divine Son, and with humble resignation embraced and adored a hundred times that Cross upon which she saw, without shedding a tear, her only Son expire. What abnegation do we not find in the most holy Virgin! The tender loving soul of this most sorrowful Mother was pierced by unheard-of dolours; indeed, who can ever describe the pains and anguish of her most sacred heart, as she stood immovable at the foot of the Cross? She knew that the Eternal Father willed that Jesus Christ should thus die, and that she should be present at His death, and this knowledge gave her strength to stand there and endure it all.

In imitation of Mary, let us resolve to die to everything and to our own will, that we may live for God alone. Jesus Christ tells us to deny ourselves, to take up our cross and to follow Him. The way of perfection is a Calvary, where it is necessary to crucify ourselves continually, in company with our Saviour; thus forcing nature to die, that grace may live and reign within us. In a word, it is necessary to strip ourselves of the old Adam, and clothe ourselves with the new Adam, and this cannot be done without suffering. I will not deceive you; Christian perfection is difficult, and very great courage is required for so high an undertaking. This perfection consists in an entire self-abnegation, and in a total renunciation of all earthly things.*

O my God! when will Our Lady be, as it were, born in our hearts? As for myself I see clearly that I am quite unworthy of such a favour; and as for you, what are your sentiments? Her Divine Son was born in a stable. Let us take courage and prepare Him a place in our hearts; a place made deep by humility, low by simplicity, and wide by charity. It is such a heart as this that Our Lady loves to visit. She dwells willingly near the manger and at the foot of the Cross. Little matters it to her that she lives unknown in Egypt, provided her Divine Child lives with her.

Whether our Lord sends us to the right or to the left, or howsoever He treats us, or makes us as a sign against which all the evils of the world are turned, we will never abandon Him until He has blessed us with eternal blessing. Let us be assured that He is never so near to us as when He appears to be furthest from us; never does He guard us with more jealousy than when He seems to abandon us, and never does He engage in combat

---

* In the way of prayer, at first everything seems painful, and with good reason; because it is a continual war against ourselves. But when we set to work, our Lord on His side assists us so powerfully, and loads us with so many favours, that all the pains and labours of this life become as nothing. —*St. Teresa.*

with us, but to take more intimate possession of our heart, and load us with His blessings. Meanwhile, let us go on ; let us walk through the valley of humble virtues, and how many roses shall we not find amongst the thorns ! Charity, which shines in the midst of the most trying afflictions, as well interior as exterior, the lily of purity, the violet of mortification, and how many more ! But the lowly virtues that are dearest to me are these three : meekness of heart, poverty of spirit, simplicity of life, together with the practices of visiting the sick, serving the poor, consoling the afflicted, and such like. However, all must be done without solicitude, and in true liberty of spirit. Our arms are not long enough to reach to the cedars of Lebanon—let us then be content with the hyssop that grows in the valleys.

SPIRITUAL FLOWERS.

There shall come forth a rod from the root of Jesse, says Isaias, and a flower shall rise up from its root. This root, writes St. Jerome, is the Mother of the Saviour; a plain and simple root, but fruitful in its unity, like the Eternal Father. The flower of this root is Jesus Christ, *like to a flower of the field and to a lily of the valley.* This flower is possessed of as many leaves as there are functions and examples. If you wish to have the flower you must first bend the stem by your prayers. If this flower rises high through the

excellence of its Divinity be not afraid; because
through excess of love its stem may be bowed.—
St. Bonaventure.

I am firmly resolved to desire no other heart
than that which shall be given me by this Mother
of hearts, this Mother of holy love. O my God!
how much do I desire not to lose sight, not even
for an instant, of this gracious Star, during the
whole course of my journey! — *St. Francis of
Sales.*

As the lily has no fixed season for its growth,
but flowers sooner or later, according to its depth
in the earth, in like manner the heart which aspires
to Divine Love will blossom very late, and with
much difficulty, if it be absorbed in earthly cares.
However, if it be attached to the world only so
far as is necessary for its engagements in life, it
will flourish in charity and spread around it
gracious fragrance.—*The same.*

EXAMPLE.

The Miraculous Medal of the Immaculate Conception.

Perhaps I can relate nothing more suitable in
regard to the origin of this celebrated medal, so
justly styled '*miraculous*,' than by transcribing the
letter addressed to the author of the book, 'Mary
Conceived without Sin,' by the spiritual Director
of the Sister of Charity to whom the medal was
revealed :

'Paris, 17th March, 1834.

'Towards the close of the year 1830, Sister M., a novice of one of the communities in Paris, dedicated to the service of the Poor, saw, whilst in prayer, a picture representing the Blessed Virgin, standing with her arms extended. She wore a white garment, a blue and silver cloak, and a veil coloured like the aurora, whilst rays of dazzling splendour issued from her hands. At the same time the Sister heard these words: "These rays are the symbol of the graces which Mary obtains in favour of mankind; and that part of the globe upon which they fall with greater abundance is France." Around the picture was written the invocation, "*O Mary, conceived without sin, pray for us who have recourse to you.*" The Sister having considered it for a moment, cast her eyes upon the other side of the picture, and saw the letter "*M*" surmounted by a Cross, and below it, the Sacred Hearts of Jesus and Mary. Then the voice said again: "*A medal must be struck according to this model; and whoever shall wear it, properly blessed and indulgenced, shall be protected by the Mother of God in a most special manner.*"

'The novice came quickly to narrate the vision to me; and I, supposing it to be a mere pious illusion, simply addressed a few words to her upon true devotion to Mary, pointing out to her that the imitation of her virtues ever was, and will be, the true means of honouring her.

3—2

' After about six months, she had the same vision, and I made her the same reply. Finally, after another interval of six months, she saw the picture again, and heard the same words, except that the voice expressed how much it displeased the Blessed Virgin that there was so much delay in having the medal struck.

' This time, however, I attached greater import-ance to the revelation, without allowing the novice to perceive it; and I began to reflect and fear lest I was not seconding the designs of her who is so justly invoked by the Church under the sweet name of " Refuge of Sinners."

' A short time afterwards I had the opportunity of seeing the Archbishop, and gave him an accurate account of these visions. He answered me that " he saw nothing whatever objectionable in this medal being struck, as it was conformable to the faith of the Church and to the piety of the faithful towards the Mother of God; and that it might certainly contribute to the promotion of her honour."

The medal was finally struck in the month of June, 1832.

' In one of the three visions, the novice asked if it were not necessary to insert some words on that part of the medal where the letter "*M*" and the Cross, with the two Hearts, are represented; but she was answered that these objects spoke with sufficient eloquence to the faithful soul.

'When the medal was struck, it was quickly circulated amongst the Sisters of Charity, who, when they learnt its origin, wore it with much devotion, and began to hang it on the necks of the sick under their charge, and these shortly experienced happy results. Three cures and three conversions were wrought in a miraculous manner in Paris, and in the diocese of Meaux. Then the desire to possess the *miraculous medal*, or the medal *that cures*, became universal. Mothers of families gave it as a New Year's gift to their children, and as a preservative to their innocence. As soon as it became known in a place, pious persons hastened to become possessed of it. But what greatly surprised and edified me, from the beginning of its propagation, was that all the children of two of our provinces agreed together to take this medal as the protection of their youth. In many places entire populations addressed themselves to their Pastor to procure it; and, at Paris, an officer purchased sixty for as many private soldiers who had asked him for it.

'Whilst the medal was miraculously propagated in all classes and provinces, the most consoling accounts were sent me by the Parish Priests, Vicar-Generals, and even by Bishops. They say that *"it reanimates fervour in populous towns as well as in the country; it gains our entire confidence; we look upon it as a means sent by Providence to enkindle faith, which in our days has so visibly decreased ; and in reality it daily awakens this faith in many hearts, in which it seemed to be extinguished ; it re-establishes peace and concord in many families ; and there is no one who wears this medal who does not experience its salutary effects."* '

Not only in France—which is specially under the protection of Mary Most Holy — did the faithful of every age, sex, and condition, rival one another in zeal and solicitude to possess the *miraculous* medal ; it spread also like lightning throughout Switzerland, Piedmont, Spain, Italy, Belgium, England, America, in the Levant, and even in China ; and we can certify that in the present day the number of these medals exceeds thirty millions. In every place it is asked for by indifferent Christians, by obstinate sinners, by the impious, by Protestants, Jews, and Turks, and worn with veneration. Heaven grant that it may not be without fruit !—that she, to whom the Church applies those words of Holy Scripture, ' *He who shall find Me shall find life, and have salvation from the Lord,*' may conduct and confirm us in the way of salvation !

Plenary Indulgences at the hour of death, and on all the principal festivals of the year, and on the feasts of the Apostles are attached to this medal when blessed by anyone who possesses the faculty.

Prayer.—O Lovely Child, who, in your happy

Nativity, didst console the world, rejoice Heaven, terrify hell, and become the relief of sinners, the consolation of the afflicted, the health of the sick, and the joy of all men, I entreat you, with all the fervour of my soul, to be spiritually born in my heart through your holy love. Attach my soul once for all to your happy service, and my heart to yours, that my life may be adorned with the virtues which will render me dear to you. O Mary! produce in me the salutary effects of your sweet name, and obtain that the invocation of this holy name may be my strength in sufferings, my hope in dangers, my shield in spiritual conflicts, and my support and comfort in the agonies of death. May it be honey to my mouth, music to my ears, and the only joy of my heart! Amen.

Aspiration.—Morning Star, pray for me.

Practice.—Visit the altar of the Blessed Virgin, after having adored the Most Holy Sacrament of the Altar.

SECOND DAY.

MARY CONSECRATES HERSELF TO GOD IN THE TEMPLE.

MARY was no sooner born than she consecrated her entire being to the service of Divine Love, and as soon as she acquired the use of her tongue she employed it in chanting the praises of the Lord. He inspired her, when she had attained the age of

three years, to leave the home of her parents and
retire into the Temple to serve Him more perfectly.
During her tender years the life of this glorious
Virgin was full of wisdom and discretion, and the
cause of astonishment to her parents, for her
actions and words were very different from those of
other children, since she had the full use of her
reason. It was therefore necessary to hasten the
period for taking her to the Temple and consecrating
her to the Divine service, amongst the other maidens
already consecrated. They, therefore, took the
little Virgin and partly led and partly carried her
to the Temple of Jerusalem. Mary certainly had
nothing to fear from the influences of her home,
but she wished to teach us by her example that we
should omit nothing, as St. Paul so earnestly
teaches, to make our calling and election sure.

All who repaired to the Temple to present their
offerings chanted as they went the Psalm : *Beati
immaculati in via qui ambulant in lege Domini*—
' *Blessed are the undefiled in the way, who walk in the
law of the Lord.*' With what grace and melody
must not our glorious Queen and Mistress have
intoned this canticle when she walked towards the
sanctuary where her God wished to prepare her to
become, not only His Spouse, but His Mother, the
blessed among all women ! The very Angels were
so pleased at the sight of such love, fervour, and
humility, that they descended in choirs to listen to
the harmony. With what joy was she not filled

when she arrived at the threshhold of the Temple, and when she mounted the fifteen steps of the sanctuary! She came to dedicate herself unreservedly to God. If her youth had not forbidden it, she might thus have addressed the holy matrons who had charge of the consecrated children in the Temple: Here am I; consider me in your hands as a piece of soft wax; dispose of me as you will, I shall never make any resistance. She was so docile that she allowed herself to be guided by others in such a manner as never to show the slightest inclination to one thing more than another. She abandoned herself totally and perfectly to the Divine Will, so that she was a marvel to all who knew her.

In order to profit in a Christian manner by the example that Mary gives us in this mystery, three points can be considered: firstly, that Mary was presented to God in His Temple from her tenderest infancy, and thus separated from her parents; secondly, that she makes a great part of the journey on foot, and the rest of the journey she is carried in the arms of her parents; thirdly, that she dedicates and offers herself entirely to God, without any reserve.

As to the first point, which is to dedicate one's self to God from one's infancy, how, you will ask, can we imitate Mary in this, for we have already passed the age of childhood, and it is impossible to recover lost time? You are deceived. If virginity can be repaired by means of humility, cannot lost time be repaired by making a fervent and good use of the present? I acknowledge that the happiness of those who have dedicated themselves entirely to God from their infancy is, indeed, enviable, and He seems to receive such an offering with special complacency. He complains, through one of His prophets, that '*men had so perverted their way, that even from their youth they had abandoned the path of salvation for that of perdition.*' Children are neither good nor bad so long as they are incapable of distinguishing good from evil. But when they have attained the use of reason, too often they turn to that which is evil. Hence God says by His prophet : *Dereliquerunt me fontem aquæ vivæ*—'*They have forsaken Me, the fountain of living water, to follow the way of iniquity.*'

Another proof of the ardent desire of the Divine Goodness for our youthful service is found in the words of the same prophet : *Bonum est viro cum portaverit jugum ab adolescentia sua*—'*It is good for a man to have borne the yoke from his youth.*' But it need not be supposed that the youth of which the prophet speaks is only that of years. When the Beloved in the Canticle of Canticles turns to her Spouse and says to Him : *Oleum effusum nomen tuum, ideo adolescentulæ dilexerunt te*—'*Thy name is as oil poured out, therefore young maidens have loved Thee,*' do you believe she speaks of maidens who are young in years? No; but of those who are young in fervour and courage, but who have consecrated to the service of Holy Love all the moments of their life and all the affections of their hearts.

It is the present time, the present moment, that we should turn to profit; because the past has escaped us, and the future is not in our power. But you ask, How can we repair lost time? You can do it by the use of fervour and diligence during the time that remains for your pilgrimage upon earth. Stags do not always run at an extraordinary speed, but yet, when pursued by the hunter, they quicken their movement and seem rather to fly than to run. This is a model for us. We must not only run, but fly in the way of perfection. Therefore let us, with holy David, beg our Lord to give us *the wings of a dove*, that we may fly without stopping, until we gain our hiding-place in the walls of the holy city of Jerusalem; that is to say, until we find ourselves united to our Lord crucified upon Calvary, through an entire and perfect - mortification of all our inclinations and affections.

Oh, how happy are those souls who follow the example of this Sacred Virgin, and dedicate themselves from their tender years to the service of God! Fortunate are they to have retired from the world before they were known to it! Like delicate flowers scarcely yet open, nor touched by the heat of concupiscence, they exhale a most sweet odour in the Divine Presence by means of their virtues and innocence.

SPIRITUAL FLOWERS.

Mary was like a most beautiful flower, which diffuses its perfume from its very first budding. Flowers differ in their method of diffusing fragrance, as, for instance, roses and carnations. Roses smell sweeter in the morning before mid-day; but carnations and pinks shed a more pleasing scent in the evening. The glorious Virgin was like a most beautiful rose amongst thorns, and although never for an instant did she cease to diffuse an odour of surpassing sweetness, yet the fragrance of her infancy was the most acceptable to the Divine Majesty.—*St. Francis of Sales.*

Chastity is the lily of virtues, because it renders men equal to the Angels; if virtues be separated from purity, they are no longer virtues. Purity is chastity, and it possesses a glory of its own, for it clothes both soul and body with its beauty.—*The same.*

As the busy bee flies to all the flowers, and sucks from each its purest juice with which to form honey, so should a religious soul observe the virtues of others, and learn, for instance, modesty from one, science from another, and obedience from a third; in a word, he should take from each one that which he perceives to be most perfect, and copy it in his own person.—*St. Antony.*

The two Invocations of St. Philip Neri.

Of the many ejaculatory prayers of St. Philip Neri to the Most Holy Virgin, two were very familiar to him. The first was, ' Virgin Mary, Mother of God, pray to Jesus for us'; the second consisted in the two words, ' Virgin and Mother.' He used to say that they contain all the panegyrics of Mary, both because they express her admirable name, and because they declare her two miraculous privileges of *Virginity* and *Maternity*, and the incomparable title of *Mother of God*. He composed a rosary with these two invocations, which he recited frequently with his penitents, and had always in his hands.   .

A pious person, who was continually tormented by evil thoughts, asked him one day for a remedy. The Saint counselled her to recite this rosary of his, which consisted in repeating these two invocations alternately, sixty-three times. She followed his advice, and in a short time recovered her peace of soul.

Prayer of St. Gertrude.—O Mary, Mother of Jesus, and my own dear Mother ! clothe me with the fleece of the true Lamb, your Son Jesus, that His love may receive me, nourish me, possess me, and sanctify me. Shining Lily, my only hope, after God, deign to speak to your Beloved Son in my favour ; say an efficacious word to Him, and faithfully and earnestly plead my cause. I beseech you, O my Mother! by your love for Jesus, to accept me as your child; be solicitous for my welfare throughout the whole course of my life, and especially at the hour of my death take me entirely under your protection.   Amen.

Ejaculation.—O Mary, Virgin and Mother! make me a Saint.

Practice.—Let all your actions this day be done in union with Jesus and Mary.

THIRD DAY.

CONTINUATION OF THE PRECEDING SUBJECT.

THE second point presented to our consideration in the presentation of Our Lady is that in order to consecrate herself to God in the Temple she was carried part of the way by her parents, and walked the remainder, being, however, always assisted by them.   When St. Joachim and St. Anne arrived at a spot where the road was level they placed the little maiden on the ground, and allowed her to walk, but even then she lifted up her little hands to clasp theirs, that she might not stumble, and when they came to the rougher parts of the road they again took her in their arms.   It should not be supposed that the intentions of her parents in allowing her to walk was to relieve themselves; they allowed it because of the satisfaction which

they experienced in seeing their little daughter
directing her first steps to the Temple of the Lord.

Now, it is in these two ways that our Lord leads
His faithful servants in their pilgrimage through
this miserable life. At times He conducts us by
the hand, making us walk with Him ; and very
often He carries us in the arms of His Providence.
He leads us by the hand when He makes us walk
along the path of the exercise of virtues, because if
He did not help us it would be impossible for us
to take one step along this blessed road.   And do
we not perceive that the steps of those who have
abandoned the paternal hand of Providence are
almost always so many falls ?   The Divine Goodness wishes to lead us by the hand along our road,
but He also wishes us to make use of our feet ; that
is to say, that we ourselves do all that is in our
power, by the assistance of His grace.   Therefore
Holy Church, like a tender mother desirous of the
good of her children, teaches us to recite daily a
prayer by which we beg God to deign to accompany
us during the whole course of our pilgrimage upon
this earth, and to succour us by His preventing and
by His accompanying grace, because without both
these graces all our efforts to make one step in the
way of virtue would be unavailing.

But after our Lord has led us by the hand
along the road of good works which require our
co-operation in order that they may become
meritorious, He carries us in His arms, producing

certain effects within us, in which we seem to take no part, as, for instance, in the Sacraments. Tell me candidly, what is it that we do in order to the reception of the Most Holy Sacrament of the Altar, which contains all the sanctity and sweetness of heaven and earth? Does not our Lord carry us in His arms in permitting us to receive Him in this Sacrament?

Oh, how happy are those souls who so pass through this mortal life as never to leave the arms of His Divine Majesty, except to do all in their power to labour in the practice of virtue, still keeping hold of the hand of their Lord! Let us never believe ourselves capable of doing the least good of ourselves. The Sacred Spouse of the Canticles teaches us this truth when she says to her Beloved: *Trahe me post Te in odorem curremus unguentorum tuorum*—'*Draw me, and we will run after thee to the odour of thy ointments.*' She says '*draw me*,' to teach us that our soul can do nothing of itself unless it be drawn, assisted, and anticipated by Divine Grace. But to show us that she corresponds voluntarily to this attraction, she quickly adds: '*We will run*,' as if she wished to say: If only, my Beloved, Thou stretch out Thy hand to draw me, I shall not cease to run, until Thou hast received me into Thine arms, and united me to Thy Divine Will.

Let us now pass to the third point: the consecration and dedication our glorious Lady made of her whole self unreservedly to the Divine Majesty; it is this, O faithful souls, that we should try to imitate. Our Lord does not certainly expect us to be more liberal to Him than He is to us; nevertheless, if He shows the greatness of His goodness to us by giving us His whole Self, is it not just that He should require of us the total dedication of ourselves to Him? But what means this total dedication of ourselves to God? It means that we make no reserve whatever in our consecration, not even of the least of our affections or desires; it is this that He requires of us. Listen, in fact, to this Divine Saviour of our souls: *Fili præte mihi cor tuum*—'*My Son,*' says He to each one of us in particular—'*My Son, give Me thy heart.*' 'Ah!' you will add, 'how shall I dare to give my heart to God when it is so full of imperfections and sins? How can He accept the offering of this heart in which He finds nothing but disobedience to His Most Holy Will?' Ah! be not troubled on this account, but offer it to Him all the same, because He does not require of you a pure and spotless heart, like that of the Angels and of Our Lady, but He says: 'Give Me thy heart,' such as it is. Ah! let us not refuse it to Him then, although it be full of miseries, weaknesses, and imperfections, for we know that all that is placed in the hand of His Divine Goodness is converted into good. Let us not fear, then, for when He holds this heart of ours in His hands He will know well how to

4

render it perfect.   To make it less unworthy of
God let us resolve to imitate Mary ; for amongst all
the Saints who are proposed to us as a model we
should in a special manner consider our most
glorious and dear Patroness, the Queen of all
Saints.   What mirror more beautiful, more precious,
or purer, can we place before our eyes ?   Is she not
the most excellent example of evangelical teaching ?
Who amongst creatures is more adorned and
enriched with every kind of virtue and grace ?
*Multæ filiæ congregaverunt divitias, tu supergressa
es universus*—'*Many daughters have gathered riches,
but thou hast surpassed them all.*'   Certainly it is
beyond all doubt that there is no Saint comparable
to her, because this glorious Virgin surpasses in
dignity and excellence not only the greatest Saints,
but the very Cherubim and Seraphim.   She
consecrated herself perfectly to the Divine service,
from the very first instant of her Immaculate
Conception.

SPIRITUAL FLOWERS.

When the senses are not well guarded, they are
mysterious inlets by which our enemies insinuate
themselves into our souls.   A glance of curiosity
changed holy King David into an adulterer and a
murderer.   How many have reason to exclaim
with Jeremiah, ' *My eye hath been the thief that has
robbed my soul of every good*'!—*Riva.*

The choice of a state of life is so important that

it constitutes the only foundation of a good or of a bad life.—*St. Greg. Naz.*

The Christian who abandons himself into the hand of God, lives for God alone.—*St. Francis of Sales.*

EXAMPLE.

The Feasts of the Blessed Virgin.

The days upon which the Blessed Virgin Mary shows herself bountiful of her favours, are the feasts celebrated in her honour; and if we desire to profit by them, we must sanctify them fervently. Let us approach the Sacraments on those days, and propose to practise some particular virtue of the Blessed Virgin, adapted to the mystery of the day. For instance, on the Feast of the Immaculate Conception, let us propose to practise purity of intention; on that of her Nativity, a renewal of fervour, banishing all tepidity from our soul; on that of the Presentation, detachment from those desires which require to be mortified; on the Feast of the Annunciation, of the Visitation, on the Feast of the Purification, obedience to Superiors; and on the Feast of the Assumption, preparation for death. Such was ever the practice of all the true servants of Mary; amongst others, of St. Bernardine of Siena, of St. Gertrude, and of St. Vincent Ferrer.

Mary herself made known to St. Gertrude, as we read in the tenth chapter of the 'Revelations' of this Saint, that she rewards this practice with

4—2

every kind of favour. On the Feast of the Assumption, whilst the Divine Sacrifice of the Mass was being celebrated, the Blessed Virgin showed the Saint a great number of young girls, whom she carefully guarded under her rich mantle. 'My dear daughter,' said she to her, 'behold here those souls who do all in their power to celebrate this festival worthily.'

Brother Gerard, one of the first lay-brothers of the Congregation of St. Alfonso de Liguori, had the most tender confidence in Mary. At the approach of her feasts he took care to adorn all the altars of the monastery, and his devotion was especially great to the Immaculate Conception. He wished that the faithful would fast on all the vigils of her feasts ; on which days his nourishment was but a little bread and water, and he gave himself the discipline to blood. During all her novenas, he performed some abstinence or good work in her honour. When he was allowed by his Superior, he spent the night preceding her festivals prostrate before her altar in fervent prayer. It is narrated by Fathers Petrella and Giovenale that the Blessed Virgin, touched by the love of her servant, appeared to him during one of those nights, and enriched him with favours of many kinds.

Prayer of St. Gertrude to the Sacred Heart of Mary.—O Immaculate Heart of Mary, I have nothing to offer you that is worthy of you ; yet how many thanks should I not render you for all the

favours that you have obtained for me from the
Heart of Jesus! What reparation should I not
offer you for my languor during Divine service!
I would wish to render you love for love : the only
good that I possess is the Sacred Heart of Jesus,
which you have yourself given to me. I offer you,
then, this treasure of infinite value—I can do
nothing more, and nothing less do you merit from
me. Accept, then, this gift, which is so dear to
you ; and nothing more do I desire except that
you will deign to accept, also, my poor heart.
Amen.

Ejaculation.—Mother of Good Counsel, pray
for me.

Practice. — Make a sincere act of contrition
for the time that you have spent away from
God.

FOURTH DAY.

FIDELITY OF MARY IN FOLLOWING THE CALL OF GOD.

LET us consider in this meditation the punctual
care with which Mary always followed her vocation.

God had uttered in her ears, or rather in the
interior of her heart, the words of the psalm :
*Audi Fili, inclina aurem tuam, et obliviscere popu-
lum tuum, et domum patris tui et concupiscet rex*

decorem tuum—'*Hearken, my child, incline thine ear
to Me ; forget thy people and thy father's house, and
the King shall desire thy beauty.*'

Ponder attentively these words : '*Hearken, child*'
—*Audi Fili.* They imply that, in order to hear
well, it is necessary to listen, first, very attentively—'*inclina aurem tuam;*' it is to the humble
alone that God deigns to make known His Will.
'*Forget thy people and thy father's house, and the
King will greatly desire thy beauty.*' This is as if
He would say, do not confine thyself to listening
to the word of inspiration, and abasing thyself in
order that thou mayest understand it, but further
strip thy heart of all affection for thy country and
thy relations, and then I shall be delighted with thy
beauty. O, holy and Divine seed which our Lord
sows in the hearts of so many ! And yet how many
there are who hear the Divine call, without making
one step to leave their country and go whither God
calls them ! Diligence is taken to examine and
consider attentively whether the inspiration comes
from God, or from the enemy of all good, or if it be
the deception of self-love ; and meanwhile, through
our own fault, the Divine vocation fails in its effect.
I do not wish to condemn the considerations
which ought to be made in order to discern well the
nature of the inspiration. By no means ; but after
having made your examen with simplicity, in
the presence of God, and recognised His voice, go
forth quickly and enter the land which He points

out to you.   Listen no longer to so many discourses
and reasonings suggested by the spirit of the world,
because procrastination under such circumstances
exposes you to very serious dangers.   Do not,
then, lull yourself to sleep, but follow diligently the
Divine attraction.

With what assiduity and with what solicitude did
not the glorious Virgin obey the sacred call of God !
She had no need of protracted self-examination,
because she was endowed with the grace of discernment.   Therefore, although but a child, she
repaired without delay whither her God led her, and
the King of Heaven, won by her beauty, chose her
not only for His Spouse, but also for His Mother.
*' Blessed are they that hear the word of God and
keep it.'*
Certainly, all are not called to follow the same
path, and yet they may all follow the Divine inspirations.   We will explain.   The Church may be
considered as the Court of a great Prince or King,
in whose kingdom are many vassals or under-lords.
All these vassals are invited to Court, and all
share in the favours of their Sovereign, but
differently.   Some are favoured in a very special
manner, and He treats them with greater confidence
than the rest, and repeats to them His secrets.
But besides the graces which He grants in general
to all the members of His Church, to some amongst
them He bestows more precious favours ; for
instance, religious persons, whom He admits into

His Cabinet—that is to say, into holy religion—in order to entertain Himself with them familiarly, and disclose His secrets to them in the closest union of Heart.

Amongst those who have received this grace, the Most Holy Virgin has been singularly privileged, Our Lord having made known to her secrets and mysteries which have been revealed to no other creature. Happy was she to have heard the word of God and kept it, and how happy also will you be, pious souls, if you endeavour, in imitation of her, to follow promptly the inspirations by which God manifests to you His Most Holy Will!

I am well aware that for many it is necessary that they should live in the world. These persons should use, but not abuse the riches, honours and dignities which they are allowed by the law of God to possess; and if they endeavour, in the use of these possessions, to conform their affections to the commandments of God, without following the counsels, they will be as truly blessed, and will attain to the joys of eternal life.

There are many persons who wish to consecrate themselves to God, but at the same time wish to reserve always something for themselves. They will say, for instance, I will give to God what belongs to God, and reserve for the world what is due to the world, without however doing what would be an offence to His Divine Majesty, or contrary to His most holy law. Such as these listen, it is true, to the inspirations of God, but do not correspond to them with their whole heart, and although they may be saved, yet they never will reach a high degree of perfection and glory.

There are others who are quite resolved to follow steadily the inspirations and Will of God, and also desire to live united to Him, but not in a *perfect manner.* Observe well that there is a great difference between being *all* given to God and *wholly* given to God. These persons of whom we speak wish to reserve to themselves the choice at least of their spiritual exercises, in order, as they say, that they may the better serve God. But to how much danger of being deceived do not they expose themselves ! Regulating themselves according to their own notions, they refuse to submit to others, and they mark out for themselves a mode of life according to their own caprices. I would say to such souls : Do you not perceive that with these ideas you do not belong *wholly* to God ? Their answer would be : But I act so in order to serve God. But this is not the example that our most Blessed Lady, the glorious Virgin, gives us. On the day of her presentation she consecrated herself to God entirely, without any reserve, and never again made use of her own will or choice. O faithful souls, you ought continually to keep before your eyes the life of our dear Lady, and meditate upon it, so as to be able to conform all your actions and affections to this perfect model. You are her children, and therefore you ought to follow her, to imitate her, and make use of her as a mirror in which you should always view and study yourselves well. The sweetness which will flow from the consideration of her virtues will be received in earthen vessels ; nevertheless, its fragrance will be none the less sweet. The balsam that is contained in an earthen vase is as sweet as that in a vase of crystal.

SPIRITUAL FLOWERS.

Most yellow flowers keep turned continually to the sun, but the *sunflower* turns not only its flowers but also its leaves towards the great luminary. In like manner the elect turn the flower of their hearts —that is, their obedience—to the commands of God's will.—*St. Francis of Sales.*

The virtues of the friends of God are ennobled and raised to the dignity of holy works by the excellence of the heart which produces them. All their virtuous actions are dedicated to God, for how can a heart that has given Him itself not give to Him all that belongs to it? Does not he who gives a whole tree give also the leaves, and flowers, and fruit ?—*The same.*

The rose possesses the property of killing by its odour all the snails that come around it. Similarly, the devout soul, who is as a rose before God, should chase away and destroy all the creeping things that gather around her heart—that is to say, the coldness

and tepidity which are an obstacle to her advance-
ment in the way of God.—*The same.*

EXAMPLE.

Lamps and Candles burnt in Honour of Mary.

It is a custom amongst Catholics to have lamps
or candles burning upon altars, or before pictures of
the august Mother of God for one, or three, or nine
consecutive days, so as to obtain spiritual or
temporal favours.   This touching practice, spring-
ing from the love of Mary, comes down from the
remotest antiquity.   Oil and wax, as all know, have
a deep signification.   The flame is a symbol of the
vivacity of our faith and of the firmness of our
confidence; fire symbolizes the ardour of charity,
and the ascent of the flame is a type of our hope.
These flames intimate that we must keep the fire
of charity ever burning in our hearts, so as to be
always ready to receive our Divine Master when-
soever He shall call us to the nuptials of the Lamb.
Lamps lighted before the statues or pictures of
Mary represent to us more specially the prayer of
intercession, which goes direct to the Heart of God.
They awaken a singular emotion in the heart of
him who has faith.   The oil that feeds the flame
has often cost the poor man the sweat of hard
labour, but he thinks little of this voluntary sacrifice,
because it was the fruit of love.   No one who has
not visited Italy, and in particular Rome and

Naples, can form an idea of the honour that is paid
to the Blessed Virgin.   You will find her image on
all the roadsides, in the public squares, houses and
shops, with lamps, often many at a time, burning
before them, and the amount of oil that is consumed
in this manner is considerable.   This is a voluntary
contribution of the poor as well as of the rich, and
it is an expense that every pious family considers as
necessary as their daily bread.   At Rome there
exists a sweet custom of writing a short prayer,
often with the indulgence attached to its repetition,
under each image or picture, and it is repeated by
the passers-by.   Who can say how many passions
are repressed, how many unhappy creatures consoled, and how many hopes aroused by this short
invocation?

Prayer of St. Germanus.—O you, who are, after
God, my powerful protectress and my true consolation in this world, you who are the celestial dew
that sweetens my pains; the light of my soul when
plunged in darkness, my guide in my journeys,
my strength in my weaknesses, my treasure in
poverty, the remedy of my wounds, my joy in all
my sorrows, my refuge in all dangers, the hope of
my life and of my salvation, deign to hear my
prayers, to take an interest in my woes, and to
show me that compassion which peculiarly belongs
to the Mother of a God Who entertains such love
and goodness towards men.   He is their Father,
and He has constituted you their Mother.   Ah!

place me then amongst the number of your dearest children, and obtain for me from God all the graces which you know to be necessary for the salvation of my soul.   Amen.

Ejaculation.—O Mary! be my guiding star.

Practice.—Examine what has been your fidelity in following your vocation, and how its obligations have been fulfilled.

FIFTH DAY.

MARY IS A MODEL TO RELIGIOUS PERSONS IN HER PRESENTATION IN THE TEMPLE.*

GOD had commanded all the Hebrews to visit the Temple, but all, rich and poor, were forbidden to

---

* It is an ancient and well-grounded tradition that Mary was led to the Temple to be presented to the Lord at three years of age, and that she dwelt in that sacred abode until the age of fourteen—that is to say, as long as was permitted by the laws of the Sanhedrim.   St. Bonaventure relates to us the life led by the Most Holy Virgin in that voluntary retirement.   'We may learn,' says this Father, ' what Mary did in the Temple from her own revelations to one of her faithful servants, supposed to be St. Elizabeth.'   Amongst other things we read as follows : ' As soon as I was left in the Temple by my parents, I determined in my heart to look upon God as my Father.   I often considered what I could do to merit His grace, and I began to instruct myself in His holy law.   But of all the Divine precepts, these three principally occupied my attention : (1) Thou shalt love the Lord thy God with thy whole heart, with all thy soul, and with all thy strength ; (2) thou shalt love thy neighbour as thyself; (3) thou shalt hate thy enemy.

'I kept the commandments in my heart, and I quietly embraced all the virtues that they contain.   It is thus enter it empty-handed : *Non apparetis in conspectu meo vacuus.* The offering, however, was not the same for all. The rich were to give according to their riches, the poor according to their poverty, and thus all were able to observe the precept. From this we may understand that when seculars come to God and offer Him the desire and will, they entertain to follow and observe His Divine

---

that I wish you to conduct yourself. In fact, the soul can possess no virtue whatever if it do not love God with all its powers, because it is from this love alone that the fulness of grace (without which virtue will never be preserved in the soul) descends to us ; but it will pass like running water and vanish if the soul *hates not its enemies,* which are *sin and vice.* He who desires to acquire and preserve grace must accustom his heart, then, to the exercise of this love and of this hatred, and it is in this that I wish to be imitated by you.'

The faithful servant of Mary, having heard these words, replied : ' My sweetest Lady, wast thou not already full of grace and virtue ?' The Blessed Virgin replied : ' Be certain that I believed myself to be the vilest sinner, and, like you, unworthy of grace. You perhaps believe, my daughter, that all the grace which I possessed was acquired without difficulty. But it was not so. On the contrary, I received no grace or favour without constant prayer, ardent desire, deep devotion, and many tears, with long afflictions, excepting, however, the grace of sanctification, which was given to me from my conception in my mother's womb, and, as far as I knew, I never said or thought of anything but what was pleasing to my God.' She added : ' Be assured also that no grace descends into the soul, except through the channel of prayer and corporal mortification. But as soon as we have given to God all that we possess, He Himself comes quickly to dwell within us, bringing with Him such inestimable gifts that the soul feels her heart to fail ; she loses the remembrance of having ever done or said anything acceptable to God, and she becomes more and more vile and contemptible in her own eyes.'—*Maria Regina e Madre Dei Santi,* by l'Abate Guyard, Vic. Gen. of Montalbano.

commandments, He will be satisfied with this offering, and if they put it in practice faithfully, they will obtain eternal life. But let those souls who are rich in means for doing great things for the glory of God, such as religious persons, beware lest they present themselves with the offering of the poor—that is, of seculars ; for God will not be satisfied with such an offering. Our Lord, in calling you, my dear sisters, into Holy Religion, enriched you with His graces, and on this account He requires much from you ; that is, He will have your offering to be of all that you are, and of all that you possess, without any reserve.

The Blessed Virgin, in her Presentation, made an offering pleasing to God ; offered not only the dignity of her person (the most excellent amongst pure creatures), but all that she possessed. How happy are the Religious who, by means of their vows, have consecrated all to God, dedicating to Him their bodies, their hearts, and all that they possess ; renouncing riches by the vow of poverty, pleasures by the vow of chastity, and their whole will by the vow of obedience ! Worldlings, you may enjoy your riches if you will, but do not abuse them, nor wrong anyone. The pleasures that Holy Church permits are lawful ; you are not prohibited in a thousand circumstances from following your own will, provided it be not contrary to that of God. But you, Religious, should offer all to God, without any reserve. He wishes your offering to

be entire, such as is the gift He makes to you
of Himself in the Divine Sacrament of the Altar.
Forget not that you cannot deceive Him, and if you
say that you wish to consecrate youselves perfectly
to His Divine Majesty, and do not really do so,
you are in danger of being punished like Ananias
and Sapphira, who lied to the Holy Ghost.

Now, the Blessed Virgin was always perfectly
obedient to the Will of God, from the first instant of
her conception, without ever changing or suspending
for a moment the resolution she had formed to
serve Him.

Do we not daily experience how changeable is
man in his good resolutions? How often, even in
one hour, do we not like and dislike the same
thing, and allow ourselves to be moved by excessive
joy or excessive sadness! This was not the case
with Our Lady; she hourly became more perfectly
united to God, and merited fresh graces, and the
more she received, the more did she render her
soul worthy to receive them. By these means she
was always strengthening her first resolution, so that
the only change that could have been perceptible in
her was the progress she made from one degree of
perfection to another, through the practice of every
virtue. It was for this purpose that she wished to
retire into the Temple, not through any need she
had of this retreat, for her perseverance was assured
by her consecration at the first moment of her
existence, but in order to instruct us, who are so

changeable and inconstant, that it is our duty to make use of every means in our power to strengthen and preserve our good resolutions.

Imitate the Most Holy Virgin also in this. Dedicate, therefore, yourselves entirely to God; and whenever you renew your consecration, you will acquire new strength and vigour in the service of His Divine Majesty. Renew your resolutions, renew them frequently and with fidelity, to the end of your life. This was the careful practice of all the Saints of both the Old and of the New Testament. Our nature is of itself weak and easily depressed when there is a question of virtuous resolutions. The earth itself has its periods of weakness, and refuses to be always yielding its produce; so it lies barren in winter. But when the spring arrives it renews itself, and having recovered fresh vigour, it gives us the benefit of its fruits.

For this reason Holy Church, like a wise Mother, puts before us from time to time, during the course of the year, special festivals, to animate us to renew our good resolutions. Who will not renew his soul on the solemn festivals of Easter, Pentecost, and Christmas, by holy affections and firm resolutions to live more virtuously? But besides the observance of all these festivals, it has ever been a laudable custom for persons more especially consecrated to God, such as Religious, to choose one day in particular during the course of the year upon which to renew their vows, and by so doing

5

to obey the great Apostle, who counsels us to confirm our vocation.

Divine Providence has permitted for our instruction, that Our Lady should renew in her Presentation the sacrifice which she had made of her whole self at the moment of her Immaculate Conception. Do you, then, religious souls, make this renewal in imitation of her, and do it with great fervour of spirit, with profound humility, and ardent charity. Place your hearts, your souls, and your entire being in the hands of this Holy Virgin ; she will present you to the Most Holy Trinity, and you will obtain a thousand blessings in this life, and will be enabled to arrive at eternal glory in the next.

SPIRITUAL FLOWERS.

Flowers fade quickly if they are much handled, but if they are not touched they may be preserved a long time.—*A Kempis.*

The root of the plant is hidden under ground and trodden under foot ; it has neither odour nor beauty, and yet it gives life to the flower. Thus a humble soul may, like Mary, be despised, it may be trodden upon, forgotten ; but this is the way for it to produce flowers and fruits for eternal life.— *Nouet.*

The lily is the symbol of chastity ; it preserves its whiteness and sweetness in the midst of thorns, so long as it is left untouched, but as soon as ever it is plucked it emits so overpowering an odour that it causes headache.—*St. Francis of Sales.*

Whiteness is not an essential property of the rose—indeed, red roses are more beautiful and of sweeter odour ; but it is the property of the lily. Let us endeavour to be what we are, and as justly and perfectly as possible, that we may do honour to our Maker.—*The same.*

EXAMPLE.

The edifying Death of St. Jane Frances de Chantal.

It was on the Feast of the Immaculate Conception of Mary that this Saint was attacked by the first serious symptoms of her fatal illness. On the eve of the feast she was in the refectory, and after the blessing of the table she knelt down, and with her arms in the form of a cross repeated twice these words : *O Mater Dei, memento mei.* She then commented upon these words thus : ' Holy Mother of God, by your Immaculate Conception, remember me and assist me always, especially at the hour of my death.' She remained for a long time afterwards in the same posture, absorbed in profound recollection.

The following day she was confined to her bed to rise no more. Her illness increasing every hour, she knew that her end approached, and thought only of preparing herself to appear before God. She received the last Sacraments with

striking fervour, and preserved her calmness and
serenity amidst the tears and sobs of all the community.   During her intense sufferings she was
heard to address the following prayer to the Most
Holy Virgin : ' O Mary, Mother of Grace, Mother
of Mercy, defend me from the snares of the infernal
enemy, and receive my soul into your hands at the
moment of my death.'   She kept a picture of her
Protectress always near her bed ; and when her
speech failed she made great efforts to turn her
eyes frequently towards this dear picture, and before
she breathed her last asked to kiss it once more,
and to have it buried with her in the tomb.

Prayer.—O Mary, the purest of Virgins ! terrified
at my weakness and at the dangeis that surround me,
I recommend to thy loving care with all confidence
the chastity of my soul and body.   Permit me not,
O Queen of the Angels, to be defiled by the least
stain after having been adorned with purity and
innocence, like a vessel of honour and glory.
Banish from my heart all sensual desires, evil
thoughts, and irregular affections.   To thy love, O
my good Mother, do I confide my heart ; purify it,
render it worthy to be offered to thy Beloved Son,
that, having here on earth imitated thee in the
most beautiful of thy virtues, I may enjoy with
thee for ever in heaven the happiness promised to
the clean of heart.   Amen.

Ejaculation.—Grant, O my God, that through
Mary I may belong entirely to Jesus !

Practice.—If you should meet with any contradiction to-day, preserve your peace of soul.

SIXTH DAY.

THE ANNUNCIATION OF THE MOST HOLY VIRGIN.

WE read in the Gospel that the Angel Gabriel visited Our Lady in the town of Nazareth ; and, as the word ' Nazareth ' signifies ' flowers,' well is the Church represented in this town ! What, in fact, is the Church but a house or a town adorned with flowers? All actions performed according to her laws are as so many flowers. Mortifications, humiliations, prayers—in short, all pious exercises are acts of virtue, which, like most beautiful flowers, diffuse a pleasing fragrance before God.   Most justly, then, may we call the Christian religion a garden of flowers, that are delightful to the sight and most salutary to those who breathe the air impregnated by their fragrance.   Our Lady herself was a flower distinguished for beauty and excellence above all other flowers—a flower of incomparable fragrance, possessed of the power of producing many other flowers: *Hortus conclusus, soror mea, sponsa*—' *Thou,*' says the sacred Spouse in the Canticles, ' *art a garden enclosed :*' a garden all studded with the most magnificent flowers that can be produced.   Now, tell me to whom belong so many charming and sweet-scented flowers, with which the Church is so gloriously adorned, but to the Most Holy Virgin, since they were produced by her example? It is through her that Holy Church is so well furnished with roses in the martyrs who were invincible in their constancy; with every kind of flower, in the confessors who were nursed in her bosom; and with sweet violets, in so many holy widows, who lowly, humble, and hidden, diffuse the most odoriferous sweetness. In fine, is it indeed not to her that belong, in a special manner, so many lilies of purity and spotless virginity, innocent souls, bright and clear as a resplendent mirror? There can be no doubt, that if so many virgins have consecrated their hearts and bodies to His Divine Majesty, by indissoluble vows, it was that they might imitate the example of the Most Holy Virgin.

She was the first to consecrate her body, her heart, and her whole self to God, by the vow of virginity. Hardly had she been *drawn* by God than she quickly drew after her a large number of souls who consecrated themselves to God in like manner, under her sacred auspices, in order that they might run in the way of inviolable chastity and virginity: *Adducentur regi virgines post eam.* You, beloved souls, were seen by the glorious Virgin, when she exclaimed: *Curremus*—' *We shall run ;*' thus assuring her Beloved that many would follow her standard, and that under her protection they might combat and vanquish every kind of enemy.

What an honour for us to be able to walk under the standard of the Queen of Virgins ! Our Lady is undoubtedly the honour, the Protectress, and model of all Christians, of men and women of all classes who live virtuously; yet, undoubtedly, young virgins contract by their virginity a closer alliance with her than other Christians, for their resemblance to her in purity enables them more easily and more closely to approach her.*

It is said that when the Angel came down from heaven to venerate the spotless Virgin, and announce to her the Incarnation of the Son of God in her most chaste womb, she was *alone* in her room. Faithful souls are here instructed to have a love of retirement from the world, but this is not enough; they ought also to retire within themselves that they may lead a solitary life, and thus render themselves better prepared to enjoy the conversation of their Beloved. Each should look upon his heart as a celestial cabinet where he lives alone with Him. O faithful souls, if you conceal yourselves thus, the Angels will know how to find you, as the Archangel Gabriel found Mary because she was alone.

* *It is the opinion of a Doctor of the Church that the Holy Virgin Mary instituted some congregations of young girls, and that when she lived at Ephesus with the Apostle St. John she gave rules and constitutions to one of them. How happy were those Religious to have been instituted by the Queen of Doctors, who gathered her wisdom from her Son, who is the Wisdom of the Eternal Father !—'Month of Mary.' St. Francis of Sales.*

Nothing should be so pleasing to holy virgins and to true Religious as this state of withdrawal, because they then contemplate better the beauty of their Divine Spouse dwelling in the depths of their hearts.   On this account the Psalmist said that 'All the beauty of the King's Daughter is within'—*Omnis gloria filiæ regis ab intus.* The greatest diligence is necessary to preserve and increase this interior beauty, and at the same time to guard it continually from everything that could tarnish it, remembering that although men see only the exterior, the Divine Spouse penetrates into the inmost recesses of the heart.   This is the motive which induces the loving spouse (I speak of a soul consecrated to the Divine service, in order to please God alone), to live retired within her own heart, and thus prepare an acceptable abode for His Divine Majesty.   It is on this account that solitude is so much recommended to religious persons ; its utility is seen by the diligence with which Our Lady practised it, and which merited for her the sublime privilege of being chosen to be the Mother of God !

Our Lord being the only rest of those who have abandoned all worldly cares in order to listen to Him speaking to their hearts in solitude, it follows that if they do not attend to the interior word of Jesus Christ that solitude becomes a long martyr-dom to them.   Instead of being the habitation of peace and tranquillity their solitude is a cause of sadness and disquiet.

Those who lead like Martha a life of great activity may still enjoy the tranquillity of Mary, if they are careful to refer all their works to God : this *one aim* being *the eye which touches the heart of the Divine Spouse.* In order not to lose the security of our habitation, we must seek it, not so much in a *cell*, as in *God Himself.* Thrice happy are they who dwell in this House, which not only belongs to God, but is God Himself, for He will be their abiding rest throughout ages of ages.

Spiritual Flowers.

Whatever flower the bee rests upon, it always extracts honey from it. So will it be with an interior soul : if she never leave her home but when it is necessary for the glory of God, she will always return to it laden with the honey of good works.—*A Father of the Desert.*

When grace speaks it is time to act, not to hold discourse. Long prayers unaccompanied by mortification are nothing in the sight of God, but time spent uselessly —*St. Teresa.*

Whoever abandons prayer casts himself into hell.—*The same.*

Holy prayer is a water of benediction, which refreshes the plants of our good desires and makes them flourish. It washes our souls from their imperfections, and extinguishes the fire of passion in our hearts.—*St. Francis of Sales.*

EXAMPLE.

St. Bernard's Love for Mary.

The luminous star of the Middle Ages, St. Bernard, who was the soul of the Crusades instituted for the defence of religion and of civilized Europe, the counsellor of Bishops, Popes, and Kings, may be said to have had infused into him at his baptism a special devotion to the Most Holy Virgin. In his tenderest infancy he leaped for joy when he saw by chance a picture of Mary, or when he heard her name pronounced. He was ever thinking of her, and wished everyone to be speaking to him always of her. To correct in him those defects which are common to childhood, it sufficed to tell him that such and such a thing was displeasing to Mary, and he immediately took care not to repeat the fault, and he eagerly embraced those practices of piety which he was told were dear to her. She, on her side, did not delay to manifest the care she took of him, and undoubtedly the great love he had for holy purity was a special gift from the Queen of Virgins. Other favours, however, were in store for him in the hands of his powerful benefactress.

On Christmas Eve the young Bernard was waiting in the church with his relations for the commencement of the midnight service, when, having inclined his head, he fell into a kind of ecstasy, and saw in spirit, by means of supernatural light, the mystery of Bethlehem, and he quietly contemplated the Divine Infant miraculously born from the virginal womb of His Mother. This vision penetrated him with so warm a feeling of gratitude towards Jesus and Mary, that he immediately promised to consecrate himself entirely to their love and service henceforth. The writings of St. Bernard breathe a tender piety towards Mary, and unite all the most beautiful and moving expressions of love and veneration for her, which were written in former ages, and he united in his heart all the affections of the most zealous of her servants. With what respect, confidence, and love towards this good Mother are we penetrated when we read the pious works that he has written for her glory! His emotion, when under the influence of these sentiments, frequently rapt him in ecstasy.

Prayer of St. Andrew of Crete.—Hail, Mary, full of grace, the Lord is with you! Hail you, O source of our joy! through you the sentence of our condemnation was changed into a sentence of benediction! Hail, O Temple of the glory of God, sacred dwelling of the King of the heavenly kingdom! You are truly blessed amongst all women, because you were chosen to be the Mother of your Creator, and all nations shall call you blessed.

O Mary, I place in you a holy confidence, and from you I expect my salvation. I shall walk without fear in the midst of all my enemies, if you will deign to number me amongst those whom you protect. Sincere love of you is the safest weapon with which to fight and overcome ; number me, then, amongst your children, for I have chosen you for my tender Mother. Amen.

Ejaculation.—*Sub tuum præsidium confugimus, sancta Dei Genitrix*—'We put ourselves under your powerful protection, O Holy Mother of God !'

Practice.—Recite to-day the *Angelus* with great fervour.

SEVENTH DAY.

THE EXCELLENCE OF THE VIRGINITY OF MARY.

LET us consider attentively the virtues that were practised by the Most Holy Virgin on the day of her glorious Annunciation. The first was virginity and purity so perfect that nothing can be compared to it amongst the purest creatures. Secondly, a most profound humility, united with a most ardent charity.

Although the angelic virtue of perfect chastity belongs more particularly to Angels than to men, nevertheless, Our Lady infinitely surpassed all the

Angels in this virtue, because it possessed three great excellences not conceded to the Angels.

The first is that in Mary it is fruitful, whilst in the Angels it is sterile. The virginity of Mary is not only fruitful in having produced and borne the sweet fruit of life, our Blessed Saviour, but it is fruitful also because it produces a multitude of virgins, for (as we observed in the preceding consideration) if so many young persons dedicate and consecrate their purity to God, it is that they may follow her example. But the pure virginity of Mary not only possesses the property of being fruitful, it can also restore virginal purity in those souls who have defiled this virtue by the contrary vice. In her lifetime she had already called many virgins to follow her, who became her inseparable companions; among others, St. Martha and St. Marcella. But it was also through her means that St. Mary Magdalen, who had been the scandal of Jerusalem, was enrolled after her conversion under the standard of virginal purity, and became like a brilliant crystal vase, capable of receiving and containing the most precious waters of grace.

The virginity of Our Lady, therefore, is not sterile, like that of the Angels, but it is so fruitful that from the moment she vowed it to God, until the present time, it has always borne its fruit. A soul that is perfectly dedicated to the service of God is never alone; many others, drawn by the sweetness of its perfumes, flock after to copy its

example. It is on this account that the Spouse says
to her Beloved: *Trahe me post te, curremus*—'*Draw
me and we shall run.*'

Secondly, the virginity and chastity of the
Blessed Virgin surpassed that of the Angels in this,
that they are chaste by nature ; and we do not,
properly speaking, praise a person for the gifts of
nature, since praise is not due where there is no
merit.   But the virginity of the Most Holy Virgin
is, on the contrary, worthy of praise, because it was
chosen and preferred by her, and consecrated by
her to God.   Although she was united in marriage
to St. Joseph, it was without any prejudice to her
virginity, because he to whom she was espoused had
also consecrated his virginity to God.

Thirdly, the virginity of Our Lady surpassed that
of the Angels, because it was subjected to the
severest trials, whilst that of the Angels could
never be tempted or tried.   In this sense St.
Augustine, addressing the Angels, says : ' It is not
difficult for you, O blessed spirits ! to be pure and
remain virgins, because you neither are, nor can be,
tempted.'

Some may, perhaps, wonder that I have said that
the purity of Our Lady was exposed to the severest
trials ; and yet so it was.   But we must not
suppose that these trials were similar to our own.
As she was all purity, these assaults could not be
like our own.   The temptations which come to us,
who, unhappily, bear their incentives within our

hearts, could never have ventured to approach that
wall of her virginal integrity.   But was it not a
great trial for Our Lady when the Angel appeared to
her in human form ?   And did she not manifest
this in the fear and perturbation which assailed her,
so that the Angel was obliged to reassure her in
these words : *Ne timeas, Maria*—' *Fear not, Mary* '?
By them he wished to remove the disquiet which
her virginal purity suffered ; it was as if he were
to say : You see me in human form, but I am
no man, nor do I come to you on the part of any
man.

Modesty, says a holy Doctor, is, as it were, the
sacristan of chastity.   The sacristan of a church
keeps an eye always to the altars, that nothing may
be stolen, and he fastens the door with care.   In
like manner virginal souls are jealous to preserve
this virtue unspotted, and no sooner do they perceive danger, or even the shadow of danger, than
they are quickly alarmed.   Thus it was with the Most
Blessed Virgin, who was not only the Virgin *par
excellence* of all in heaven and on earth, but also the
most humble of all, and she manifested in this
mystery of the Annunciation, the most sublime act
of humility that a pure creature could make.
When she heard herself called by the Angel *full of
grace*, and received the announcement that she
should become the Mother of a Son Who was to be
both God and Man, she was troubled, and filled
with fear ; because, although she had conversed

familiarly with the Angels, she had never heard
them utter a single word in her praise.

The Most Holy Virgin would here teach us the
dangers to which purity is exposed by the desire of
praise.   Humility is the inseparable and necessary
companion of virginity, which could not long be
maintained in a soul that was not humble.   It
is true that in persons who live in the world one of
these virtues may subsist without the other, as we
see in the married life, but in regard to virgins, it
must be absolutely asserted that one who does not
profess both these virtues has neither of them
except in appearance.

Our Lady, being reassured by the Angel, and
having understood what her Lord had decreed to
work within her, made a sublime act of humility,
saying : *Ecce ancilla Domini, fiat mihi secundum
verbum tuum*—'Behold the handmaid of the Lord,
be it done unto me according to Thy word.'   It
was thus she expressed herself at the very moment
when she saw herself raised to the sublimest dignity
that can be imagined.   An incomparable dignity,
indeed, is that of Mother of God, but it does not
disturb the humility of Mary.   Although she is
raised above all creatures, nevertheless she simply
declares that she is, and ever will be, the servant of
His Divine Majesty ; and to show the truth of her
protest she adds : *Fiat mihi secundum verbum tuum :*
'Be it done unto me according to Thy word.'
She abandons herself to the Divine Will, and pro-

claims that of her own choice she would never have come forth from her state of humility and lowly self-esteem. How well did the Most Holy Virgin know that humility is ever the inseparable and necessary companion of virginity!

Although, as we have said, humility and virginity can dwell singly in persons who live in the world, yet such a separation can never be made between humility and charity, these virtues being absolutely inseparable. They are like the ladder of Jacob, by which the Angels ascended and descended. This was not done simultaneously, but alternately; the Angels descending first, and then ascending afterwards. Similarly, as soon as humility has abased us, charity quickly raises us up towards heaven. It might seem that the virtue of humility in some degree removes us from God, Who is at the summit of this mysterious ladder, because it causes us to descend very low in self-abasement. On the contrary, however, in proportion as we lower ourselves we become more and more worthy to mount towards the summit of this mystical ladder of perfection, where our Heavenly Father awaits us. Our Lady, then, obtained the dignity of Mother of God by abasing herself, and acknowledging herself unworthy of it; for scarcely had she protested her lowliness, and abandoned herself, by an act of incomparable charity, to the Divine Will, than the mystery was accomplished. If we thus regulate our conduct, and, in imitation of Mary, unite virginity with humility, we shall be certainly helped by charity. This Divine gift will lift us up the mystical ladder of Jacob, and introduce us into the presence of the Eternal Father, Who will enrich us with every kind of heavenly consolation. We shall sing canticles of Divine praise with our most holy Patroness, and eternally glorify Our Lord for the grace we have obtained to imitate her virtues, and fight under her standard.

SPIRITUAL FLOWERS.

Humility made the Son of God descend from Heaven into the immaculate bosom of Mary, and by the same virtue we may also cause Him to descend into our souls.—*St. Teresa.*

It is not humility to acknowledge ourselves to be miserable, for this needs but a little understanding of our condition, but to *wish* and *desire* to be treated as such is true Christian humility.—*St. Francis of Sales.*

We ought never to make use of our heart, eyes, and words for the indulgence of our own humours and inclinations, but only for the service of the Celestial Spouse.—*The same.*

EXAMPLE.

The Love of St. Alphonsus for Mary.

The love of St. Alphonsus Liguori for the Blessed Virgin Mary was so burning that he desired to inflame with it the hearts of all mankind. He was often heard to say: 'O men, what are you doing? Why so much affection for earthly creatures, for false deceivers, who make you lose both body and soul, both Paradise and God? How is it you love not Mary, who is ever most amiable, most loving, and most faithful; and who, after having enriched you with consolations and graces in this life, will obtain for you from her Divine Son the eternal glory of Paradise?'

He loved her so tenderly from his childhood, that one day he said to her quite simply: 'O my sweet Virgin Mary, I do not wish that there should be anyone in the world who loves and honours you more than I do;' and this desire of his heart was fully gratified. He thought of her even in sleep, and made use of this tender aspiration: 'O Mary, how beautiful you are! O how beautiful you are!' No one could speak to him without receiving a recommendation to be devout to Mary. 'Be devout to the Holy Virgin Mary,' he would say; 'whoever is devout to her will certainly be saved.' He inculcated the pious practices of visiting her images, reciting the Rosary, and fasting in her honour, on Saturdays and on the vigils of her festivals. But in a special manner he wished all to recite, every morning and evening, three *Ave Marias* in commemoration of her Immaculate Conception and perpetual virginity, adding this ejaculation to each Ave Maria: 'By your sacred virginity and Immaculate Conception, O Mary, obtain for me purity and sanctity of soul and body.' He gave pictures of her to everyone, saying: ' Here is the image of your Heavenly Mother; give her your love and confidence.' At other times he repeated: ' Love the good Virgin much, because Mary is the Mother of perseverance; and whoever loves Jesus and Mary will become holy.'

Prayer.—O Mary! you are truly the valiant woman in whom the Lord found rest, and whom He has chosen to be the depositary of all His treasures. The universe honours you as the most pure sanctuary of the Divinity, the true Temple of the Lord, in which was begun the salvation of the world, and in which took place the grand reconciliation between God and man. You are that privileged field which sin could not enter and devastate; you are that magnificent garden in which Our Lord planted all the flowers that adorn His Church. You, O Mary, are the Paradise of God, whence springs the fountain of living water which waters and fructifies the earth: obtain for me, by your powerful intercession, that, being washed in this-most pure water, I may be admitted with you to the nuptials of the Immaculate Lamb. Amen.

Ejaculation.—Most pure Virgin, pray for us.

Practice. — In temptations against holy purity invoke Mary, Virgin and Mother.

⁻ EIGHTH DAY.

THE VISITATION.

THOUGH Mary had thus humbled herself before God, she did not stop there, because she knew that humility and charity do not attain their highest degree of perfection until, for God's sake, they are exercised in behalf of our neighbour. True fraternal charity proceeds from the love of God, and in proportion as this increases, the love of our neighbour becomes more intense. The Apostle of Charity teaches us this truth, when he says : *Qui enim non diliget fratrem suum quem vidit, Deum quem non videt, quomodo potest deligere ?*—' For he that loveth not his brother whom he seeth, how can he love God whom he seeth not?' If we desire, then, to show our love to God, we must love our neighbour, we must serve him, help him, and relieve him in his necessities according to our power. How profoundly was the Blessed Virgin penetrated with this truth ! No sooner had she heard that her cousin had conceived in her old age, than she arose and went with haste (the Gospel says, *cum festinatione*) over the mountains of Judea to the city of Ephrem.

Consider that Mary is become the Mother of the Son of God, and having with all humility and sweetness obtained leave of her Holy Spouse to go and visit her cousin Elizabeth, she bade a painful adieu to all her neighbours. With great eagerness did the Most Holy Virgin undertake her long and fatiguing journey, as the Gospel says, she *went with haste !* The first movements of Him Whom she bears in her womb increased her fervour, and she began her journey with haste but without mental flurry. The Angels are ready to accompany her, and St. Joseph gladly conducts her. One would wish to have known something of the conversation of these two great souls, and willingly should we listen to the account thereof. It is probable that the Holy Virgin conversed only of Him Whom she bore within her, and breathed only for her Saviour. St. Joseph, on his side, thinks only of his Redeemer, Who moves his heart with a thousand sentiments and affections. As wine locked up in the cellar acquires the scent of the flowery vines, so the heart of this Holy Patriarch insensibly participates in the perfume and the vigour of the Divine Infant Who blooms in His beautiful vineyard. The profound humility which Mary exercised in serving one who was in every respect her inferior, is indeed most worthy of our admiration. It is true that Elizabeth was of noble birth, because she was of the royal race of David, and was, moreover, united in marriage to the High Priest of the tribe of Levi. However, this nobility is nothing in comparison with that of the Most Holy Virgin, whose incomparable greatness can only be expressed by the title of Mother of God—*Mater Dei*—and yet where can

we find more profound humility? Her humble
heart is not satisfied with calling herself the handmaid of the Lord, but she leaves her house, and
for three entire months is as a handmaid to her
venerable cousin. The Gospel, moreover, gives us
to understand that when the Divine Mother entered
the house of Zacharias she was the first to give the
salutation, and this through her great humility: *In-
travit in domum Zachariæ et salutavit Elizabeth.*

Remark also the conduct of Our Lady amidst
the praises and blessings which Elizabeth bestowed
upon her. Assuredly it was very different from that
of women in the world, who instead of humbling
themselves when they are praised, become more
puffed up. Was it not vanity that possessed our
poor mother Eve, who, on hearing that she was
created to the image and likeness of God, became
thereby so presumptuous that she strove to become
equal to Him, and gave ear to all the suggestions of
the infernal enemy? But as the Most Holy Virgin
had come into the world to regain all that Eve had
lost by her vanity and pride, she thinks only of the
abyss of her nothingness, and calls herself the
handmaid of the Lord, although proclaimed by the
Angel His Mother; when she is declared by Elizabeth to be the most blessed of women, she replies
that her blessings are accorded because the Lord
has looked down upon her lowliness and her little-
ness: *Quia respexit humilitatem ancillæ suæ.* What
an excellent sign is humility of heart in a soul that

has made progress in the spiritual life! When such souls humble themselves before God and before all creatures, in proportion to the greatness of the favours received, and place all their happiness, like Mary, in this alone, that the Divine Goodness has looked down upon their lowliness and misery, it is a sure indication that the graces of God are not received in vain.

The effects of grace in the heart of the Most Blessed Virgin were a profound humility and a burning charity towards God and towards her neighbour. The Apostle St. Paul in relating to us the love that our Saviour bore to the virtue of humility, says that 'He humbled Himself unto death, even to the death of the Cross—*Humiliavit semetipsum usque ad mortem, mortem autem crucis ;* and he would have us learn from this that we should not be satisfied to have practised this virtue in some particular circumstances, nor for a certain time, but that we must practise it always and on all occasions. We must practise this virtue not only *until death* but *unto the death of the Cross ;* that is to say, unto the perfect mortification of ourselves, humbling our self-esteem and our self-love. Let us not deceive ourselves by a certain appearance of humility ; as, for instance, in speaking of our imperfections, or in performing external acts of reverence and humility, for the virtue of humility does not consist in this. True and Christian humility makes us esteem ourselves absolutely as nothing, as unworthy to live, as deserving only of universal contempt. It moves us to embrace generously the precept of our Saviour, that we renounce ourselves if we wish to follow Him : *Si quis vult post me venire, abneget semetipsum.*

Spiritual Flowers.

Humility is the root of every virtue. As the flower receives its nourishment from the root, and withers when it is cut off from it, so virtue, however perfect it may be, languishes and dies if it be not rooted in humility.—*Nouet.*

Bees suck honey from the lily, the iris and the rose ; but they draw it also from the smallest flowers, such as rosemary and thyme. Indeed, they gather more honey from the latter, and it is of a better quality ; because more closely confined in the smaller flowers and better preserved. Thus is charity practised, both more frequently and with more humility, in lowly exercises of devotion, and consequently with greater perfection and holiness.—*Francis of Sales.*

Example.

The Pilgrimage of St. Francis of Sales to Loreto.

St. Francis of Sales was always thinking of the honour of the Most Blessed Virgin, and had made a vow from his youth to visit the holy Chapel of Loreto. In his travels through Italy, made by order of his father, his great desire was to fulfil the

promise he had made to venerate the Most Holy
Virgin in the Sanctuary where she had received
the visit of the Angel and the sublime dignity of
becoming the Mother of God, and he did so with
wonderful piety. He was rapt in admiration in
beholding those walls that had enclosed such
wonders. He prayed motionless for a long time
before the Altar of the Queen of Heaven, thank-
ing her devoutly for all she had done for himself,
exhorting her to continue her holy protection, and
renewing his promise to imitate her angelic virtue
of purity during his whole life. Ineffable were the
graces and consolations that he then received ; his
mind was illumined by celestial light, and his heart
was inflamed with such ardent charity, that from
that moment nothing appeared to him impossible,
when there was question of the glory of God and
the salvation of souls.

Prayer of St. Germanus.—Hail Mary ! you are
the hope of Christians, and it is in this quality that
I turn myself to you. Receive, O tender Mother,
the prayer addressed to you by a poor sinner, but a
penitent sinner, who honours you, and who, after
God, places in you all his hope for his conversion
and salvation. I am indebted to you for so many
graces, but grant me, I beseech you, one grace
more. Confirm me and establish me in the grace
and love of your Divine Son. You are the consolation of the afflicted ; deign, then, to intercede in
my favour with your Divine Son, my Saviour,

Jesus, that He may deliver me from the burden of my sins, dissipate the darkness of my understanding, remove every irregular affection from my heart, and restrain all the efforts and temptations of my enemies, that, being aided by this grace, I may henceforth so order my life that, under your protection, I may arrive at the happy port of eternal life.   Amen.

Ejaculation.—O Holy Virgin ! may I always remember you, and have recourse to you in all my necessities.

Practice.—Visit the altar of Mary, either in the church or in your room, to obtain from her sorrow for your sins.

NINTH DAY.

THE CHARITY OF MARY IN THE VISITATION.

WE must not imagine that the Blessed Virgin Mary was moved to undertake this long journey to visit her cousin, St. Elizabeth, by curiosity to know if what the Angel had told her were true, for she had not the slightest doubt of it.   Our Blessed Lady was moved by a secret impulse of God, Who wished to commence the work of Redemption and the sanctification of souls in this visit, by the sanctification of the infant St. John.

The most ardent charity and most profound humility animated her, and gave her wings to fly

across the mountains of Judea, and these two
virtues were also the cause of her journey. As
St. Ambrose says, charity or grace knows no
delays nor cold deliberations: *Nescit tarda molimina
sancti spiritus gratia.* It need not therefore surprise
us if the Most Holy Virgin, filled as she was with
charity (because she bore in her womb Him Who
is Love itself), should exercise it in continual acts
towards God, to Whom she was closely united by
the sacred bond of perfect love, and towards her
neighbours, whom she loved so tenderly and
sincerely that she sighed for the salvation and
·sanctification of the whole world. She went with
all alacrity, because she knew with what happy
results her visit would be attended, in the person
of St. John, and also because she wished to con-
gratulate her cousin who, notwithstanding her age
and sterility, had conceived the long-predicted
precursor of the Word Incarnate. She went that
they might rejoice together, and excite each other
to glorify the God of all mercy, and to thank Him
for so many favours and benedictions.

St. Luke would teach us by the words, *Exurgens
Maria abiit cum festinatione in montana in civitatem
Juda*—' Mary arose and went into the mountain
country with haste, into a city of Judea '—the care
and readiness with which we also ought to correspond to the Divine inspirations. As it is the work
of the Holy Spirit to banish all tepidity and
negligence from the heart, so He would have us

execute His Divine Will with all care and diligence, and He is offended by any kind of delay. The virginal purity of Mary, which so dearly loved solitude, also caused her to go with haste, for the best protection for virginal purity is to appear as little as possible in the tumult of the world.

Having reached the house of Zachary, she entered it. She saluted Elizabeth. The Evangelist does not relate that she saluted Zachary also, for her love of purity was so great that she spoke little with men. Let virgins learn from this that they cannot take too great care for the preservation of this virtue.

Who can imagine the sweet fragrance of this most beautiful lily in the house of Zachary during the three months that she remained there? How well did she spend every instant! What honey, what precious balsam, must those sacred lips have distilled in the few but excellent words that they uttered! Indeed, Mary could speak only that which filled her heart, and *that* was Jesus!

Let us consider the meaning of the words, that 'Elizabeth was filled with the Holy Ghost'—*Et repleta est Spiritu Sancto Elisabeth*—that Elizabeth, who had already received the Holy Ghost with all His gifts, received a new fulness and a new increase of grace by this visit. Although the Lord grants His graces to the just *in full measure*, yet, as the Gospel says, this measure can be so augmented as to overflow on all sides: *Mensuram bonam confertam et coagitatam et superaffluentem dabunt in sinum vestrum.*

Let us well understand this important truth. The grace of the Holy Ghost can never be granted to us in this life in such full measure that it cannot be augmented ; therefore, let us beware of saying : 'It is enough ; I am sufficiently enriched with graces and virtues. *Mensura conferta est —* the measure is filled up, further progress in mortification is unnecessary.' He who should speak thus would only show too clearly'his misery, or, rather, his presumption, and the great danger to which he exposes himself. *Omni habenti dabitur et abundabit, ei autem qui non habet et quod videtur habere auferetur ab eo.* This text signifies that to him who has received much—that is to say, who has laboured much, and never gives up—much shall be given. Such a one believes that he has never done enough ; but, conscious of his own misery, he continues to labour with holy and sincere humility. *He, then, who possesses much, shall receive with usury, and superabundantly ;* but from him who profits not by the grace received, letting it lie idle and fruitless, because he believes he is rich enough, *from him shall be taken that which he thinketh himself to possess and that which he does not possess.* This means, that graces already received shall be taken away, because he has not traded with them, and those which have been prepared for him shall not be bestowed upon him, since he has rendered himself unworthy of them by his negligence. All this, however, is not to be understood of *sufficient* grace, which is never denied by God to anyone, but of *efficacious* grace, which, by a just judgment of God, is not granted to tepid and ungrateful souls.

The thirst for riches and honours, by which worldlings are tormented, never allows them to say, *Enough.* And yet they ought to be contented with a little, for experience teaches us that the highest dignities and honours and great wealth frequently occasion the loss of souls. It is in regard of such temporal matters that we should say, *I have sufficient.* But, with regard to spiritual goods, let us never believe that we possess them in sufficient abundance, so long as we remain in this land of exile, but let us make every possible effort *to advance day by day from virtue to virtue.*

Experience teaches us that plants and fruits do not attain maturity until they have produced their seeds, which are necessary for the reproduction of their species. In the same way our virtues will never be sufficiently perfected, or reach their maturity, until they produce within us an ardent desire to make further progress. This desire is the spiritual seed which produces new degrees of virtue.

SPIRITUAL FLOWERS.

Mary is a most beautiful rose, which dared not open its petals even to the gentle breeze of an Angel !—*St. Ambrose.*

How precious and how delicate a flower is purity ! A sigh, a look, a word is enough to wither it ! On this account chaste souls continually distrust themselves, and flee from the slightest occasions of danger.—*Nouet.*

The rose is the symbol of love and charity; its petals are red, and formed like a heart. Such should be the actions of the spouses of Jesus Christ. They should have as many hearts as they have petals—that is to say, hearts full of love, and like petals in the little esteem they should have of their actions.—*St. Francis of Sales.*

EXAMPLE.

Consecration of the Saturday to Mary.

Holy Church is ever desirous to maintain a tender devotion in the hearts of the faithful towards the Most Blessed Virgin, and from the earliest ages of Christianity she has encouraged the consecration of the Saturday to her. It is related that there was in the church of Santa Sofia at Constantinople a picture of the Mother of God which was veiled during the rest of the week, but on Friday evening the veil was raised without human aid, and lowered

on the evening of Saturday.   Thus did Almighty
God manifest His Will that *Saturday* should be
dedicated to Mary.   It was on Saturday she took
so great a part in the work of our redemption,
and it was fitting that on the morrow of the day
when she so bitterly wept over the sorrowful scene
of Calvary we should remember her tears shed for
us in a special manner.   Again, on Saturday God
rested from His work in the creation of the world,
and the Church consecrates this day to her, to
honour the mysterious repose of the Holy Ghost
in her Immaculate Heart, and that of Our Blessed
Saviour in her chaste womb.   Saturday is the
introduction to Sunday—the symbol of eternal
rest—and the Holy Virgin is truly invoked under
the title of 'Gate of Heaven'—*Janua Cœli.*

Saturday, moreover, is the day between Friday,
the day of mourning, and Sunday, the day of joy—
and the Holy Virgin is the mediatrix between God,
Who is Eternal Beatitude, and man, who is subject
to endless evils and miseries.   Mary is the way to
arrive at Jesus, and Saturday is a prelude to the
solemnity of Sunday.   Saturday is as a magnificent
portal consecrated to the Mother of God, by which
we enter the Sanctuary of God Himself.   The
Saints held this day in great esteem—on it they
redoubled their pious exercises—and many begged,
as a signal favour, that they might die on a
Saturday.

Prayer.—O Sovereign Queen of Angels! you

7

are the Mother of Orphans, as your faithful servant, St. Bonaventnre, says: *Mater Orphanorum.* Sinners are truly orphans—for they have had the misfortune to lose their God, the most tender of Fathers. To you, therefore, I have recourse, O Mother of Mercy. I have had the misfortune to lose my true Father, by sin; and yet, since you have not abandoned me, O my Mother, I feel a lively hope that through your goodness you will deign to intercede for me, and reconcile me to my Father, Whom I have so grievously offended. O Holy Virgin! he alone can perish who does not have recourse to you. I confess, indeed, that I am a most unworthy sinner, and, nevertheless, to you do I fly, animated by sweet confidence in your love. Your mercy is greater than all my miseries; and, although my iniquities are enormous, they will never exhaust the treasures of your Son's mercy, nor your own. I sincerely detest, from my heart, all my sins, and hope, through your intercession, for a general pardon. Amen.

Ejaculation.—O Mother of God and my Mother, the confidence I place in you is to me a pledge of my eternal salvation.

Practice.—Let all your prayers and actions this day be offered in suffrage for the holy souls in Purgatory.

TENTH DAY.

BY THE VISIT OF MARY, ELIZABETH IS FILLED WITH THE HOLY GHOST.

LET us continue our Meditation on the sweet mystery of the Visitation.

The visit which this incomparable Virgin made to St. Elizabeth was not useless, nor, like the visits of worldly people, a matter of ceremony. Such visits result in harm to the conscience, in offences against chastity or charity. The Most Holy Virgin was induced to visit her cousin Elizabeth from pure motives of charity, and the days she spent with her were not employed in useless occupations, but in praising and magnifying God. How holy, pious, and devout was not this visit! It filled the whole house of Zachary with the Holy Spirit, and admirable effects were produced in St. Elizabeth. The first effect was humility. As soon as Our Lady appeared in the house of her cousin the Saint was filled with astonishment at such a favour, and exclaimed: *Unde hoc mihi ut veniat Mater Domini mei ad me?*—'Whence is this to me, that the Mother of my God should come unto me?' This is the virtue that the Holy Ghost first produces within us; a profound humility, which forces us to annihilate ourselves in the sight of the infinite greatness of God, and acknowledge our own baseness and worthlessness.

The second effect was to confirm St. Elizabeth in faith, as is gathered from the words she addressed to the Most Holy Virgin: 'Blessed art thou that hast believed; blessed art thou among women, and blessed is the fruit of thy womb'—*Beata es quæ crededisti; benedicta tu inter mulieres, et benedictus fructus ventris tui.* Indeed, one of the chief operations of the Holy Spirit is to ground us in faith and convert us entirely to God, and make us acknowledge Him as the Source of all the graces and blessings granted to mortal beings.

Truly may St. Elizabeth have said, you are blessed amongst all women, but your blessedness proceeds from the Fruit of your womb, the God of blessings. We do not usually praise the fruit on account of the tree, but the tree on account of the excellence of its fruit. Thus, although we ought to render to the Most Holy Virgin a worship or veneration beyond that which we render to the Saints, yet our homage and veneration should never equal that which we give to God. God alone should be sovereignly adored; but, as the Most Holy Virgin is the Mother of Our Saviour, and a co-operator in our redemption, she is worthy of such a special worship as all true Christians have ever given to her. When the Holy Spirit dwells within us, we love and praise God alone above all things, as our Sovereign Creator; and after Him, Mary, His Most Holy Mother.

The third effect that the Holy Ghost produces in those upon whom He descends is a complete change of heart, as is represented in the joy of the Baptist yet unborn : *Ecce enim ut facta est vox salutationis tuæ in auribus meis, exultavit infans in utero meo*—'Behold, as soon as the voice of thy salutation sounded in my ears,' said Elizabeth to Our Lady, 'the Infant leaped in my womb.' Thus was St. John sanctified, going forth as it were out of himself, and casting himself before his Maker. And so it is with those who receive the Holy Spirit : they go out of themselves and lose themselves in God ; that is to say, they live no longer according to nature and the senses, but they follow the inspirations of grace. If you desire, then, to know whether you have received the Holy Ghost, examine your actions.

It was through the intervention of Most Holy Mary that St. Elizabeth received the Holy Spirit. This teaches us that we should make use of her as a mediatrix with her Divine Son in order to obtain heavenly graces. It is true that we can address ourselves directly to God in our petitions, without employing the mediation of the Most Holy Virgin or the Saints ; but this is not according to the order ordained by God, Who wished that there should be a communication between us and His Saints. Hence the Church militant and triumphant form but one Church, directed and governed equally, though differently, by God Himself ; and

He wishes us to have recourse to Him through the Most Holy Virgin and the Saints, and He bestows the most precious graces upon us by their intercession.

For the concluding point of this meditation we may add that it is of the greatest advantage to our souls to be visited by the Most Blessed Virgin; and her visits are always accompanied by many blessings and graces, as in the case of St. Eliza-beth. O God! you will say, I do, indeed, desire that she would deign to honour me with one of her visits during prayer, since her visits fill the soul with sweet consolation. However, we must bear in mind that Mary often visits us with inspira-tions and interior lights, to aid our progress in perfection ; and these are precisely the visits that we are unwilling to receive.

Endeavour to receive Holy Communion devoutly, and you will contract a spiritual relationship with the Most Holy Virgin, since the Most Precious Body of Our Saviour, which we receive in Holy Communion, was formed by the Holy Ghost of her most pure blood.

In this manner, and by the imitation of her virtues, the relationship which you will contract with her will be much more excellent and more pleasing to her than that of Elizabeth, which was merely of flesh and blood. Our Lord says : 'Whosoever shall do the will of My Father Who is in heaven, he is My brother, and sister, and mother' (Matt. xii. 50).

In order to have some share in the visits of this Holy Virgin, we must not look for consolations, but generously resolve to accept even contempt and sorrow. In fact, Mary did not visit St. Elizabeth until she had suffered the ignominy and humiliation of her sterility. It is impossible to lead a devout life without trouble, and merit is in proportion to suffering. Finally, if we desire to receive the favour of this visitation, we must be transformed ; we must die to self, and live only to God and for God: in a word, we must humble ourselves profoundly, according to the example of St. Elizabeth. Be faithful then, pious souls, in this exercise, during this short and miserable life, that you may afterwards chant eternally in heaven with the Most Holy Virgin : *Magnificat anima mea Dominum !*—'My soul doth magnify the Lord!'

My God ! how ashamed I am to be still so full of myself, when I have so often come to Holy Communion ! O dear Jesus ! may we always bear Thee in our hearts, that we may no longer breathe but Thee ? How is it that I am so little united to Thee, since Thou art always in me ? Why do I stray so far from Thee, whilst Thou art always close to me ? Thou dwellest in my heart, how is it that I do not abide in Thine ?

Spiritual Flowers.

Chastity is the unblemished beauty of the Saints, which, like the rose, adorns the soul and body, and fills them with sweet and pleasing fragrance.—*St. Ephrem.*

A slight breath of wind suffices to make the flowers fall from the trees in spring ; and sometimes one flattering word, of itself, is enough to ruin a chaste soul, which is infinitely more delicate and tender than any flower.—*Nouet.*

As the bee gathers from flowers the dew of heaven and the sweetest juice of the earth, forming it into honey and carrying it to its hive, so the Priest takes from the altar our Blessed Saviour (the true Son of God, Who descended like dew from heaven, and came forth from the Virgin Mary as a flower from the earth of our humanity), and places Him in your mouth, and He becomes to you a delicious and spiritual food.—*St. Francis of Sales.*

Example.

Devotion of St. Thomas Aquinas to the ' Ave Maria.'

The most tender devotion towards Mary was, as we may say, innate in St. Thomas Aquinas. One day, when he was a little child, his nurse observed that he kept a piece of paper in his hands, which she wished to take from him : but the child resisted

with loud cries, and made every effort to retain
it. This singular resistance excited the curiosity
of his pious mother, the Countess Theodora.
She therefore took hold of the piece of paper,
opened it, and found, to her surprise, written upon
it the Angelical Salutation. Whilst she was reading
it, the infant redoubled his cries and tears, so that
she was obliged to return it to him. Thomas had
no sooner received it, than putting it into his
mouth he swallowed it with great eagerness. This
fact foreshadowed the devotion which the Saint
ever had for the Angelical Salutation, on which he
has left us a most pious and learned commentary,
full of the praises of Mary.

Prayer.—Holy Virgin and my tender Mother!
You are the channel by which the graces of God
reach us ; you are the depositary of all celestial
treasures, and you yourself declare to us that you
possess all the wealth of heaven, to enrich those
that love you : *ut ditem diligentes me.* O Divine
Mother! you see that my poverty is great, and my
indigence extreme ; but remember, I beseech you,
that I trust in you, and hope that you will be
moved to compassionate my miseries, and to
obtain for me a remedy. I love you, O Holy
Virgin ; you are, after God, the great object of my
affections. Have compassion on me then, and
never abandon me to the snares of the enemies of
my salvation, but succour me during the whole
course of my life, and above all at the moment of

my death, so that I may come one day to your feet, in the abode of eternal happiness.　Amen.

Ejaculation.—O Holy Virgin, help those who groan in misery !

Practice.—Mortify self-love, by some act of obedience or meekness.

ELEVENTH DAY.

HUMILITY OF MARY.

THE Blessed Virgin Mary surpassed all the Angels and Saints in perfection and merit; and of all creatures none as she was so pleasing to God. Who, indeed, ever possessed so ardent a charity and so profound a humility?　Where shall we find humility equal to that which appeared in Mary when, in answer to Elizabeth, she confessed that the cause of her happiness was that the Lord had deigned to regard the humility of His handmaid, and that therefore all generations should call her blessed ?—*Quia respexit humilitatem ancillæ suæ ; ecce enim ex hoc beatam me dicent omnes genera tiones.*

Many Doctors of the Church are of opinion that, when Mary said, 'the Lord hath regarded the humility of His handmaid,' it was not her intention to speak of her virtue of humility, because, although she was profoundly humble, she did not believe herself to be so ; but that she thought only of her lowly state, her baseness, and abjection as a crea-

ture of God, and of the nothingness from which
she had been drawn.   There are others, however,
who hold a contrary, and perhaps more probable,
opinion, and say that Our Lady intended to speak
of her virtue of humility, being well aware that it
was this virtue that had attracted Our Saviour to
her chaste womb.   We may well believe that Mary
was aware that she possessed this virtue, and that
she had no fear of losing it, being intimately persuaded that it was the effect of the grace of God
within her and not of her own merits.

Indeed, we find the great St. Paul acknowledging
that he possessed the virtue of charity, and in such
decisive terms as would seem in others presumptuous rather than humble.   He writes : ' Who
shall separate me from the charity of Christ?'—*Quis
me separabit a charitate Christi?*   ' Shall tribulation,
or distress, or hunger, or nakedness, or danger, or
persecution, or the sword ?   I am sure that neither
death nor life nor Angels shall be able to separate
us from the love of God, which is in Christ Jesus
our Lord.'   See Rom. viii. 35-39.

Notice the confidence with which this great
Apostle speaks when he protests that there is no
power in the world, or in hell, that is capable of
separating him from the charity of his God.   He
believed that he possessed this virtue of charity;
and in speaking thus he confided entirely in grace,
and in his own merits *by grace.*   The glorious
Virgin knew well that the virtue of humility has

more power to attract the Heart of God to our hearts than all other virtues. The Divine Spouse in the Canticles seems to signify this, when he expresses his admiration for the beauty of the footsteps of his beloved : *Quam pulchri sunt gressus tui in calceamentis, filia principis !*—' How beautiful are thy steps in shoes, O Prince's daughter!' (Cant. vii. 1), and then enumerates her other beauties. Judith did not captivate Holofernes so much by the rare beauty of her countenance and the splendour of her attire as by her sandals, or her shoes, which were probably embroidered with gold.

In like manner the Eternal Father, considering the variety of virtues that adorned Our Lady, was in admiration of her beauty ; but when He cast His eyes upon her sandals He was so pleased that He sent His Only Son to become Incarnate in her chaste womb. What is signified by these sandals or shoes of Mary but her humility ? These articles are the least valuable part of our attire, and the soonest covered with dust. Now, the spirit of true humility continually abases the souls who possess it, and annihilates them in their own eyes, and keeps them under the feet of everyone. Such is the property of this virtue of humility, which is the foundation of the whole spiritual life. It was this lowliness that the Lord looked upon in the Most Holy Virgin with so much complacency, and this look of His formed her whole greatness : *Quia respexit humilitatem ancillæ suæ, ecce enim ex hoc beatam me dicent omnes generationes.*   All generations shall call her blessed *because* God had regarded her.

Whichever of the two significations given to these words : God hath regarded *the humility of His Handmaid* be accepted, we find that the Holy Virgin always spoke with so much humility as to leave no doubt whatever that she considered all her happiness to proceed from her Lord having looked upon her lowliness.   On this account the words of the Spouse of the Canticles are applied to her : *Dum esset Rex in accubitu suo nardus mea dedit odorem suum*—'While the King was at his repose, my spikenard sent forth the odour thereof.' The plant on which the spikenard grows does not grow up high like the cedars of Lebanon.   But lowly as it is, it delights all by the sweetness it diffuses around.   What a precious plant was the Most Holy Virgin, who never sought to exalt herself, although enriched by God with the most signal favours !   She was always penetrated by the sense of her own abjection and nothingness ; and in virtue of this humility she spread around, like the spikenard plant, so sweet a perfume that it ascended to the Throne of the Divine Majesty, and attracted the Son of God to descend and take flesh in her immaculate womb.

We see, then, how dear humility is to God ! Our Saviour taught this truth in His memorable reply to the woman who exclaimed aloud : *Beatus*

venter qui Te portavit et ubera quæ suxisti—'Blessed
is the womb that bore Thee, and the paps that
gave Thee suck.' 'Yea,' said Our Lord, 'rather,
blessed are they that hear the Word of God and
keep it'—*Quinimmo beati qui audiunt verbum Dei et
custodiunt illud.* That is to say: 'My Mother is
indeed blessed on account of having borne Me in
her womb; but more blessed is she on account of
the humility with which she listened to the words
of My Heavenly Father, and kept them.' And
this He again taught when He said that they who
heard the Word of God and practised it were to
Him as His Mother and His Brethren.

SPIRITUAL FLOWERS.

Jesus Christ built His throne upon the ruins of
the world. Before the fruits of grace can be
gathered the flowers of prosperity must fall.

The present moment's grace may be that which
will decide our eternity.—*Nepveu.*

The Heart of Mary is a garden of delights, in
which we can gather the most precious fruits.
This most beautiful garden is closed against the
impure spirit; it is full of Divine perfumes,
cultivated by a Heavenly Hand, and adorned with
the most charming flowers of virtue. Of these
there are three which particularly attract our
admiration, and fill the house of God with the
sweetest fragrance—they are the violet of humility,

the lily of chastity, and the rose of charity.—*St. Bernard.*

The less you seek after praise and your own interests, the more do you deserve to be praised and rewarded by God.

EXAMPLE.

Origin of the Rosary.

The Rosary of the B. V. M. in its present form was instituted by St. Dominic. But as early as the year 1094 Peter the Hermit had invented a kind of rosary of beads of wood, upon which the Crusaders, who were generally uneducated men, recited a certain number of *Paters* and *Aves*, varied according to the solemnity of the feasts.

Historians also relate that even before that time pious persons were in the habit of reciting a series of *Paters* and *Aves* upon knotted cords. In the East it was the custom to present crowns of roses to persons of distinction. St. Gregory Nazianzen, moved by ardent piety towards the Mother of Our Redeemer, offered to her, instead of a material crown of roses, a spiritual crown of prayers. It consisted of a long string of the highest praises and most glorious titles and excellent prerogatives of Mary.

St. Bridget, Patroness of Ireland, who lived in the fifth century, developed this pious idea of St. Gregory by substituting for those prayers which were unknown to the people the more popular and more beautiful prayers of the *Credo*, the *Pater*, and the *Ave Maria*. And to regulate the number of prayers to be recited, the Saint adopted the method of the anchorets of threading beads of stone or of wood together in the form of a crown or chaplet.

The word 'Rosary' signifies a crown of roses, and the prayers, the expression of the heart's affections, of which it is composed, are spiritual roses with which we adorn the head of our dear Blessed Mother.

It is said that a holy solitary was watching one day a poor old woman reciting her rosary with great devotion, when he observed an Angel by her side holding a golden thread, upon which he strung a rose for every *Ave*, and a lily for every *Pater;* afterwards he placed this garland in the form of a crown upon the head of the old woman, and disappeared, leaving behind him a sweet fragrance of roses. This fragrance was often perceived in former days in churches, after the recital of the Rosary.

Prayer.—O Mary, my good Mother! obtain for me an ardent love for your Divine Son, my Saviour Jesus Christ. From Him you can obtain all that you desire; obtain, then, for me the grace to be always so united to the Divine Will that. I may never again be separated from it. I ask you not, my Mother, for earthly goods, nor honours, nor riches; but I ask of you that which you have much more at heart, the grace to love my God.   Is it possible that you should refuse to assist me in a work which is so agreeable to you ?   No ; you will help me, my good Mother—you will pray for me. Pray then, O Sacred Virgin, and cease not to pray for me, until you see me in heaven, out of danger of losing my God, and certain of loving Him throughout eternity.   May I be able to thank Him for ever, with you, my good and charitable Mother, for so great a mercy.   Amen.

Ejaculation.—Make me like unto you, O Mary, who were so sweet and humble of heart.

Practice.—Make an act of external humility in union with Mary.

TWELFTH DAY.

THROUGH THE BLESSED VIRGIN MARY, ST. JOHN THE BAPTIST RECEIVES THE MOST SPECIAL GRACES.

WHO could number all the graces and favours showered upon the house of Zachary, when the Holy Virgin entered it ?   If Abraham received many graces for the hospitality he gave to three Angels; if Jacob was the cause of so many blessings to Laban, an idolater, in whose house he dwelt; if Lot was saved from the fire of Sodom, for having given shelter to two Angels ; if the Prophet Elias filled with oil all the vessels of the poor widow who entertained him ; if Eliseus raised to life the

8

son of the Sunamitess his hostess; if Obededom
obtained so many favours from Heaven, for receiving into his house the Ark of the Covenant—how
great and precious must have been the graces and
blessings poured upon the house of Zachary for
having lodged for three months the Angel of the
great Council, the Divine Prophet, the real Ark of
the Covenant, Our Lord Jesus Christ inclosed
in the immaculate womb of Mary! Who could
understand the Divine sweetness poured into the
heart of Elizabeth during the time of that Divine
visitation? How profound must have been her
meditation on the mystery of the Incarnation, and
what thanks must she have offered to God for all
the favours bestowed upon her. But, above all,
very special favours were conferred by Our Lord
upon His precursor St. John Baptist.

Firstly, according to the common opinion of
the Fathers, St. John received the use of reason;
secondly, from that moment he was sanctified;
and thirdly, he was filled with the knowledge of
God and of His Divine mysteries. Even then he
loved his Saviour, he adored Him, and leaped
for joy in His presence, as we learn from Elizabeth
herself, in the words she addressed to the Holy
Virgin: *Ecce enim ut facta est vox salutationis tuæ
in auribus meis, exultavit infans in gaudio in utero
meo*—'Behold, as soon as the voice of the Salutation sounded in my ears, the Infant in my womb
leaped for joy.'

Such extraordinary joy was not surprising. Jesus Christ, speaking to the Jews, says: *Abraham frater vester, exultavit ut videret diem Meum*— 'Abraham, your father, rejoiced to see My day.' All the prophets desired ardently the promised Messiah, and rejoiced that at His coming their predictions would be fulfilled. We may well believe, therefore, that St. John rejoiced at the presence of this long-desired Messiah, in the immaculate womb of the Holy Virgin, Who had come to visit him and begin the work of Redemption, delivering him from original sin. It would not have been fitting that he, who was chosen to prepare the way of the Lord, should, at his birth, bear the stain of original sin. On this account, therefore, Our Lady repaired to the house of St. Elizabeth, that the Child, Whom she bore and Who was the Sanctifier of souls, might, in this visit, purify the glorious St. John from original sin and sanctify him. This He did with such fulness of grace that many Doctors are of opinion that he never sinned even venially. The charity, of which the heart of our glorious Queen was full, caused her to co-operate in this work of sanctification. No wonder that she should have been so ardent in love and zeal for the salvation of men when she bore in her bosom Charity Itself, the Saviour and Redeemer of the world! All faithful souls should rejoice when they are visited by our Divine Saviour in the Most Holy Sacrament of the Altar, or by the

interior graces which are so often vouchsafed
them, or by the many inspirations and loving
words which He addresses to them when knocking
at the door of their hearts. Under what an obligation are they not to correspond to so many favours,
and with what care and fidelity should they not
fulfil the Most Holy Will of their Divine Saviour!

O my dear Sisters, Daughters of the Visitation
of Our Lady and of St. Elizabeth, since you have
Mary for your Mother, you should have nothing
so much at heart as to imitate her particularly in
her humility and charity. These are the two
virtues which especially animated her when she
visited the house of Zachary. Like her, you
should visit, diligently and joyfully, your Sisters,
when they are suffering, and endeavour to aid each
other in your spiritual and temporal infirmities.
Be most careful and diligent in those things in
which humility and charity are most required.
To be numbered amongst the Daughters of Our
Lady, it is not sufficient to live in a house of the
Visitation and wear the Religious habit. If you
would not wrong such a Mother, you must imitate
her in her virtues and the sanctity of her life. Be
careful, then, to conform your life to hers. Be
mild, sweet, humble, charitable, good ; magnify
Our Lord continually with her, and be assured,
beloved souls, that, if you fulfil your duties with
humility and fidelity during the whole course of
your life, you will, after death, be admitted to the

.Holy Virgin in heaven, singing, ' *Magnificat anima mea Dominum.*'*

SPIRITUAL FLOWERS.

A soul dedicated to God entirely, in act and in will, deserves that God should give Himself entirely to her.—*St. John of the Cross.*

We ought always to have our eye fixed upon the Will of God alone, recognising it, and with all joy, or at least courage, following it carefully in all our actions. But even this is not enough; we should also love this Will of God, whatever it may cost us. —*St. Francis of Sales.*

It is a highly valuable exercise of piety, to follow always the Will of God, instead of our own natural humours and inclinations.—*The same.*

EXAMPLE.

Conversion of the celebrated Pianist, Hermann Cohenn.

The compassionate mercy of the Most Holy Virgin has at times been admirably displayed in

* As soon as the Most Humble Virgin heard herself praised by St. Elizabeth, she humbled herself, and referred all the glory to God in that most beautiful and admirable canticle of the *Magnificat*, which far surpasses the canticles by the women of the old Law. It is far more excellent than that of Judith'.; more beautiful than that of the Sister of Moses, after the passage of the Red Sea ; more sublime than that of Deborah and Baruch, after the victory gained over the enemies of the Hebrew people. The canticles of Zachary and of Simeon, with all those of the Old Testament, cannot be put in comparison with this Divine Canticle.

behalf of the Sons of Israel.   To the name of the
Abbé Ratisbonne, so well known to the servants of
Mary, we must add that of another Jew, converted
by the Mother of Divine Grace.

Hermann Cohenn, a German by birth, and a
Jew in religion, had acquired great fame in Paris
as a pianist and composer of music.   He says of
himself: ' I was courted and applauded in society,
and as I possessed understanding beyond my years,
I soon had instilled into me all the fearful doctrines
that the powers of hell have taught in the earthly
hell of Paris.   Atheism, pantheism, socialism,
licentiousness of manners, etc., all found a place
in me, so that I had become one of the most
zealous propagandists, and therefore a great favourite
of all the new prophets of hell. . . .'

Whilst this second Saul was thinking out ingenious projects for the perversion of innocent
hearts, he was requested by the Prince of Moscow
to take the direction, during his absence, of a
choir of singers who were going to sing the praises
of the Blessed Virgin Mary at a church in Paris
during the month of May of 1847.   Although he
was a Jew, still he consented ; and it was there,
before the Altar of Mary, that grace awaited him.
Whilst he was rendering external honour to the
august Mother of God, she pleaded his cause
before her Divine Son.   His moment of grace and
benediction came at the very moment when he
was looking with scorn and derision upon the piety

of the faithful. . . Suddenly he feels an invisible weight upon his shoulders, which forces him, in spite of the obstinate resistance of his will, to bow his head and bend his knees ; his mind is quickly illuminated by the light of Faith, and he feels his heart opening to the salutary impressions of grace. It would take too long to narrate the many obstacles which hell opposed to his conversion, but at last he triumphed over all, and on the Feast of St. Augustine, he was washed in the waters of Baptism, with the most heart-felt emotion ; and upon the Feast of the Nativity of Mary, had the ineffable consolation of making his first Communion, and of receiving the Scapular.

Some time afterwards, finding himself called to Religion, he retired into a community of Marist Fathers, that he might there meditate seriously on his vocation ; and finally, by the counsel of his Director, he chose to enter the austere Order of Carmel.

Having visited Rome and obtained the necessary dispensation, he was afterwards ordained Priest, and consecrated himself entirely to the glory and honour of Jesus and Mary.

He employed his great musical talent for the honour of the Queen of Angels. In order that all Christian tongues might bless the mercy of that Divine Mother, who had delivered him so wonder fully from the darkness of error, he composed *a collection of hymns for the month of May, and for the principal festivals of the year*, set to music for the organ or pianoforte.

The following extract from the dedication of these compositions will show his tender devotion to the Blessed Virgin : 'Morning Star ! you appeared to me in the obscure night, in which I was lost ! Health of the sick, you cured the mortal wounds of my heart ! Refuge of sinners, you opened to me an asylum in your Immaculate Heart ! . . .'

Glory then to Mary, and to the sweet and salutary devotion of the month of May, which procured us a new brother in Christ, and a new masterpiece of the grace of God and of the mercy of Mary !

Prayer (from St. Augustine and St. Bernard).— Remember, O most compassionate Virgin Mary ! that it was never heard in any age that anyone who implored your protection has been abandoned by you. Animated by this confidence, I have recourse to you, O Mother of God, Virgin of virgins. Do not despise my prayers, Mother of the Divine Word, but graciously hear and answer me.

O Mother of God ! you pray for all, and above all, for sinners ; deign, then, to pray for me, a more obstinate sinner than any other, and therefore a more worthy object of your pity ! You see plainly the urgent need I have of your intercession ; therefore interest yourself in my regard, and obtain for me, from your Divine Son, the grace of sincere conversion and holy perseverance. Amen.

. *Ejaculation.*—I place myself for the whole of my life under your protection, O Mother of my God! O show that you are my true Mother!

Practice.—Be very attentive in all your exercises of piety during the day.

THIRTEENTH DAY.

THE TRIALS AND CONSOLATIONS OF THE BLESSED VIRGIN.

WE can never meditate too much upon the great and cruel sorrows with which the heart of the august Virgin Mary was afflicted during the whole course of her life; yet she was the most holy of creatures, the most beloved by God. 'You,' exclaims St. Chrysostom, 'who bitterly weep and lament, under the contradictions and afflictions that assail you, are you not ashamed to desire and seek for such a happiness as even the Holy Family did not enjoy? Ponder, I beg of you, the vicissitudes and changes to which they were exposed!'

Mary receives the glad tidings that, by the operation of the Holy Ghost, she should conceive a Son, the Lord and Saviour of the world. What a joy to her heart is this! and what rapturous delight filled her soul at the moment of the Incarnation of the Word in her most chaste womb!

But this celestial joy is quickly followed by sorrow. Her Spouse, St. Joseph, is alarmed at the prodigy, and thinks of secretly abandoning her. Oh! the affliction of Mary when she sees the perplexity of St. Joseph, whom, through her humility and modesty, she is unable to comfort. After this most excruciating trial, the Angel discloses the celestial secret to her Spouse, and orders him to remain with her. What consolation fills the heart of these two Angelic Spouses at this announcement! But God had prepared new afflictions for them. They must abandon their happy retirement, and journey to Bethlehem in obedience to the order of the Emperor Augustus. Faithful souls, lose not sight of Mary in this mystery; remain near this Mother, and abandon her not for an instant, whilst she journeys from Nazareth to Bethlehem. Without any painful solicitude, but with most ardent desires, she awaits the birth of the Blessed Fruit of her immaculate womb. You will see this beautiful Lady, the fortunate Daughter of Sion, beg hospitality, and not find a shelter in the whole of Bethlehem, although she is the Mother of the King of Glory. However, she blushes not for her poverty and misery, but considers it rather an honour to have to endure it.

Many holy affections are awakened in our hearts by this Divine birth; but we are especially taught the spirit of perfect detachment from all worldly pomps and worldly gratifications.

It seems as if there were no mystery that so much unites tenderness with austerity, love with rigour, bitterness with sweetness, as this mystery of the Nativity. Where can we find a poorer, and yet a more illustrious birth, or a Mother so blessed? She who gives birth to the Son of God has certainly no need of the consolations of the world!

Let us then delight to dwell near the sacred manger, where the Saviour of our souls so powerfully speaks to us in His silence and teaches us so many virtues; and let the joy and consolation of the Son and of the Mother form all the happiness of our souls! How well it becomes Mary to caress this Infant! How enchanting her charity in allowing all who wish it to look at Him, to touch and embrace Him! Do you also ask her to give Him to you, and she will do so.

O my Jesus! what a sweet night is this! The Church sings that the heavens everywhere distil honey. It would seem that those blessed Angels, who make the air resound with their song, gather this celestial honey from the breast of the sweet Virgin Mary, and from her chaste Spouse St. Joseph.

What is there that we can give to our little King that we have not received from His Divine abundance? Let us, then, give Him our hearts, which He prizes above all. O Saviour of our souls, transform our hearts into gold, through charity; into myrrh, through mortification; into incense,

by prayer; and then receive us within the arms of
Thy Divine Protection, and let us hear Thee say,
from Thy Sacred Heart, 'I am thy Salvation for
ages of ages.'

SPIRITUAL FLOWERS.

'A bundle of myrrh is my Beloved to me. He
shall abide between my breasts' (*Cant.* i. 12), in
order that I may incessantly inhale its bitterness.

The afflictions of this life are like the flowers
that precede the fruits of glory; and the blood
which we shed is as a royal unction which consecrates us to immortality.—*St. Greg. Nyssen.*

The rose grows amidst thorns; and the most
beautiful and most solid virtues grow amidst the
severest contradictions.—*St. Francis of Sales.*

No one will be crowned with roses, if he be not
first crowned with the thorns of Our Saviour.—
The same.

Our actions are like roses, which, though more
pleasing when fresh, are yet sweeter and more
agreeable when faded. Thus, although works performed with consolation are more pleasing to us;
yet if they be done in the state of aridity, they
have a sweeter odour, higher value before God.—
The same.

EXAMPLE.

A Fortunate Mistake.

The following is related by an eye-witness of the event: 'One evening, in December, 1855, a Priest named B——, having returned to his house after a hard day's work, sat down and began to recite his Office, when he heard a knock at his door. He opened it, and saw a young girl, who asked him to go and visit a dying lady, living at No. 28, —— Street. . . . The good Priest was ready to interrupt his prayer to follow the little messenger, but she told him there was no hurry, provided he went in the course of that evening; so he wrote down the address of the sick person, and told her to say that he was coming shortly.

'After finishing his Office, the good Priest went to the street named, and entered No. 18, thinking this was the number mentioned. It was a wretched house, and as there was no one in charge of the door he walked in, groped up the poor staircase, and knocked at the first door that he came to. A man opened it, and at the sight of the ecclesiastical dress, fell into a passion, and to the inquiry made as to whether this were the house of the sick lady, he made an impudent answer, and shut the door in the face of the Priest. Patient and mild, like his Divine Master, the Priest knocked at the next door, and met with no better reception. He then went up to the second story, where he found a boy playing in a passage. "Can you tell me, my child," said he, "where I can find a poor lady dangerously ill, who lives in this house, and is called G——?" "Yes; down there, Reverend Sir; my father said that she would not be able to live through the night; but I do not think that you have said her name correctly." "Never mind the name; lead me, I beg of you, to her door."

'The Priest, preceded by the child, entered the room and found a woman in her agony; a man about fifty was sitting near her bed, and at the sight of the Priest he immediately arose, evidently annoyed. "Are you Mr. G——?" said the Priest; "how is your sick wife?" "No," replied the man bluntly, "I am not; who has sent you here to meddle with other people's affairs?" "I was requested to come," replied the Priest with surprise. "I was told that a poor lady, named G——, was seriously ill, and wished for the last consolations of religion. I may have mistaken the street, or the house, or room; but undoubtedly this sick woman has much need of my ministry. The Divine Mercy has certainly led me here, and allowed this mistake to occur." "Yes, man of God!" murmured the dying woman, "yes, it is God Who has led you hither." "Nothing of the sort," said the husband angrily; "for ten years no Priest has set his foot in my house; you shall not confess my wife. I am her master; mind your own business." "You are much mistaken, sir,"

answered the Priest, firmly and mildly; "the first
Master of your wife is God, and you have no right
over her soul. If she desire, I shall hear her confession, and I can only withdraw when she freely
and of her own will refuses my ministry." Then,
approaching the sick woman, he said: "Madam,
do you desire to be reconciled with God, and die
a Christian death?" The poor woman raised her
hands to heaven, and shed tears of joy, exclaiming:
"Blessed be the Divine Goodness that has allowed
this mistake! for three days I have been asking
my husband for a Priest, and he has answered me
only with insults. I do truly wish to be reconciled
to my God, Who has had so much compassion on
my poor soul." "Do you hear, sir?" said the
Priest to the husband; "be pleased to leave me
alone with her for a few moments." These words,
pronounced with much firmness and resolution,
forced the man to retire, although he did so
grumbling.

'The dying woman then pointed to a rosary
hanging over her bed, and said: "See, this has
saved me; I had the weakness to fear my husband
more than God, and to avoid disturbances and
quarrels, for ten years I have given up every
practice of religion. One only thing have I preserved—the love of the Most Holy Virgin, and
confidence in her intercession. I have recited her
Rosary almost every day; it is she alone who has
led you here, and she, the true Mother of Mercy

and refuge of sinners, saves my soul." The Priest was deeply moved by this touching narrative. He consoled the sick woman, helped her to make her confession, and then told her to prepare to receive the Holy Viaticum and Extreme Unction, whilst he went to give notice thereof to the Parish Priest.

'On leaving the house he looked at the address which the little girl had given him, and saw that the number was not 18 but 28. Blessing God for this fortunate misunderstanding he hastened to No. 28, where he found the sick lady expecting him. After complying with the duties of his sacred ministry here also he immediately went to the Parish Priest to see about the other Sacraments which the two sick persons required; but meanwhile, the poor woman at No. 18 died. She had received the pardon of her sins by the sacramental absolution, and the fervour of her will would assuredly supply before the God of All Mercies for the other succours of religion. ·

'The man of God, full of faith and gratitude towards the Most Holy Virgin—the refuge of sinners and consolation of the afflicted—then proceeded to fulfil the duties of his sacred ministry towards the other dying lady.'

This most touching fact shows once again the treasures of benediction that result from piety towards the Most Blessed Virgin, and the great Mercy of Our Adorable Saviour towards those who love His Holy Mother.

Prayer of St. Bernard.—O Mother of Mercy! even when on earth you were deserving of our veneration and confidence; but now that you are raised to the highest heavens your faithful servants look to you as the help of all nations. We beseech you, then, All Holy Virgin, to succour us by your patronage and prayers. Your prayers are more dear to us and more valuable than all the treasures of earth; they are so efficacious that they obtain from God the abundance of His graces; so powerful that they suppress and bring to naught all the efforts of our enemies, who labour for our destruction. Scatter them, O Mother of Mercy! confound all their designs, strengthen our weakness against their malice, and show yourself the true Mother of all the faithful who place their confidence in you. You are all my hope, and will be so as long as I have breath. Amen.

Ejaculation.—I place all my confidence, after God, in you, O Mary, my dear Mother.

Practice.—Bear patiently, and in a spirit of penance, all the contradictions you may meet with this day.

FOURTEENTH DAY.

MARY AT BETHLEHEM.

GOD resolved to confer on mankind the most signal and loving benefit of the Incarnation, and came down upon earth into the desert of this world like

9

a celestial manna, that He might become our
food, during our journey to the promised land of
Paradise. Our adorable Saviour rendered Himself
visible to us at His birth, as a beautiful little
Infant, lying in a manger, and this was in the
night, when the world was covered with darkness.
The Divine Nature of Our Lord Jesus Christ is
represented by the honey contained in the manna—
because honey is a celestial liquor gathered by the
bees from flowers, and it is not distilled from their
sap, but collected by them as it descends from
heaven with the dew. In like manner the Divine
Nature of our adorable Redeemer came down
from Heaven, at the moment of the Incarnation,
upon this blessed flower of the earth, the Most
Holy Virgin, and, having become united with a
human nature, preserved it in the bosom of the
Most Chaste Mary, as a sweet hive, during the
space of nine months.

But let us consider more at length this miracle
of Divine Mercy.

The Most Holy Mother of God gave birth to
her Divine Son as the stars produce their light ;
and on this account her name Mary truly signifies
Star of the Sea, or Morning Star. The star of the
sea is the Polar star, towards which the mariner's
needle continually turns ; and through this star
those who navigate the ocean know how their
course is directed.

The Patriarchs, Prophets, and Fathers of the

Church turned their eyes towards the Most Holy Virgin, and she was ever the Polar Star and the chosen Port for all poor mortals who navigate the sea of this miserable world, and by her means they may avoid those shipwrecks which occur so often on the rocks and precipices of sin.

Mary was, also, that beautiful Morning Star which brought the joyful news of the coming of the Sun of Justice. The Prophets knew well that a Virgin would conceive and give birth to a Son, at once God and Man, through the operation of the Holy Ghost, and would still remain a Virgin, though she became a Mother : *Ecce Virgo concipiet et pariet Filium et vocabitur ejus Emanuel.* How should He Who selected her for His Mother, on account of her virginity, impair her integrity? How could the Eternal Word, Purity itself, lessen the virginal purity of His Mother? From eternity He is generated and virginally produced in the bosom of His Father ; and although receiving from Him the Divinity, it is not divided, but the Word is always one and the same God with the Father. The Most Holy Virgin here on earth also produces virginally her Divine Son, Our Lord. There is this difference, however, that He will never again enter the bosom of Mary, but He will be eternally generated in the bosom of His Father, being One with Him, in virtue of the unity of the Divine Essence.

This Divine generation may indeed be made

9—2

the foundation of our meditations on the mystery
of Our Lord's Nativity ; but it does not admit of a
curious inspection, nor should we weary our mind
by endeavouring to examine into that which is too
sublime for our weak understanding : *Generationem
ejus quis enarrabit ?* — 'Who shall declare His
generation ?' says the Prophet Isaiah.

But now, after having considered the virginal
purity of the Most Holy Virgin in giving birth to
her Divine Son, let us turn our eyes to this Divine
Infant, and see how He allows Himself to be
cared for by His Holy Mother, as if He could
not do otherwise. Why is this ?   It is to teach
us how to act, Religious especially, who are
bound by the sweet chains of the holy vow of
Obedience. Our Lord certainly could not make
bad use of His Will, or of His liberty, being the
Eternal Wisdom ; nevertheless He concealed His
knowledge, and all His perfections as God and
those of His perfect human intellect, under the
swathing bands of infancy. He keeps hidden under
the veil of holy obedience to the Eternal Father,
Who had willed that He should be, as St. Paul says,
in all things like to His brethren, excepting sin.
Behold our Model ! Let us often visit this Child,
lying in a manger; and let us learn from Him how
to act in all things according to His Most Holy
Will.

But shall we visit Him empty-handed ? The
shepherds took with them some of their little

lambs to present to Him. What can we offer more acceptable to this Divine Pastor of our souls than our hearts as a little offering of our love and the choicest part of our spiritual flock. How dear will this offering be to Him! He will look upon us with mercy in return for our gift; and we shall gladden the Most Holy Virgin, who so much desires our welfare. Let us take with us from her Divine Infant one of His precious tears, the sweet dew of Heaven, and place it on our heart, that it may henceforth feel no other sorrow than that which rejoices this Blessed Infant—that is, sorrow for sin! We should all be like so many simple shepherds watching over the flocks of our affections, ready to adore this our Infant Saviour, as soon as the Angels call us. We should offer Him, as a pledge of our eternal service, the finest lamb we possess; that is, all our love, without any reserve or exception.

Oh, how happy shall we be, and what great consolation shall we receive, if we thus visit the Saviour of our souls!

As the manna had the taste of every kind of food, so this Divine Infant contains in Himself every kind of consolation. Each one can find in Him what he desires, and proportionate to his capacity, provided that he possess the requisite dispositions.

SPIRITUAL FLOWERS.

No flower could be a better emblem of the resplendent virtue of Mary and her singular privilege than the lily; whose three petals may signify that she was a Virgin in her conception of Jesus, a Virgin at His birth, and a Virgin ever afterwards. —*Nouet.*

Mary is the Mystical Lily without spot, in which the Eternal Word espoused our nature.—*The same.*

The flower falls from the tree when the fruit is formed; but the Mother of God, who is the tree of life, preserves her flower and her fruit, and by an unheard-of miracle unites maternity to virginity.— *The same.*

As the lily lifts its stem on high, so the soul who often receives Jesus Christ should direct its hopes towards heaven in imitation of Jesus, Who is the Flower of the field and the Lily of the valley. The virtue of such a soul has roots deeper than the cedars of Lebanon, which defy the winds and the storms. In the fruitfulness of her good works and in her charity towards the poor, her glory is like that of the olive. The fragrance of her holy life and of her sweet conversation is spread around like the odour of the flowers which bud forth on Mount Lebanon in spring-time.—*St. Cyril.*

EXAMPLE.

The Devotion of the Saints to the ' Angelus.'

1. St. Alfonso di Liguori omitted no favourable opportunity for showing his tender devotion to the Most Blessed Virgin. Whenever he heard the clock strike, whatever might be his occupation or conversation, he interrupted it to recite the Angelical salutation, saying that one *Ave Maria* was more valuable than the entire world. He was most exact in the recital of the *Angelus.* As soon as he heard the sound of the bell, he went down on his knees, even when he happened to be in the public streets. When he became deaf he desired to be warned of the ringing of the bell, and even when at his meals he would break off and kneel down to recite it. Often was he rapt in ecstasy during this prayer from the fervour of his devotion.

2. St. Charles Borromeo, who was so celebrated for piety and learning, was not ashamed, when Archbishop of Milan, to descend from his carriage or his horse in the open streets to recite the *Angelus* in honour of Mary.

3. St. Vincent de Paul, wherever he might be, or in whatever society, even at court, would recollect himself, and kneel down as soon as he heard the sound of the *Angelus.* He considered himself happy to be able to give public testimony of his filial love of the Most Holy Virgin Mary,

and those who were present always followed his example.

All who devoutly recite the *Angelus* on their knees morning, noon, and evening at the ringing of the bell gain a hundred days' Indulgence each time, and if they continue to say it at least once a day during the course of a month, they may gain a Plenary Indulgence on the usual conditions. Those who are unable to hear the sound of the bell may gain the same Indulgence by reciting the *Angelus* at the time that it is usually rung. As to those who are much engaged, and who wish to supplicate the Blessed Virgin thrice a day, they can supply for the *Angelus* the following invocations: Virgin before the birth of your Divine Son, pray for us; Virgin at His birth, pray for us; Virgin after His birth, pray for us. Lastly, those who do not know the prayers can say the *Paters* and *Aves* in memory of the Incarnation of the Word in the womb of Mary.

Prayer of St. Anselm.—We beseech you, O Queen of Heaven and Sovereign of the Universe, by the grace which Our Lord conferred upon you in raising you to so sublime a degree of glory, to intercede for us, that the fulness of grace with which you were enriched may render us one day partakers of your glory and happiness. O Mother, full of mercy, interest yourself in our behalf, that we may be able to enjoy the ineffable happiness for which our God deigned to inclose Himself for nine months in your most holy womb. If you deign to pray for us to your Divine Son, you will be assuredly heard. Let the bowels of your maternal mercy speak in our favour. If you, our tender Mother, have no compassion for us, what will become of your most miserable children? What will be our destiny when your Divine Son, as Judge of the living and the dead, will call us to His judgment-seat? Have pity on us then, O Mother of Mercy! Amen.

Ejaculation.—See, O Mary, the many dangers by which we are surrounded, and have pity on our miserable condition.

Practice.—Let all your actions be done this day for the sole end of pleasing God, that you may thus be able to offer Him the tender lamb of your love.

FIFTEENTH DAY.

THE UNION OF CHARITY AND HUMILITY IN THE HEART OF MARY AT THE INCARNATION.

GOD is One; hence He loves unity and union, and hates all that is not in accordance with this unity. The reason is this—that as He is perfect in all His attributes, He must have a sovereign love for all that is perfect, and unity is perfection. He must also be averse to all disunion, because whatever is disunited is so far imperfect.

As then God wished to show us how dear to Him is union, He effected three distinct modes of union in the Most Holy Virgin on the day of His Incarnation.

Firstly, He united the Divine to the human nature ; and so admirable and sublime is this union, that it infinitely surpasses all that human or angelic intelligence can comprehend.   Nor could the Seraphim or Cherubim have ever imagined anything so wonderful.   Indeed, two opposite extremes were to meet—the Divine Nature, which is essential perfection, and human nature, the deepest misery : the contraries being the greatest that can be conceived.   Nevertheless, God in His Wisdom and infinite Goodness was able to find a method of uniting the two natures so intimately through His Incarnation in the womb of Our Lady that in one Person man was made God and God became Man, without disparagement to His Deity.

The second union was that of Maternity with Virginity.   This certainly is most admirable and beyond all the laws of nature.   A virgin becomes a mother, and remains still a virgin after maternity. This miraculous and supernatural union could only be effected by the omnipotent hand of God, Who granted this privilege to Mary ; and as this union has been effected in her alone, so she alone will be eternally both a Virgin and a Mother, and the Mother of a Son Who is both God and Man.

The third union accomplished by God in our

glorious Lady was that of the most ardent charity with the most profound humility.

Reflect on these two virtues, and you will ask how it is possible that charity can be united with humility, if the nature of one is to soar on high, and that of the other to abase itself? Naturally, indeed, it is impossible; but God, Who is One, and Who loves and desires unity, manifested the greatness of His power by uniting these two dissimilar virtues in the soul of Mary.

In her, charity was so united to humility that one depended on the other, and whilst her charity continues humble, her humility is ever full of charity. Charity raised her soul above all creatures, and humility abased it below them all, and yet the union of these two virtues was continuous.

To what a high degree of humility and charity did not the Most Holy Virgin attain at the moment of the Incarnation! Ponder her words to the Archangel : *Ecce ancilla Domini, fiat mihi secundum verbum tuum*—'Behold the handmaid of the Lord, be it done unto me according to Thy word.' No sooner did she hear herself proclaimed the Mother of God, the Queen of Angels and of men, than she abased herself beneath all, saying : 'Behold the handmaid of the Lord!' This is a great act of humility.

The Most Holy Virgin in that moment had so clear a knowledge of the misery and nothingness of human nature, and of the infinite distance between

God and man, that, seeing herself raised above all
creatures, she abased herself beneath them all,
considering her own nothingness and the infinite
greatness of God Who had chosen her for His
Mother. True it is, then, that Mary never humbled
herself so profoundly as when she pronounced
these words: *Ecce ancilla Domini*—' Behold the
handmaid of the Lord !'

But see how the Most Blessed Virgin united the
most perfect charity to her humility when consent-
ing to the proposal the Angel made her in the
Name of God : *Fiat mihi secundum verbum*—' Be
it done unto me according to Thy word '—were
her words ; and thus, by charity, she was raised
above the Cherubim and Seraphim, and at that
very moment the Eternal Son of God took flesh in
her virginal womb, and she became His Mother !

Let us learn from the example of Our Lady that
humility does not merely consist in diffidence in
ourselves, but it must be accompanied by confidence in God. This confidence in God is produced by this diffidence in ourselves and in our
own powers. This confidence is also the source of
generosity of soul, of which Our Blessed Lady
gives an example on this occasion when she says
the words: ' Be it done unto me according to Thy
word.' It is true, would she say, that I am unworthy of this grace, in regard to what I am only
in myself; but as all that is good in me is from
God, and as that which you announce to me is

His Most Holy Will, I believe that it can and will be done, and, therefore, let it be accomplished in me !

Humility conceals the virtues of a soul, in order the better to preserve them ; nevertheless, when charity requires, it allows them to be known for their increase and perfection. Thus it resembles those plants which close their beautiful flowers at night and open them only when the sun is high, so that people speak of those flowers as sleeping during the night. Humility, in the same way, conceals all our virtues, and never allows them to appear, except for the exercise of charity, which, being a celestial, Divine gift, not an acquired virtue, is truly as a sun amidst all the virtues, and should always rule over them. Hence the humility, which is prejudicial to charity, is undoubtedly a false humility.

SPIRITUAL FLOWERS.

Let us have a supreme contempt for all that is not God. Oh, how sweet it is to abandon one's self into His hands ! Daily experience proves to us that the less we trust in our miserable efforts, the more does God work in us by His omnipotent virtue. All consists in being a docile instrument in His hands, and seemingly dead.—*P. Milley.*

It is good to leave Our Lord sometimes to serve others for His sake ; and we should do so, if we can

prevent our devotion from causing annoyance.—
St. Francis of Sales.

As the olive, when planted in vineyards, com-
municates its savour to the vine, so charity com-
municates its perfection to the virtues amidst which
it flourishes. It is also true that when the vine is
engrafted on the olive, it not only receives its taste,
but also its sap; thus we should not be satisfied
with the possession of charity and with the exercise
of all other virtues, but it is necessary that all our
virtues be accompanied and produced by charity,
and be attributed to this virtue alone.—*The same.*

EXAMPLE.

The Efficacy of the 'Salve Regina.'

The following appeared in the French journal,
the *Univers:* 'We have already announced the
departure of five Nuns of the Cross, on their way
to apply their admirable spirit of unselfishness to
the exercise of works of charity in the Diocese of
Natchitoches, in America.

'After a painful misfortune at sea, these worthy
Sisters have landed at Havre. They were to set out
from this port, and in a letter addressed to the
Bishop of Saint Brieux, the Mother Superior of the
Sisters of the Cross thus writes:

'"Our Sisters started about eleven, on the morning of the 10th of November, 1856. They had

received the blessing of our Chaplain, and did not expect ever to return; but Divine Providence had disposed otherwise. The steamer was already before Cherbourg, when, at about eleven o'clock in the night following their departure, a fearful noise was heard throughout the steamer. All the passengers were called to go on deck, and they came up exclaiming: 'We are lost! We are lost!'

' "One of the boilers had burst, and the explosion had wounded six men and set fire to the vessel. 'Have you a Priest on board?' said a lady to one of our Sisters. 'No,' she replied. 'So much the worse,' said the lady, 'because our death is certain.' 'No, madam,' calmly and confidently replied Sister Mary Agatha; 'let us invoke the Most Holy Virgin, and she will save us.' Our Sisters immediately went down on their knees, with their hands crossed on their breast, and recited the *Salve Regina.* Many passengers and sailors joined them, and their cries reached the heart of the Mother of God. A few moments after, when the Sisters, who had gone down into a cabin, were continuing their prayers, they were informed that the fire had been miraculously extinguished, and that there was no further danger. No one doubted that their salvation was owing to the prayers which had been addressed to the Blessed Virgin Mary." ' —*Univers,* 30th November, 1856.

Prayer. — O most humble of Virgins, holy Mother of God, Mistress of life and Lady of the universe, teach me humility and the true love of this precious virtue. How great is the pride of my heart, who am but dust and ashes ; I have eagerly sought for the praises of men, when shame and confusion for my innumerable infidelities should have made me feel my nothingness ! Take pity on me, O Holy Virgin; banish the proud thoughts that arise in my soul, and let me imitate your humility here on earth, that I may be worthy to experience, with you, the truth of these words : 'The humble shall exult in the abundance of peace.' Amen.

Ejaculation.—Pray for us, O most humble of all Virgins !

Practice. — Endeavour to-day to neglect no opportunity of practising humility and charity.

SIXTEENTH DAY.

THE PURIFICATION OF THE BLESSED VIRGIN.

LET us meditate attentively upon the virtues of which Mary gives us so moving an example in the mystery of her Purification in the Temple. First of all, what more profound humility can be imagined than that practised by Our Saviour and Our Lady in their visit to the Temple ? He comes to be offered, like all the sons of sinful men ;

she, to be purified like all other women. With regard to our adorable Redeemer, it is of Faith that He, being essential purity, could not be under the obligation of this Law, which was promulgated for sinners. With regard to the Most Holy Virgin, what need had she to purify herself, who, from the instant of her Immaculate Conception, had been endowed with purity so excellent, and with such a fulness of grace, that the highest Seraphim and Cherubim could not be compared to her? And yet, behold, the Son and the Mother, notwithstanding their incomparable purity, present themselves in the Temple, as if they were sinners like other children of Adam! O truly wonderful act of humility! If the value of this act increases in proportion to the dignity of the person who humbles himself, how full of useful instruction to souls tending to perfection is the humility practised by the Sovereign Creator of all things.

He shows us that this virtue was so dear to Him that He preferred death rather than relinquish its practice; for after teaching that there can be no greater love than to give one's life for the object beloved, He lays down His life for the exercise of humility. By submitting to die He, the immortal God, practised the most excellent and most sublime act of humility that can be conceived. Some persons deceive themselves by regarding humility as a virtue necessary merely to novices and beginners in the spiritual life, and the practice

of which can be laid aside after some advance.
But our adorable Saviour shows us how erroneous
is this opinion, by humbling Himself unto death.

Oh if we could well understand the necessity of
perseverance in this virtue ! How many, after
beginning well, have miserably fallen away because
they did not persevere in the practice of humility !
But Jesus Christ did not say he who *shall begin,*
but he who *shall persevere* until death, shall be
saved : *Qui perseveraverit usque in finem hic salvus
erit.*

Genuine virtue may be distinguished from that
which is only apparent, as true balsam is distinguished from false. Balsam is tested by drop-
ping it into water ; if it sinks to the bottom of the
vessel it may be considered very pure and precious.
We may know if a person be truly piudent, generous and noble, by observing if these virtues tend
to make him humble, modest, submissive ; for in
such a case they are truly valuable gifts ; but if
they stay only on the surface, and love to show
themselves and to win admiration, they are so far
false and counterfeit.

The Angels, and, after them, our first parents,
prevaricated through pride. Upon this account,
Our Lord, like a wise and loving physician of our
souls, applied the remedy to the root of the evil,
and came into the world to plant in the place of
pride the beautiful and useful virtue of Divine
humility, become very necessary on account of the

contrary vice being so general. Indeed, so common an evil is pride, that humility can never be sufficiently inculcated ; and on this account, our adorable Saviour and our Immaculate Lady would obey the law, not made for them, to teach us to esteem this virtue. For us, who deserve only humiliation and contempt, to abase ourselves is no great thing. However, humiliation acquires an inestimable value when embraced by Jesus Christ and His Most Holy Mother ; and this humiliation was continual with them throughout the whole course of their life. Wherefore the Apostle, speaking of the humility of Our Redeemer, said that ' He humbled Himself unto death, even to the death of the Cross '—*Humiliavit semitipsum usque ad mortem, mortem autem crucis.* But if we miserable creatures humble ourselves on some slight occasion, we quickly seek by every means in our power to indemnify ourselves for the transient exercise of this virtue, and the very thought of persevering in the practice of it alarms us. We are convinced, it is true, that we are very imperfect, and yet we desire to be looked upon as holy and perfect, notwithstanding the example of Mary, who consented to be clothed in the semblance of a sinner, although confirmed in grace and possessed of a more than angelic purity.

Observe any other daughter of Eve, and see how eagerly she seeks for honour and esteem ; and although this defect be common to all mankind in general, it seems to be more marked in the female sex. Now, Our Lady and glorious Mistress is not the Daughter of Eve according to the spirit, but only according to the flesh, and therefore she always persevered in the most profound humility, and could say in her sacred Canticle of the Magnificat that on this account ' All generations would call her blessed '—*Beatam me dicent omnes generationes.*

How beautiful is it to behold the Holy Virgin presenting herself and the Infant Jesus in the Temple, and making her offering of two doves ! Happier is she than all the princes of earth ! And what shall I say of the aged Simeon, who takes the Divine Infant in his arms ? Let us also embrace Him, let us live and die in these tender embraces.

Place this sweet Jesus in your heart, like another Solomon upon his ivory throne. Let your soul follow His steps, that you may hear the holy words He continually breathes. Remember that your heart should be like ivory in purity and firmness ; firm in its resolutions, and pure in its affections.

Spiritual Flowers.

Anything we do, however little, will have an inestimable value if it be done for the love of God. —*St. Teresa.*

It is an exalted degree of perfection to assimilate

and conform ourselves to the spirit of the sacred Infancy of our most humble and most obedient Saviour.—*St. Francis of Sales.*

Whoever wishes to acquire virtue, and does not possess humility, is like to one who carries dust in his hands when there is a high wind.—*The same.*

EXAMPLE.

Punishment of the Profaners of a Sanctuary of the Blessed Virgin.

The holy Hermitage of Voiron did not escape the profanations of the heretics. They invaded it with arms in their hands, as if they were going to besiege a fortress; they ill-treated and expelled the Monks, took away the sacred vessels, the papers, documents, indulgences, etc., committed horrible sacrileges, and at last set fire to the place and entirely destroyed it, and rolled the remaining stones down the mountain.

This atrocious impiety was not left unpunished, for soon afterwards all who had taken part in the destruction of the hermitage perished miserably. It is remarkable, however, that in spite of all the devastation effected by these impious men, they could not gain their principal object, which was to carry off the statue of the Most Holy Virgin, which was preserved miraculously.

John Burgnard, a native of Chablais, who had embraced the heresy of the Bernese, and was the leader of these profaners, had no sooner reached the hermitage, than he mounted the Altar to carry away the statue of the Most Blessed Virgin. He threw a rope round its neck, and descending from the Altar was walking out of the Church, dragging the statue after him, and uttering at the same time these words : 'Come along with me, come along with me, little black woman' (the face of the statue was black); 'if you are as powerful as the Papists say, let me now have a proof of it. Why do you allow yourself to be thus shamefully dragged on the ground ? Why do you not defend yourself?' He had no sooner uttered these blasphemies than the statue became immovable. The wretched man, finding that he was unable to drag it further, turned his head round to see what was hindering him, and by a second miracle his head remained turned in that direction, so that he could never again place it in its right position ; and, moreover, he became crippled in an arm and a shoulder. Being obliged to leave the statue, he left the spot with great difficulty, and bore the chastisement of his impiety throughout his life, giving an undeniable proof of the sovereign power of the Queen of Heaven. But more terrible is the fact that he persevered in heresy, and died in despair in the presence of many of the parishioners of Bons. Amongst these were Michael Novello and Claude

Ippolito Cortager, who gave testimony of this fact on oath A.D. 1629.

His Highness Duke Charles Emmanuel, when at Tortona during the time that St. Francis of Sales was converting the people of Chablais, verified the fact we have related, and ordered the secretary of the Town Corporation to register it, that the miracle might be transmitted to posterity. (See ' Life of St. Francis of Sales,' by Augustus de Sales.)

Prayer.—Holy Virgin ! when you presented your Divine Son to the Eternal Father, you became dear to all the Heavenly Court. O present also our hearts, that, fortified by grace, we may never fall into mortal sin !

Most humble Virgin ! when you placed the adorable Jesus in the arms of the aged Simeon, you filled his soul with heavenly sweetness. O place our hearts in the hands of God, that He may fill them with His Divine Spirit ! Most diligent Virgin, you co-operated in the redemption of the world, when you redeemed your Son Jesus with two turtle-doves ; be pleased to redeem our hearts from the slavery of sin, that they may be always pure and holy before God. Most clement Virgin ! when you heard from the lips of the holy Simeon the prophetic announcement of all your dolours, you submitted yourself quickly and perfectly to the Will of God. O help us to support

always with patience and resignation all the tribulations of life !

Most merciful Virgin ! bymeans of your Divine
Son you illuminated, the Prophetess Anna with
supernatural light, so that she magnified the mercies of God and acknowledged and proclaimed
Jesus as the Saviour of the world.   O fill us with
heavenly grace, that in the abundance of joy we
may be able to reap the precious fruits of Redemption.   Amen.

Ejaculation.—O Mary ! watch over me.

Practice.—Take every possible care to-day not to
commit any sin, however venial it may seem.

SEVENTEENTH DAY.

MARY, THE MODEL OF PERFECT OBEDIENCE, IN THE MYSTERY OF THE PURIFICATION.

LET us consider in this meditation how our
adorable Saviour and His Most Holy Mother
united perfect obedience to profound humility.

Our Lord preferred the death of the Cross
rather than fail in obedience. ' Jesus Christ,' says
the great Apostle, ' was obedient unto death, even
to the death of the Cross'—*Factus obediens usque
ad mortem, mortem autem crucis.* And what signal
obedience did not Mary exercise at the death of
her Son, the only object of her heart's affection !

She stood firm and constant at the foot of the Cross, pierced with the sword of sorrow, perfectly resigned to the Will of the Eternal Father. All the actions of Our Divine Saviour were regulated by obedience, as He Himself declared, saying : 'I am come not to do My Will, but the Will of Him that sent Me'—*Descendi de cœlo non ut faciam voluntatem meam sed voluntatem ejus qui miset Me.* Thus He teaches us that the Will of His Heavenly Father was the sole guide of all His thoughts. Notice Our Lady's life, and you will always see her obedient. So highly did she esteem this virtue of obedience, that she obeyed the command to espouse St. Joseph, although she was bound by a vow of virginity. She always persevered in the practice of this virtue, and as the mystery of the Purification shows us, she presented herself in the Temple, that she might observe the Law she was not bound to observe. Thus her obedience was the more precious as it was voluntary. Indeed, this is the only virtue that she has recommended to the practice of mankind. The Gospel tells us that when she spoke to the attendants at the marriage of Cana, she said to them : 'Whatsoever He shall say to you, do '—*Quodcumque dixerit vobis facite.* Here she teaches the practice of holy obedience, which is inseparable from the virtue of humility, because it springs from this virtue. Only those who are truly humble subject themselves to the Will of God

Our Lady had no fear of being disobedient, because she was not obliged to obey the Law, but she shunned its very shadow.   Many would have misunderstood her conduct, if she had not gone to the Temple to offer her Divine Son and perform the ceremony of her Purification.   She would, therefore, remove all suspicion of disobedience, and at the same time teach us not merely to avoid sin, but also its very appearance, and the occasions which may expose us to it.   Let us learn, also, not to be satisfied with the testimony of our conscience alone, but to try to remove from others every occasion of thinking ill of us and of our actions.

The example of Our Saviour and of His Most Holy Mother should animate us to submit not only in those things that are commanded us, but in those that are merely of counsel, that we may thus become more dear to the Divine Goodness. O God! is it then so great a work to subject ourselves to obedience, when for this alone we have been sent into the world, and when the Supreme King, to Whom all things should be subject, practised it?

We must learn then from the example of our adorable Saviour and of His Most Holy Mother, to be docile, pliable, and easily ruled, not only for a certain time, and in some actions, but even unto death.   But two fundamental conditions of this virtue of Obedience must be observed.   These are—firstly, that to obey perfectly we must love

God Who commands; and secondly, we must love the action that is commanded. All the faults committed against obedience proceed from the want of one of these conditions. Many love the thing commanded, but not God Who commands it. For instance, some will perform their devotions, not out of obedience to the Will of God, but on account of the consolation they experience in this exercise. In this there is nothing but self-love; and it will be perceptible by the repugnance, or discontent, which is felt in the performance of those observances that are not according to our inclinations. In this case, it is plain that it is not God Whom we love, but only the thing that He commands. If we loved God Who commands, our hearts would be indifferent as to our occupation, because in all we should be equally sure to find the Will of God.

Others will love God Who commands, but not the action commanded. These will say: I know very well that it is the Will of God that I should do this or that, but I feel so great a repugnance, that I cannot resolve to do it, and were I to strive to obey, the person who, in the name of God, desires me to perform the action, enjoins it so ungraciously, as to rob me of all the satisfaction I might experience in an act of obedience.

The source of all our difficulties is that we obey readily only when our superiors accommodate themselves to our natural inclinations. On all other occasions, the smallest obligations appear to us difficult and disagreeable.   It is therefore evident that we do not regard God Who commands us through another, but we look at the person who speaks to us in His Name, to see how he is clothed so to speak; that is to say, we look only at his external deportment.   O God! what a mistake! We ought to submit to the Will of God in obedience, without any exception, and from whatever quarter the order may come; and not only love God Who commands, but also the thing that is commanded; *taking the command and placing it upon our heads*—that is, in our inmost heart, to execute it with all fidelity and sincere goodwill.

Spiritual Flowers.

Bless God for having given you Mary as your Mother.   Imitate her, and consider what a blessing it is for you to have so powerful an advocate in Heaven.—*St. Teresa.*

Humility cannot subsist without love, nor love without humility—and one can never be acquired without the other.—*The same.*

The more we mortify our natural inclinations, so much the more do we merit to receive supernatural inspirations.—*St. Francis of Sales.*

Example.

A Conquest of the Blessed Virgin's.

Father Paul Stub, a Barnabite, became a conquest of grace, and an Angel in virtue and learning, through the intercession of the Blessed Virgin Mary. He himself thus relates his conversion in his excellent book for the Month of Mary, entitled 'The School of Mary':

'A Protestant youth set out from the North, in 1826, to take a post at Genoa, in the family of the Consul of Sweden and Norway, who was a very good Catholic. But the wife of the Consul, fearing that this youth might by his conversation have an evil influence on a nephew who lived with them, went to the sanctuary of Our Lady of Graces, and made the following prayer to the Queen of Heaven and Earth :

"'O Mary ! if you see that this Protestant youth will become a Catholic and be virtuous, then let him arrive, but if otherwise, send his ship to America."

'The ship arrived safely at Genoa, and the boy entered on his situation. He was edified by the examples of virtue that he witnessed, but had no thoughts whatever of becoming a Catholic—until after some time, when he was in trouble, calling to mind the devotion which Catholics bear to Our Lady, he said to her : "O Mother of Jesus ! it is

the first time that I invoke you, but if you do me
the favour I desire I will invoke you all my life."

'The favour was obtained most completely, and
after that time the young man began to pray to
God to know the truth, entered upon the study of
religion, and became a Catholic in 1829, to his own
great joy and that of many others.   He afterwards
took the Religious habit, and has since exercised
his zeal for the glory of the Most Blessed Virgin
in preaching ; and, to give her a new proof of his
gratitude, he composed this little book in her
honour.'

Prayer.—Most pure Virgin ! obtain for me the
grace to understand henceforth the Divine sweetness
of union with God.   May my adorable Saviour
abide with me under the veil of Faith as He dwelt
with you in the seclusion of a hidden life !   May
He live in me through the union of my heart with
His adorable Heart as He lived in you, forming
one heart and soul with you !   Oh that henceforth I
may know how to love, to desire, and to relish only
Jesus !   May He alone, during the whole course of
my life, be my strength, my life, the heart of my
heart, the soul of my soul, that after having been
frequently nourished with His virginal Body, which
was conceived and born of you a Virgin, I may be
able to say with the Apostle : '*I live now, not I,
but Christ liveth in me.*'   Amen.

Ejaculation.—My heart is prepared to obey you
in everything, O my Mother !

Practice.—Let everything you do to-day be done in the spirit of obedience.

EIGHTEENTH DAY.

THE FLIGHT INTO EGYPT.—TRUST IN PROVIDENCE.

THE unspeakable joy which Mary and Joseph experienced after the birth of Jesus was of short duration.

The Angel of the Lord came again to visit Joseph in sleep, and said to him, ' Arise, and take the Child and His Mother and fly into Egypt, and be there until I shall tell thee, for it will come to pass that Herod will seek the Child to destroy Him.'

See how the heavenly messenger treats Mary and Joseph, precisely as if they were true Religious! How many pretexts might they not have found to be dispensed from obeying? Could we not wait till to-morrow? might they have said. What provisions have we for so long and tedious a journey? Who knows what we may have to suffer from the Egyptians, the declared enemies of the Israelites? Who will give us shelter in that country? These and a thousand other excuses would have been made by us had we been in their place. But perfect models as they were of submission and of confidence, they set out without delay, certain that God would provide for all their necessities. And so it proved, for they found lodging and food, either by means of the trade exercised by St. Joseph, or by the alms bestowed upon them.

That we may not lose even one of the many instructions given us in this touching mystery, let us consider first that Our Lord, the Eternal Wisdom, does not Himself take the charge of His Family. Being perfect God and perfect Man, He already possessed the use of reason, and from the first instant of His Conception He could have made known to Joseph and to His Blessed Mother all that was to happen to them. However, God the Father had conferred upon the Angel Gabriel the care of the Holy Family, and therefore Our Lord would take no part in it. The Angel commands and is obeyed most faithfully, although he was inferior to Jesus and also to Mary, who, as Mother of God, was endowed with greater graces and perfections than all the celestial spirits.

But this is not all. Observe the order that reigns in this Holy Family. Who can doubt that Our Lady was superior to St. Joseph in discretion, as well as in all the other qualities required for good government? And, nevertheless, the Angel does not inform her of all that is to be done, but he informs her Spouse, St. Joseph. It might appear strange that he addresses himself to him rather than to Mary, the Mistress of the house, who carries the Treasure of the Eternal Father. Had she not every reason to be offended at this proceeding of the Angel, who seemed thus to ignore her? She could undoubtedly have said to her Spouse, ' Why should I go into Egypt, when neither my Son nor the Angel have made it known to me ?' But Our Lady is silent, and obeys with all simplicity, without being in the least concerned that the Angel had only spoken to St. Joseph. She knew well that all had been ordained by God ; she does not even inquire the reason, but the knowledge that such is the Will of God is sufficient to secure her prompt submission. It is thus God acts towards men—to teach them holy and loving submission. A merely human mind does not wish to yield and to adore the secret mysteries of God and of His Most Holy Will until it is able to ascertain *the why and the wherefore of this and that.* A thousand reasons are brought forward as of greater discernment or experience, and so on ; but they only cause disquiet, ill-temper, and complaints. From the time we begin to criticise everything disturbs us. Let us be satisfied to know what God wants of us, and let this suffice. But (some will say) who can assure us that such is the Will of God ? This shows that our hearts would prefer that God should manifest everything directly to us by means of secret inspirations, or that He should send an Angel to announce to us His Will. And yet he did not thus reveal it even to Our Lady, but wished her to come to the knowledge of it through St. Joseph, to whom she was subject, as to her superior.

11

Our self-love would like to be instructed sometimes by God Himself by means of ecstasies, visions, etc. We indulge ourselves in follies such as these that we may not be subject to the common and ordinary path of subjection to our rules and our superiors. Let it suffice for us to know that God wills our obedience without reflecting on the mental capacities of those who command us, and we shall accustom ourselves to walk with all simplicity in the happy road of holy and tranquil humility, which will render us pleasing to God. O! how many wonderful examples of obedience to the Will of God did not this glorious Virgin leave us during her whole life, and, above all, in her flight into Egypt! Whither, O glorious Virgin, do you direct your steps with that little Infant in your arms? I am going into Egypt, she replies. But why do you go there? Because it is the Will of God. For how long? As long as it pleases God. When will you return? When He shall command me to do so. But when you return will your heart be more happy than at present? O no, certainly not. And why? Because I fulfil the Will of God equally in going, in remaining there, and in returning. When you return, will you go into your own country? She replies, I know no country but the accomplishment of the Will of my God in everything.

O admirable example of obedience! Let us, in imitation of the Blessed Virgin, endeavour to

submit to authority at all times and in every cir-
cumstance, whether it be pleasing to us or not.
Let us go with all simplicity even as far as Egypt
—that is, into the midst of enemies—because God
Who sends us there will know how to protect us,
and assuredly we shall not perish. On the contrary,
if we remain in Israel with our enemy, self-will, it
will certainly be the destruction of us. In imitation of Mary and Joseph, let us answer the suggestions of the enemy of our soul when he urges
us to disobedience in these words : *Deus providebit*
—'God will provide.' O my God ! happy we if
we could accustom ourselves to answer our heart
always thus when it becomes anxious, and thus
banish all solicitude and trouble. Great indeed
is the confidence which God asks of us in His
Paternal care and Providence ; but why do we
refuse it to Him when we know that no one has
ever been deceived in Him, but, on the contrary,
has always reaped therefrom the most copious
fruits? And was not this the promise which Our
Saviour made to His Apostles when He urged
them to this loving confidence? 'Your Father in
heaven knoweth that ye have need of these things.'

SPIRITUAL FLOWERS.

Obedience has the property of changing the
flower of our desires into the fruits of good works.
Shun singularity as far as possible, and do not

make yourselves different exteriorly in any way
from others.—*St. Teresa.*

As the best honey is gathered from the flowers
of the thyme, which is a small and bitter herb, so
when virtues are exercised in the bitterness of the
most humble tribulations, they become truly
excellent.—*St. Francis of Sales.*

As the sun gives its heat no less to a rose amidst
a thousand other flowers than if it were alone, so
Our Lord does not diffuse His love the less upon
one soul because He also loves an infinity of others.
The power of His love never diminishes on account
of the multitude of rays that it diffuses, but is
always unchangeable in its immensity.—*The same.*

EXAMPLE.

The Excellence of the ' Hail Mary.'

The first *Hail Mary* pronounced by an Angel
produced the greatest of all miracles, and was the
source of the salvation of sinful men. If our redemption began with the Angelic Salutation, it
follows that our salvation depends in a special
manner upon this prayer. If it gave birth to the
fruit of eternal life upon this dry and barren earth
when it was brought by the messenger of Heaven,
it will, if we recite it devoutly, give birth to Jesus
Christ in our soul. It is a celestial dew which
fertilizes souls, and those that are not refreshed by

it do not produce fruit but only briars and thorns. The Most Holy Virgin made the follow-ing revelation to the Blessed Alan : ' Know, my son, and do not forget to make it known, that it is a probable sign of damnation to have tepidity, aversion, and negligence in the recital of the Angelical Salutation which brought salvation to the world.'

I know nothing, O Mary, says Thomas à Kempis, that is so glorious for you and so con-soling for us as the Angelical Salutation : its sweet-ness is so great that no words can express it. Most certain it is, says another servant of Mary, that this prayer never ascends to Heaven without obtaining great favours for the body as well as the soul ; because this tender Mother always responds with some grace when we salute her with the *Hail Mary.* The Blessed Virgin promised St. Gertrude as many favours at the hour of her death as she had recited *Ave Marias* during her life ; and she also counselled St. Bridget to recite this prayer to obtain the pardon of some acts of impatience. We know that this Mother of Mercy taught St. Dominic the Holy Rosary as the most efficacious means for obtaining the conversion of heretics and sinners. And, in fact, the historians of that period relate that the first-fruits of this new devotion were manifested by the abjuration of more than a hundred thousand heretics, and the conversion of an incredible number of sinners.

Let us also quote the beautiful words of a Saint. The '*Ave Maria*,' well recited, is the enemy that puts the devil to flight, and the weapon that kills him.   It is the sanctification of the soul, the gladness of Angels, the melody of the predestinated, the Canticle of the New Testament, the joy of Mary, and the glory of the Most Holy Trinity. The *Ave Maria* is a celestial dew that fertilizes the soul, a beautiful rose which we present to Mary, and a precious pearl which we bestow upon her. Finally, it is the most magnificent eulogium which can be offered in her honour, and the attractions it possesses have so much power over her heart, that she is constrained to love him who recites it well.'

Another great servant of the Immaculate Virgin says of himself, that whenever he pronounced these words, *Hail Mary*, the world in his eyes lost all beauty, he felt an increase of Divine love, a more fervent devotion, more firmness in hope, greater joy, and a renewal of virtue and strength in his whole being.

Prayer of St. Bernard.—O sovereign Mistress of Angels and of men, to you do we turn our eyes! We must all appear one day before the Eternal Judge; alas! how shall we dare to present ourselves before Him, loaded as we are with so many sins, and who shall appease His just indignation? No one, O Mother of Mercy, can so assuredly do this but you who loved Him so much, and who were so tenderly loved by Him.   Open then, O Mother of

Grace, your compassionate ears to our sighs, and the bowels of your mercy to our tears ; to you do we run as to our dear Mother. Ah ! appease the just indignation of your Divine Son, and restore us to His favour. You do not abhor the sinner, nor do you reject him, however unworthy he may be, if, repentant, he implores your patronage. To you, then, do I have recourse, O my Mother ; animate me to hope, sustain my weakness, abandon me not for a single instant, and reconcile me to my Eternal Judge, that I may be able to find mercy at the moment of my death. Amen.

Ejaculation.—*Monstra te esse matrem* — Show me, O Mary, that you are my mother !

Practice.—Whatever contradiction you may meet with this day, accept it with resignation, and with the reflection that *God wills it.*

NINETEENTH DAY.

MARY, AT THE MARRIAGE OF CANA, TEACHES US THE BEST METHOD OF PRAYER.

' THERE was a marriage,' says St. John, ' in Cana of Galilee, and the Mother of Jesus was there. And Jesus also was invited and His disciples.'

Let us consider the goodness of our adorable Saviour in not refusing the invitation to the wedding. He had come to redeem and reform man, and therefore would not assume a rigid and austere

manner. He was always gentle and courteous, so
as to draw men to follow Him. His presence at
the wedding was a restraint upon all levity and
excesses that so often occur on these occasions.
O faithful souls ! what modesty must have reigned
at these nuptials, in the presence of Our Lord and
of the Most Holy Virgin ! The failing of the wine
was pre-ordained by the Will of God, Who wished,
by a miracle, to manifest His power to those
assembled, and in particular to His Apostles. The
Most Holy Virgin, in her wisdom and prudence,
knowing that the wine failed, was moved by the
most ardent charity to find an expedient for sup-
plying it. And how does she act? Well aware of
the power and goodness of her Divine Son, and of
His charity and mercy, she was certain that He
would supply what was required, all the more as
the married couple were not rich, and she knew
He took pleasure in relieving the poor and con-
versing with them. She turned, therefore, to her
Divine Son ; and notice well how Our Blessed Lady
acted, and what she said : *Vinum non habent*—
‘ They have no wine.’   These words imply, ‘ These
good people are poor, and although their poverty
is pleasing and dear to You, nevertheless, in itself,
it is a misfortune, and is often the cause of confusion before men. You are Omnipotent, and can
relieve their wants, and I doubt not Your charity
and mercy will make some return for the kind
invitation they have given us to assist at this feast

by providing for them in their present need.' The Holy Virgin, however, did not utter so many words when she asked this miracle ; she was most skilled in the art of praying well, and made use of the shortest and most suitable method that could be found, saying : ' They have no wine.' Mary speaks to Our Lord with the greatest possible reverence. She does not address Him in terms of arrogance or presumption, like many thoughtless and indiscreet persons when they ask, but she simply represents to Him the need of the guests, sure that He would hear her petition. What an excellent manner of prayer is this, to expose our necessities simply to God, and then abandon ourselves into His adorable hands, certain that He will succour us in that way which is most to our advantage ! For instance, to say to Him : Lord, behold one of Thy poor creatures, who is desolate, afflicted, full of aridity, of miseries and sins, but Thou knowest my wants, and it is enough for me to manifest to Thee my state. To Thee it belongs to deliver me from so many miseries, in the manner and at the time that thou knowest to be most conducive to Thy glory and my salvation.

We may ask God, also, for temporal blessings ; of this there is no doubt ; for Our Lord Himself has taught us, in the *Our Father* to ask first that *the Kingdom of God may come* as the *end* to which we aspire, and that *His Holy Will be done* as the sole means to attain this *end ;* and afterwards to ask Almighty God to *give us our daily bread* (*Panem nostrum quotidianum da nobis hodie*). Therefore Holy Church has authorized particular prayers for temporal blessings; for peace, in times of war; rain, in seasons of drought, and so on; and also special Masses for procuring relief in times of pestilence, and in other necessities. No doubt we can have recourse to God in all our wants, both spiritual and temporal, in two ways : by merely exposing to Him our necessities, as did the Most Holy Virgin, or by asking Him for that grace which in particular we require, but always with this condition, that *His Will be done and not ours.* And yet, in general, even when spiritual persons ask God for His holy love, which softens and lightens every difficulty, they take care not to include in their petition those virtues that mortify nature.

Spiritual Flowers.

However slight the services we render to the Blessed Virgin Mary, they are always dear to God, and He rewards them with eternal glory.—*St. Teresa.*

When you find yourself in any great difficulty, do not take any step without having first considered eternity.—*St. Francis of Sales.*

He who is capable of exercising mildness in sufferings, generosity under ill-treatment, and peace amidst discord, is almost perfect. Mildness, sweetness of heart, and evenness of temper are virtues as rare as is the virtue of chastity.—*The same.*

EXAMPLE.

The Advantages of the ' Hail Mary.'

After having considered in the preceding example the esteem in which this prayer was held by the Saints, let us now consider its advantages.

Mary rejoices greatly when she is addressed in the Angelical Salutation, as she herself revealed to St. Mechtild, saying that of all the honours that can be rendered her none is more pleasing, or gives more joy, than this prayer, to which are added the words, ' Holy Mary, Mother of God, pray for us sinners,' etc. This prayer reminds her of the obligation she is under to have compassion on poor sinners, to pray for them, to love them. Sinners are the occasion of all her happiness, ' because,' said she, ' I should not have found grace if they had not lost it ; I should not have been chosen to be the Mother of the Saviour if it had not been necessary to save them ; and lastly, I should not have received such an abundance of graces had it not been necessary that I should become the Mother of Mercy and the Refuge of Sinners.'

But the recitation of the *Hail Mary* does not form the joy of Mary alone ; it is also the joy of the Angels and of the Saints. Blessed Alan says that the words of this prayer convey joy to all the inhabitants of heaven. The Angelical Salutation is the distinctive salute of the Angels to Mary ; and these blessed spirits enjoy a special delight in offering it to her frequently every day. But whilst this admirable prayer causes all Paradise to exult with joy, and is a source of grace to faithful souls, it is also the terror of the demons, who take flight as soon as they hear it pronounced. When the *Hail Mary* was brought from heaven by an Angel, the earth leapt for joy, on account of its approaching deliverance. But hell seemed already to foresee the formidable presence of the Omnipotent Who was to destroy the empire of Satan ; and it trembled with fear when this salutation was uttered. No wonder, then, that the impious, who are children of the accursed spirits, should adopt their sentiments and hate all that relates to the mystery of the Incarnation, and speak contemptuously of the Holy Rosary and of devotion to the Blessed Virgin. However, experience shows us that the more a soul gives signs of predestination, the more does she love, relish, and gladly recite the *Hail Mary ;* and the more she loves God, the more does she love this prayer. ' I have no surer secret for ascertaining if a person love God,' says the venerable Louis Marie de Montfort, 'than to examine if he love to recite the *Ave Maria* or the Rosary.'

Prayer.—Help us, O Mother full of mercy, and do not allow the multitude of our sins to weaken your love for us. Remember that our adorable Saviour deigned to take from you a mortal body, not to condemn but to save sinners. If it were for your own personal glory alone that you were chosen to be the Mother of God, it might be said that our eternal salvation, or damnation, matters but little to you ; but it was for the salvation of all men that your Divine Son clothed Himself with our flesh. What advantage would accrue to us from your happiness and power if you did not make use of your power to render us partakers of your happiness? You know the need we have of your assistance; and therefore we recommend ourselves earnestly to you. Help us, that we may not have the misfortune to lose our souls, but may eternally love and serve your Divine Son with you in His kingdom of glory. Amen.

Ejaculation.—Obtain for us, O Mary, by your powerful intercession, the grace not to lose the place which Our Saviour has prepared for us in Paradise.

Practice.—Ask Mary to obtain for you from God all the graces you are in need of to-day.

TWENTIETH DAY.

THE PETITION OF MARY AT THE MARRIAGE OF CANA WAS FULL OF CONFIDENCE.

LET us endeavour, by the Divine assistance, to discover all the lessons contained in the petition of Mary and in the answer of Jesus.

Mary turns to Jesus, and says to Him : *Vinum non habent*—'They have no wine ;' and He replies : *Quid mihi, et tibi est, mulier ? Nondum venit hora mea*—'Woman, what is there in common between Me and thee ? My hour is not yet come.'

This reply at first sight seems harsh, and it surprises us, coming from such a Son and addressed to such a Mother. Is it possible that so respectful a Son should reject with asperity a prayer made with so much reverence and humility by the most loving and the most loved of Mothers ? Has the creature no part with her Creator from Whom she receives her being and her life ? Has the Mother nothing to do with her Son, nor the Son with the Mother, from whom He received His Body and His Blood ? These words seem, as I have said, somewhat strange, and are difficult to understand ; indeed, they have been misinterpreted by some who, having kept merely to the letter, have unhappily originated several forms of heresy. However, the reply was most loving, and the Holy Virgin, who

well understood its genuine sense, considered herself the happiest of Mothers. This she expressed,
with a heart full of confidence, in her answer to
the waiters. 'You have heard,' she said, 'the reply
my Son has made me, and perhaps, not understanding the language of love, you fear that He is
indignant at my petition; but it is not so, fear not;
whatsoever He shall say to you, do ye'—*Quæcum-
que dixerit vobis, facite.*

The opinions of the Doctors upon the words of
Our Blessed Saviour are various; many think that
His meaning was: 'It does not belong to us to
meddle in this affair; as we are merely amongst
the invited, we should not observe what is required
or not required at the wedding.' However, the
greater number of the holy Fathers of the Church
think that Our Lord thus replied to His Most Holy
Mother, in order to teach those of high position in
the Church not to make use of their influence in
favour of their relations, in things which are contrary
to the law of God or to the perfection of their state.
To give this lesson to the world, He made use of the
tender Heart of Mary, and, in doing so, He certainly gives us a very great proof of His love.
His words signified that He knew well the tenderness and perfection of the love His Mother bore
Him, and the firmness of her will, and therefore was
well assured that the apparent harshness of His
words would in no way trouble her soul. On this
account the Most Holy Virgin did not lose con-

fidence when she received His answer, but said to
the waiters : 'Whatsoever He shall say to you, do
ye.'   Our Lord loves most tenderly those who
abandon themselves, like His Most Holy Mother,
completely to His care, allowing themselves to
be governed by His Divine Providence, without
caring whether the result be sweet or bitter,
certain that the parental Heart of God will never
permit the least thing to happen which will not
turn to their advantage, if they have a perfect
and filial confidence in Him.   We ought, then, to
imitate this example of Mary on all occasions,
whether prosperous or adverse ; allowing ourselves
to be led by the Divine Will without ever seeking
the accomplishment of our own.   It is true that
great confidence is necessary to enable us to
abandon ourselves thus unreservedly to Divine
Providence ; but, if we do so, Our Lord takes care
of everything, and conducts all for our advantage ;
while if we reserve something to ourselves, not
confiding entirely in Him, then He abandons us.
It is as if He were to say : You believe that you
are capable of succeeding without My succour,
therefore I shall withdraw, and you will see what
will be the result.

This perfect abandonment must be grounded
upon the infinite goodness of God, and upon the
merits of the Passion and Death of Our Lord
Jesus Christ, and accompanied by a firm and

perfect resolution to give ourselves entirely to God leaving all things to His loving Providence.

SPIRITUAL FLOWERS.

In Arabia Felix, not only the plants which are called aromatical are sweet scented, but all plants without distinction, because they all experience the influence of the sun's intense heat. So all the works of a soul that is replenished with charity or the virtue of holy love, even the very least, have a most pleasing fragrance before the Divine Majesty, Who rewards them with an increase of charity.—*St. Francis of Sales.*

If you sincerely love God, you will often speak of Him. As bees gather honey only with their mouths, so your tongue will be always honeyed with the words you speak of your God ; and never will your mouth taste such sweetness as when you sing the praises and blessings of His Most Holy Name. —*The same.*

As some herbs, when well masticated, produce so great sweetness as to appease hunger and thirst, so one who receives from God the celestial manna of interior consolation cannot in any way desire the consolations of the world, though it be only to receive a momentary satisfaction.—*The same.*

EXAMPLE.

Further Advantages of the ' Hail Mary.'

Let us glory, says a pious author, in repeating this salutation with the Angel Gabriel, the Apostles, the Martyrs, and all the Christian world. Let this *Ave Maria*, which comes to us fragrant as a Canticle of heaven, and repeated by as many echoes as there are faithful souls on earth, be sweet to our lips, and sweeter still to our hearts. It is a rare and enviable favour indeed to be able to salute a queen, and yet every day, at every moment, men and women, old and young, all of every condition, can salute the Queen of heaven and earth, who contains in her hands all the treasures of God, and can be sure of being always heard, and that each salutation addressed to her will meet with a corresponding benefit. . . . But can the sinner also dare to approach her? Yes, certainly; let him also come with humble confidence and salute her who is his refuge, for she will in no wise be offended by his prayer; and if the *Hail Mary* from his lips be a cry of sorrow and repentance, it will become omnipotent, and will obtain mercy, pardon, grace, and salvation.

Hail Mary !—*Ave Maria !* . . . A sweet and beautiful word it is, which heaven sent to earth, and earth again returns so frequently to heaven !

The *Ave Maria* is the universal prayer of each

and all. The infant begins to lisp it, and on his knees, with his hands raised to heaven, says *Ave Maria !* The aged, weakened by infirmity, may be incapable of reciting long prayers, but they will always have sufficient strength to repeat devoutly the *Ave Maria.* This is the favourite prayer of just souls. Oh, how many times in the day does it rise from their hearts full of burning love, and ascend, like purest burning incense to the throne of Mary ! *Ave Maria !* . . . it is also the prayer of sinners, and perhaps their only prayer. In the great number of these there are some, alas ! who have forgotten all other prayers, but they still know and repeat the *Ave Maria.* Yes ; amidst the universal wreck of all other prayers and practices of religion, the *Ave Maria* or *Hail Mary* has remained for them ever a means of salvation. . . . How many poor wrecked souls have been led back to the haven of salvation by this means !

Prayer.—O Jesus ! only Son of God, Who from the bosom of Thy Eternal Father, descended into the bosom of Mary, Thy Mother, receive the homage of my adoration and love. Through Thee I go to Thy Father, and through Thy Mother I come to Thee. Like the spouses at Cana, I dare not address my prayer directly to Thee, but I fear nothing when I direct it through Thy Blessed Mother. O Lord ! well Thou knowest that I have no wine, no courage, nor strength, nor holy and generous resolutions ; I have lost all ! Ah !

say not to Thy Mother, who intercedes in my
favour : 'Woman, what is there in common between us ?' because I know for certain that she is
all-powerful over Thy filial Heart.   Add not ' My
hour is not yet come !'   Ah, no ; Thy hour, O my
God, to benefit those who pray to Thee, through
Thy Blessed Mother, is ever at hand.   O Lord !
behold, the vessel of my heart is full of the insipid
waters of earth ; change this water into the
delicious wine of holy affections for heaven,
where the Saints celebrate the nuptials of the
Lamb amidst eternal joys.   Amen.

Ejaculation.—Succour my weakness, O most
powerful Virgin !

Practice. — Endeavour to preserve confidence
in God, when He delays the graces you desire.

TWENTY-FIRST DAY.

MARY OBTAINS THE FIRST MIRACLE FROM JESUS BY HER LIVELY FAITH.

THAT we may conceive a just idea of the power
the Most Holy Virgin possesses over the Heart of
Jesus, let us meditate upon those other words
which He addressed to her at the marriage of
Cana : *Nondum venit hora mea*—'My hour is not
yet come.'

Without discussing the opinion of certain Doctors,
who think that Our Lord, by these words, meant to

say that the wine was not yet wanted, I shall call your attention to this reflection : that there are certain times ordained by Divine Providence upon which our conversion and salvation depend.

It is certain that God had from all eternity determined the hour and moment when He would work the great miracle of His Incarnation, and give to the world the first sign of His power, but yet this determination could be accelerated by prayer.

The greater number of the Fathers assert that Mary, by her loving sighs and aspirations, merited the acceleration of the Incarnation of Our Lord. Not, indeed, that He became Incarnate before the time that He had determined, but that, from all eternity He foresaw that the Holy Virgin would beg Him to hasten the time of His coming into the world ; and therefore, in consideration of the great merit of her intercession, He ordained to become Man sooner than He would have done had He not been petitioned to do so. The same may be said of the first miracle, wrought by Our Lord at the wedding of Cana. *Nondum venit hora mea*—' My hour is not yet come,' said Jesus to His Holy Mother, ' but as I can refuse you nothing, I shall hasten to hear your prayer.'

Oh, how precious is that hour in which Divine Providence wills to impart to us those special graces and blessings that are necessary for our salvation. Happy the soul who awaits this hour patiently, and who endeavours to prepare herself for it when it arrives. The Samarian woman assuredly was converted at this hour, and upon its arrival will depend also our own conversion and spiritual regeneration. We will now consider how Our Lord acted when He worked this miracle.

In the hall were seven stone urns, prepared for the purification, practised by the Jews. Our Lord ordered them to be filled with water, *Implete hydrias aqua;* and as the waiters had already been directed by Mary to follow punctually the orders of her Divine Son, they filled them 'up to the brim,' as the Sacred Text expresses it. Afterwards Our Saviour said something interiorly, not understood by anyone, and the water was instantly changed into most excellent wine. These words which He spoke were similar, without doubt, to those by which He drew all things out of nothing, or by which He gave being and life to man, or by which, also, at His last supper with His disciples, He changed wine into His adorable Blood, and thus instituted the Most Holy Sacrament of the Eucharist, giving to us, through it, that most excellent wine which nourishes us for eternal life.

This fact in the Gospel shows us, moreover, the great confidence we should have in the powerful intercession of Our Lady. But in order that she may represent our necessities to her Divine Son, we must invite her and our adorable Saviour to our banquet, because wine can never fail when

Jesus and Mary are present; this Mother of Mercy being ever prepared to ask it for us, and her Divine Son ever ready to bestow it.

However, if we desire Our Lady to intercede with her Divine Son that He may change the water of our tepidity into the wine of His fervent love, we must imitate the waiters at the marriage of Cana, and do all that Our Lord shall tell us. Obey Him, then, with fidelity, O ye servants of God, fill your hearts well with the penitential water of repentance, and He will change it into the wine of His holy love. In order to obtain the spirit of fervour, nourish your mind with holy thoughts; make frequent ejaculations, and, as a general rule, if you wish to be recollected in time of prayer, avoid dissipation during the day, and waste no time in useless reflections upon yourself, or on what happens around you. Keep yourself in the presence of God, and repose in the loving arms of His Providence. Bless this adorable Providence continually during life, and you will glorify It eternally in heaven, with all the Saints and blessed spirits.

SPIRITUAL FLOWERS.

The Spouse in the Canticles says that her hands distil myrrh—a liquor which preserves from corruption; her eyes are like those of the dove, in their purity; from her ears hang pendants of gold, as a sign of chastity; her lips are vermilion, the symbol of her modesty in speech; and her nose like the tower of Lebanon, of incorruptible wood. Such should be the devout servant of God— chaste, pure and unspotted in her whole soul and body.—*St. Francis of Sales.*

Clasp Jesus closely to your breast; let Him be a beautiful and sweet bouquet of flowers upon your heart, so that whoever approaches you may be conscious of the perfume, and know that the fragrance of your life should be of myrrh—the symbol of mortification.—*The same.*

Keep always close to Jesus Crucified, in spirit, in meditation, and in reality by Holy Communion. As he who is accustomed to lie down upon a certain species of herb becomes chaste and pure, so your soul and your heart will be very quickly purified from every spot and from every unruly desire when Our Lord, Who is the true Lamb of God, reposes upon your heart.—*The same.*

EXAMPLE.

Most pleasing to Our Blessed Lord is our Devotion to His Mother.

St. Teresa relates the following :

'Don Bernadino de Mendoza, to testify his devotion to the Most Holy Virgin, came to offer me his house, at Pico de Olmos, near Valladolid, for a

Convent of Our Lady of Carmel. To say the truth, I felt some repugnance to found a religious house far from a town, yet the offering had been made so cordially, and for so holy a purpose, that I considered I ought not to refuse it, and thus deprive the young gentleman of so much merit.

'About two months afterwards he was seized by a mortal illness, deprived of the power of speech, and died without having been able to make his confession. The Divine Master then said to me: "His salvation, my dear daughter, was in great danger; but I showed him mercy, in reward of the house he had made over for the foundation of a Convent consecrated to My Mother, under the title of Carmel. However, he will not be released from Purgatory until the first Mass is celebrated in that Convent."

'From that time my mind was ever occupied with the thought of his sufferings. The foundation of Valladolid could not be formed as quickly as I desired. One day, when I was stopping at St. Joseph's, at Medina del Campo, whilst I was at prayer, Our Lord said to me: "Make haste, because this soul suffers much." After this nothing could induce me to delay. Being arrived at Valladolid, although the house was unhealthy, I prepared some cells, just for the time being, and provided merely what was absolutely necessary. When Sunday arrived, notwithstanding the delay of the formal authorization, permission was granted to have Mass celebrated on the spot which was destined for the Church. I did not, indeed, believe that the promise of Our Lord regarding this gentleman would be fulfilled then; on the contrary, I was persuaded that the words, *until the first Mass,* related to that Mass when the Blessed Sacrament would be reserved for the first time in the Church. But when the Priest turned towards us, with the sacred ciborium in his hand, to communicate us, and I had approached the Altar to receive the sacred Host, I saw the gentleman by the side of the Priest, full of joy and resplendent with light. He thanked me for all I had done to deliver him from the flames of Purgatory, and then ascended to heaven.

'Oh, how precious is any service, however small, that we are able to render the Most Holy Virgin! Who can tell how pleasing it is to Our Lord, and how mercifully He rewards it?'

Prayer.—O Mother! full of love and clemency towards us, you are penetrated with the same sentiments as your Divine Son, and you also say with Him: 'Whenever the sinner returns to me with sincere sorrow for his offences, he always finds me ready to receive him with kindness and tenderness. I think not of the malice, or the number of his sins, but I only look at the desire he has to be converted; and I am always disposed to implore a remedy for his wounds, because I am, in deed and in name, the Mother of Grace and of Mercy!'

O Mary! since you never reject the sinner who returns to you with a resolution to amend, and since you have the power, as well as the will, to obtain the cure of all the wounds of the heart, behold me at your feet, full of confidence. Behold, I beseech you, the deep and cankered wounds of my soul, and if you will deign to offer your prayers to your Divine Son for me, I shall hope every thing for my eternal salvation. Amen.

Aspiration. — Through your intercession, O tender Mother, I hope to obtain the eternal happiness of heaven !

Practice.—Let all the good works of this day be directed to obtain the conversion of sinners.

TWENTY-SECOND DAY.

MARY CHOSE THE BETTER PART.

WE read in the Gospel that Martha, into whose house Our Lord had entered, was busy and troubled about many things in her anxiety to serve Him, whilst her sister Mary remained at His feet, listening to His words. Martha was concerned about Our Lord's bodily comfort, but Mary, laying aside every other thought, nourished her soul with the sacred instructions of her Divine Master. A soul, recollected interiorly before God, is sometimes so sweetly attentive to the goodness of her Beloved as not even to be aware of its attentiveness, so simply and gently is it exercised. Such souls are like those who navigate rivers the waters of which flow on so calmly that they neither see nor feel any motion. This delightful repose of the soul is called by St. Teresa 'The Prayer of Quiet.'

Martha, moved by a slight sentiment of envy (which is an almost universal vice, affecting even devout souls), complained thus to Our Lord: 'Master, hast Thou no care that my sister hath left me alone to serve? Speak to her, therefore, that she help me.' Our Lord, Who is Infinite Goodness, would not reprehend her seriously, although He knew the imperfection of her senti-ments, but He called her by name, gently and affectionately (for the whole Gospel is love), and said to her: 'Martha, Martha, thou art careful and troubled about many things; but one thing is necessary. Mary has chosen the better part, which shall not be taken from her!'—*Martha, Martha, sollicita es et turbaris erga plurima; porro unum est necessarium. Maria optimam partem elegit, quæ non auferetur ab ea.*

Whilst Martha was thus busy serving Our Divine Saviour, Mary had but one thought—to remain with Him and hear His words. This was also the one thought of Our Blessed Lady, the Most Holy Virgin. Observe her at Bethlehem, where all her efforts to find a lodging were vain; she says not a word, utters no complaint, but retires into a stable and places the newborn Infant in a manger! After a few days the Magi come to adore Him, and she receives in silence the praises addressed to her. She flies into Egypt, but shows no sign of grief; she returns to Judea without any manifestation of joy. On Calvary, at the feet of her Divine Son, she opens not her mouth, but listens to His words, for to hear them is all her desire. Indifferent to all things else, 'happen what will,' says she, 'whether He console me or afflict me, I am equally contented, provided I be near Him and possess Him.'

Thus does a soul abandoned to the Will of God remain in His arms, like a child on the bosom of his mother. When she places him on the ground he walks, and when she takes him again in her arms he allows himself to be carried, and is in no way troubled to know whither he is taken. Thus the soul cultivates tranquillity of heart, and advances continually in union with the Divine Goodness.

The exercise of union with God can be practised by means of short but frequent aspirations of the soul to God, such as : 'Ah, Jesus, who will give me to be but one spirit with Thee? I renounce all creatures and desire Thee alone, for this is the one thing needful. Ah! plunge my soul into the ocean of Thy Goodness, from whence it proceeds, and make me, O Lord, wholly Thine. Draw me, and I will run after Thy attractions, casting myself into Thy paternal arms, and never again withdrawing myself from them.'

A soul immersed in God dies not. How could it die if immersed in Him Who is life? It lives, then, but not in itself. As the planets do not shine in the presence of the sun, but the sun shines in them, so does it live, not, indeed, a natural life, but the life of Jesus Christ, Who lives in it.

In imitation of the Blessed Virgin we must make it our whole study to unite ourselves to Our Lord by advancing in perfection. Let us not, however, forget that our best means for attaining to this is to remain tranquil, and place all our confidence in Him Who alone can give increase to that which we have sown and planted. Our Lord desires from us a peaceful solicitude, which will lead us to obey those who direct us and walk with all fidelity in the paths they point out. We should abandon ourselves in all things to His Paternal care, and maintain peace of soul as far as possible, because Our Lord reposes in tranquil and peaceful hearts. When the waters of a lake are not agitated by the wind, the firmament with its stars is so vividly represented therein that, looking down into the deep, we can see its beauty as perfectly as if we were looking up to the heavens. So also when our souls are tranquil and undisturbed by superfluous cares or distractions, we are then well prepared to receive within us the image of Our Lord. But if the soul be disquieted, darkened, and agitated by the various tempests of the passions, and allows itself to be guided by them, and not by reason, which renders us like to God, it cannot reflect the beautiful image of Jesus Christ Crucified and His most excellent virtues, nor can He rest in the soul. We must abandon the thought of ourselves to Divine Providence, for anxiety of mind and the desire to know if we advance in virtue is not pleasing to God, and serves only to satisfy self-love, which is a great busybody that seeks to have a hand in everything. One work well done with peace of mind is more meritorious than many works performed with agitation and anxiety.

SPIRITUAL FLOWERS.

When the lily springs up from the earth it produces a number of long leaves, but as it grows higher the leaves near the flower are fewer and much smaller. These leaves represent our words. The more a soul progresses in the way of God and of perfection the fewer are her words.—*Père St. Jure.*

As the bees go all round their hive gathering honey here and there, and when they have collected it take pleasure in working it up, on account of its sweetness, so we meditate that we may acquire the love of God ; and then we contemplate Him, and are attracted by His goodness through the sweetness which His love causes us to experience. Hence the soul is never satiated with considering and looking upon the Divine Beauty. —*St. Francis of Sales.*

The occupations that are necessary for each one in his state of life are no hindrance to piety, but increase it and adorn the work of devotion. The nightingale loves its own melody when it is silent as much as when it sings; the devout heart also cherishes Divine love no less when it is distracted by the external duties of life than when it prays. Its action and its contemplation, its occupation, as well as its repose, equally chant the canticle of love. — *The same.*

EXAMPLE.

Beauty of the ' Ave Maris Stella.'

In this hymn are celebrated all the prerogatives of Mary. She is the powerful Mother of God and the most glorious of Virgins—*Dei Mater alma atque semper Virgo*—and at the same time the most sweet and humble of Virgins— *Virgo singularis inter omnes mitis.*

The Most Holy Virgin performs the function of advocate with her Divine Son in our favour, and offers Him our prayers—*Monstra te esse Matrem.*

She is the Gate of Heaven. She loosens the chains of sinners, guides the blind in the way of virtue, removes every kind of evil from us, and asks in our name for every grace necessary for us to reach the port of eternal life.—*Solve vincla reis.*

Nothing is more appropriate to inspire us with a tender confidence in Mary than the *Ave Maris Stella,* for its verses contain considerations of time and eternity. Let us, then, repeat it often, and Mary will load us with benedictions, as many miraculous facts in the lives of the Saints attest. Indeed, this Queen of Heaven herself showed how dear to her is this hymn when she appeared one day to St. Bridget, and thus addressed her: 'My Son, the Sovereign Master of heaven, of earth, and of hell, can Himself alone suppress all the powers of evil, from whatever source they may arise. I shall henceforth be a shield of defence for you and for the others against all the attempts of the enemies of your souls and bodies, on condition, however, that all your community meet together to sing every evening the *Ave Maris Stella.*'

The Saint did not fail to fulfil punctually the will of the Most Holy Virgin, and her example was followed by her Confessor, and her daughter, St. Catherine of Sweden, who caused this pious practice to be adopted by all the convents of the Order of St. Saviour. Let us then be glad to salute our most amiable Mother frequently with this hymn of the holy Abbot of Clairvaux. However, we must not be satisfied with merely singing it; let us also carry it in our minds and in our hearts; and, above all, strive to be penetrated with all the

13

affectionate sentiments it contains. Let us pray to St. Bernard to recommend us himself to the Queen of Angels, and obtain for us that she may be to us all that she was to him to the last instant of his life.

Most Blessed Virgin ! be my strength, my guide, my Mother ! and let me never become unworthy to bear the beautiful title of Child of Mary. *Monstra te esse Matrem.*

Prayer.—O Holy Virgin and Mother of God ! deign to succour those who implore your assistance. Cast an eye of compassion upon us, and be moved at the sight of our miseries. O Mother of Grace ! have you forgotten men in their tribulations and need, by reason of the sublime dignity to which you have been raised ? No, without doubt your heart will be ever interested in our favour, nor can your great mercy ever forget misery so profound as ours. Turn then towards us, and consider the many dangers to which we are continually exposed. God Almighty has constituted you the depositary of His power and of His graces ; pour them upon us in abundance, we beg of you. The more powerful you are, the more do I trust, O Mother of Mercy, that you will be singularly merciful to your afflicted children who have recourse to you. Amen.

Ejaculation.—O Mary ! you are able to succour me, and I hope your goodness will not refuse me this favour.

Practice.—Endeavour to recollect yourself frequently during the day, that you may act with greater purity of intention.

TWENTY-THIRD DAY.

THE BLESSED VIRGIN DID NOT NEGLECT THE DUTIES OF MARTHA.

THE conduct of Martha and Mary give us another touching subject for our meditation. These two sisters well represent to us Our Lady. Like Martha the Blessed Virgin Mary received her Son Our Lord into her house, and into her most chaste womb, when He came into this world, and with incomparable care she always served Him whilst He lived on earth, in reward of which He exalted her in heaven to an unparalleled glory. Like Mary, she listened to His words in uninterrupted silence, ✦and occupied herself only in loving Him. This glorious Virgin exercised admirably in the course of her life the offices of both of these sisters. But as regards the office of Martha, with what care and attention did she not serve Our Lord when an Infant! What diligence did she employ in avoiding the anger of Herod, and all the dangers with which His life was threatened !

Take notice that Our Lord reprehended Martha because she was disturbed and troubled, not because she was careful. Our Lady, like Martha,

took great care to serve our Divine Master well—
but her care was devoid of all disquiet and anxious
trouble.   The Saints in heaven are zealous for the
glory of God, but are not disquieted.   The Angels
are careful in all that regards our salvation, and
God Himself has care of His creatures, but always
in peace and undisturbed calm.   To us, miserable
creatures, however, this is difficult.   Some become
suddenly disturbed because they cannot do what
they desire; others wish to console and visit
the sick, but if they meet with some hindrance
they are immediately troubled; others will have a
great affection for mental prayer, and although this
relates only to God, yet even here human nature
enters, and they will be disturbed and troubled if
they are constrained to occupy themselves in some
other employment.

Now would Martha have been so much troubled
if she had had no other end in view than to please
Our Lord ?   No, certainly ; because one only
kind of food, well prepared, was sufficient for His
nourishment, and, moreover, because she saw that
the whole pleasure of her Divine Master was to be
listened to, as was done by her sister Mary.   But
Martha mingled a little self-esteem with her desire
to provide all that was necessary for our Divine
Master; and this moved her to wish that her
hospitality, in receiving those who honoured her
with their visits, should be recognised.   The good
lady believed that by this external service she

would become a great servant of God, and surpass others ; and through love for her sister she wished that she also should be solicitous to serve the Beloved Master, and thus, as she thought, acquire more merit. But our Divine Redeemer was more pleased with the practice of Mary, into whose heart He poured forth, through His divine words, graces surpassing all conception. This was the truth He wished also to inculcate, when He said, that those alone were blessed who should have listened to His word and practised it.

All that anxious restlessness and eager desire to do something for Our Lord, which some devout persons look upon as real virtue, is then a manifest error, reproved by our Divine Master, when He said : *Porro unum est necessarium*—' But one thing is necessary.'

You may ask, in reply, But how are we to prevent being uneasy when we are under an obligation of practising virtue? This solicitude is certainly not blamable, provided it be not over-anxious and troubled. Invoke frequently the one beautiful Dove of the Heavenly Spouse, that she may truly obtain for you the heart of a dove, and that you may not only be a dove in your flight towards heaven, by prayer, but also a dove in your nest, and with all those who surround you. Unite the office of Mary with that of Martha : diligently fulfil the duties of your state. Often cast yourself at the feet of Jesus, and say to Him

from your heart : O my Divine Master, whether I
go or stay, I am all Thine and Thou art all mine.
Thou art my only Spouse, and all that I am going
to do shall be for Thee.

As the birds have their nests in which to hide
themselves when needful, so our heart should
select and take possession of some spot every day,
either on Calvary or in the Sacred Wounds of Our
Lord, or near Him, whither it may retire on every
occasion to defend itself in temptations and re-
create itself after the many exterior affairs of the
day. Happy the soul that can truly say to Our
Lord : You are my house of refuge, my secure
home ; my roof, in time of rain, and my refresh-
ment under burning heats.

A remedy, however, against so many anxious
cares and troubles is to copy the practice of Mary,
because it was praised by Our Lord Himself, Who
called it the best and the one thing necessary.
Now, this one thing necessary is nothing else than
the exercise of Divine Love, which, as it contains
in itself the perfection of all other virtues, produces their acts in due time and place, according
to circumstances. In one word, then : *Possess holy
Charity, and no virtue will be wanting to you,
because all virtues are comprised in Charity.*

Spiritual Flowers.

The Most Holy Virgin Mary is compared to
an orange-tree laden with fruit, and diffusing the

sweetest odour of Lebanon. This means that all her thoughts, words, and actions were so perfect that, like an exquisite perfume, they delighted both Heaven and earth : and that, like the pomegranate, they wore the crown of perfection.—*Père S. Jure.*

The bee sucks honey from flowers without injuring them, and leaves them as entire and fresh as he found them. Devotion has this higher excellence, that it adds new beauty to all that it touches.—*St. Francis of Sales.*

Remember that when the bees make honey, they take bitter food ; so, also, we can never make acts of greater patience and sweetness, nor form better the honey of excellent virtues than by eating the bread of bitterness and living a life of tribulation.—*The same.*

EXAMPLE.

The 'Magnificat.'

The *Magnificat* is the first Canticle of the New Testament and the most magnificent Canticle of Holy Scripture. It presents us with most sublime ideas of the greatness of God, and is sung on solemn festivals, whilst Priests stand and incense the Altar.

We recite the *Magnificat* to thank God for all the graces bestowed upon the Most Holy Virgin. It is the only work she ever composed, and contains mysteries far surpassing our understanding. Hence this proverb was familiar amongst the ancient authors when they spoke of one who meddled with things beyond his capacity ; such a one would *correct the Magnificat.*

The Blessed Juliana had a special affection for this Canticle. Speaking of it one day to the Superior of a convent, she declared that she would not sacrifice the sweetness she experienced in reciting it for all the gold that the convent could contain. She repeated it nine times a day, in memory of the nine months that the Most Holy Virgin bore the Redeemer of the world in her womb ; and she desired ardently that all would follow her example, believing it impossible that Mary would not hear those who share in the joy she manifests in this Canticle.

Cardinal J. de Vitry, in the life of Ste. Marie de Ogniez, relates that when this Saint was near death, and was singing the *Magnificat,* the Mother of God appeared to her and told her to receive Extreme Unction, and she remained by her bedside in company with her Divine Son until the Saint expired.

St. Anselm relates of himself that when he was afflicted with various infirmities, which occasioned him the most acute suffering, he was perfectly cured by reciting the *Magnificat.*

Prayer.—August Mother of God, you are the Queen of Mercy, and I am the most miserable of sinners, and consequently your subject. You should then have greater compassion for me than for anyone less sinful. *Eia ergo advocata nostra, illos tuos misericordes oculos ad nos converte.*

O, our refuge and our advocate, turn one look of mercy towards us; interest yourself in our behalf; be moved to compassion for our evils, and obtain their cure. Deliver us from our miseries, and we shall never cease to sing the hymn of praise to your mercy, of which we have experienced the salutary effects. Amen.

Ejaculation.—Pray for me, O Mother of Grace, O Mother of Mercy !

Practice.—Whilst you fulfil the duties of your state in imitation of Martha, endeavour to have your mind and heart turned to Jesus as Mary had.

TWENTY-FOURTH DAY.

MARY IN HER SLEEP.

WE can begin to love God in this life, but it is only in the next that we shall be able to love Him perfectly. In the expression *we* I do not intend to speak of the Most Holy Virgin, because she is the Daughter of beautiful Love, the one only dove, the perfect Spouse. Yes ; the charity of Mary surpassed that of the Seraphim. 'If all the daughters have gathered riches, thou hast surpassed them all.'

The Saints and Angels are compared to stars,

but Mary is beautiful as the moon, distinguished amidst the Saints as the moon amidst the stars. As her charity surpasses in heaven that of all the blessed, so did she exercise it with greater excellence on earth ; for never having sinned, even venially, her love never met with any obstacle, and thus increased at every instant. What progress, then, must she not have made in the exercise of holy love? Say not that the Most Holy Virgin, like all men, was subject to the necessities of life. It may be said, in the words of the Canticles, that her sleep was the sleep of Love, the celestial Spouse saying, '*I adjure you, daughters of Jerusalem, that you stir not nor awake my love till she please.*'

The Queen of heaven and earth granted to her chaste body that repose only which was necessary to restore its strength, in order to serve God more perfectly ; and we may say that her sleep never interrupted the exercise of holy love, because it proceeded from an act of most excellent charity. Does not St. Augustine teach that we must love our body, that it may serve us in those works which God requires of us, and because it forms part of ourselves, and is one day to share our eternal felicity ?

The Most Holy Virgin, indeed, had other reasons to love her body with a virtuous love, because it was not only pure, submissive, and docile to all the functions of holy love and embalmed by Divine sweetness, but it was, moreover, the living source of the Sacred Body of Our Saviour. Thus it belonged to her in an incomparably singular manner, so that before yielding to sleep she could truly say to it, ' Rest from your fatigues, O throne of the Divinity, tabernacle of the new Covenant, ark of all Sanctity; recruit your strength through the repose which I allow you to take.'

Ah ! sweet Jesus ! what must have been the thoughts of your Most Holy Mother whilst sleep refreshed her body and her heart was watching ! We may imagine that her most frequent thought was of her Divine Son, Who had so often slept upon her bosom as the lamb reposes upon the soft wool of its mother. She would also feel that she rested in His adorable side, opened by the lance on Calvary, as a white dove rests in the cleft of a rock. Thus her sleep, which was a sweet repose and an agreeable solace to her body, became a kind of ecstasy to her soul, through the spiritual effects and operations it produced.

If she also represented to herself her future glory, like Joseph, the saviour of Egypt, and saw herself clothed with the sun and the moon under her feet —that is to say, surrounded by the glory of her Divine Son, and resplendent with the glory of the Saints who form her crown as she rules over the universe, of which she is the Queen ; or if, like Jacob, she foresaw the wonderful fruits that Angels and men would obtain through the Redemption, O ! conceive, if possible, children of Mary, the delights caused by such spiritual entertainments !

There is one kind of diamond which has this special property—that nothing can diminish its fine water or the brilliancy which nature has given it. The Heart of the Virgin Mother, like this diamond, never ceased to glow with the sacred fire of love that she had received from her Divine Son.   However, though the brilliancy of precious stones does not diminish, yet it does not increase ; whilst the love of the Most Holy Virgin never remained in the same state, but made continual and incredible progress until she entered heaven.   With good reason, then, is Our Lady called the Mother of pure Love — that is to say, the most lovable amongst all creatures, and the most beloved by her only Son, Who is loved by her as the most lovable and loving of Sons.

SPIRITUAL FLOWERS.

Forgetfulness of God is the sleep of the soul. The soul has been asleep all the time that it has forgotten its God.—*St. Augustine.*

The sleep of the Saints is a prayer before God. —*St. Jerome.*

It is great blindness and misery to seek repose where it is impossible to find it.—*St. Teresa.*

EXAMPLE.

Devotion to the 'Salve Regina.'

St. Bernard is celebrated for his love of the Blessed Virgin and for the praises he has rendered to her. His language is of such sweetness, that it surpasses that of all preceding ages for beauty and tenderness in discoursing of the Blessed Virgin Mary. This saint seems to have gathered together and made his own all the most loving affections of the most fervent servants. Mary was his ruling thought, and he could not restrain the transports of his heart when he spoke of her. The very mention of her name sufficed to render him ecstatic. With good reason, then, did Peter the Abbot of St. Remigius, at Rheims, say to one of St. Bernard's adversaries: 'If you have the courage to touch the pupil of Mary's eye, write against St. Bernard.'

This Saint was commissioned to preach the second general Crusade throughout Europe, and when he had traversed France, Belgium and the Rhenish countries, he retired to the Abbey of Effinghem, to recollect his soul in that pious solitude. One evening the Monks were moved to tears by a discourse of St. Bernard's in praise of Mary, and they begged him to intone the *Salve Regina*, which they sang every evening before her image. As the Saint could not excuse himself, he devoutly intoned the *Salve* with his powerful voice, and was accompanied by all the Monks. When the sweet words *Et Jesum benedictum fructum ventris tui, nobis post hoc exilium ostende* had been sung, all were silent (because at that time the anthem ended with these words). However, the inspired voice of Bernard continued, and he gave expression to the sentiments of his heart in the three invocations with which it is now concluded : *O clemens, O pia, O dulcis Virgo Maria !* These words were afterwards adopted by the whole Church.

It is in commemoration of this event that the *Salve Regina* is solemnly sung every evening in the Cathedral of Spire.

St. Vincent de Paul used to say that no prayer is so suitable to us miserable exiles in this valley of tears as this : *Salve Regina, Mater misericordiæ . . . Ad te clamamus, exules filii Hevæ.*

St. Philip Neri, having heard the confession of a famous criminal, spoke thus to him : 'My son, I shall require but little from you, and if you fulfil it I assure you that you will be saved. Promise me to place all your confidence in the Most Blessed Virgin, the Mother of Divine Grace, and for this purpose recite the *Salve Regina* seven times every day in her honour, and kiss the ground the same number of times, saying : " I may die this moment." ' The penitent made the promise and kept it. He died holily fourteen years after, full of gratitude and love towards his good Mother Mary.

Prayer.—Most amiable Heart of Mary, object of the complacency of the adorable Trinity, and worthy of the veneration of Angels and of men ; Heart like unto that of Jesus Christ and its most perfect image; Heart full of goodness and compassion for our miseries ! Oh, break the ice of our hearts, turn our affections towards the adorable Heart of Our Saviour, and impress on them the love of your virtues. Watch over Holy Church, protect it, and be to it an impregnable fortress, so that it may be secure amidst all the assaults of its enemies. Be you our way to God, our succour in our trials, our consolation in sufferings, our strength in temptations, and our refuge in persecutions. Above all things assist us at the point of death, when hell will exert all its efforts for our eternal ruin. Let us then, indeed, experience the power you have over the Heart of Jesus, that we may find a secure asylum in the bosom of His Mercy, and then, with you, praise Him throughout ages and ages. Amen.

Ejaculation.—I sleep, O Mother, but my heart watches.

Practice.—Endeavour to be reflecting upon some eternal truth when you fall asleep.

TWENTY-FIFTH DAY.

MARY ON CALVARY IS THE MOTHER OF ALL CHRISTIANS.

OUR Beloved Saviour had instituted the Sacrament of Love that He might remain amid His children. He had poured forth all His Blood for us, and He wished moreover to bequeath us a legacy in the last Testament of His Love.   But what more could He give us?   He casts a compassionate look upon His tender Mother, who stands immovable at the foot of the Cross with His beloved disciple.   It is not to enrich her with His grace, for she already possessed it most excellently; nor is it to promise her glory, she was sure of it; but it is to infuse into her heart, before He died, a more tender and ardent love for men than she yet possessed.   'Woman,' says He to her, pointing to the beloved disciple, '*behold your son!*'   What an exchange was this !   The servant instead of the Only Son—the creature in place of the Creator ! And yet she does not refuse it, well knowing that she accepted for her children, in the person of John, all the followers of the Cross of Jesus, and that she was to become the beloved Mother of all Christians.

Although Our Lady gave birth to none but our adorable Saviour, yet, in a spiritual sense, she brought forth all Christians in the Person of Our Saviour; because this Blessed Seed has begotten us all by His death. A seed when planted produces a tree, from which are produced other seeds, all of which may be said to belong to the original fruit from which the tree came forth. Thus, as the Most Holy Virgin brought forth this mystic Seed, which when cast on earth, budded and brought forth many other seeds, she has consequently brought us all forth and has become the Mother of us all. How much we ought to love the Son and the Mother! for they are our Divine parents, and it is impossible to love one without loving the other.*

As Holy Church wishes to teach us to go to Jesus through Mary, she directs that the Angelical Salutation should follow the *Our Father*, that we may thus petition, through her, for all benefits, both spiritual and temporal, as far as these latter are conducive to our eternal salvation. We also implore the intercession of Mary in order to receive the Holy Ghost, as it was through her that St. Elizabeth received His gifts.

Honour and revere with especial love the holy

---

* Happy the soul who, like a good child in regard of her parents, sees only Jesus and Mary, converses only with Jesus and Mary, and whose only joy and desire in this world is to know Mary in Jesus and Jesus in Mary. This is a wonderful means, given us by God, of spending our lives holily during our sorrowful sojourn in this present life.—(J. J. OLIER.)

14

and glorious Virgin Mary, for she is the Mother of Our God and Saviour Jesus Christ, and therefore our most excellent Mother. Let us then have recourse to her as little children ; let us cast ourselves upon her bosom on every occasion, and at every moment, with perfect confidence. Let us appeal to her maternal love, endeavour to imitate her virtues, and cherish in our heart the true sentiments of children.

In the ancient Law much honour was paid to the Ark, in which were preserved the manna, the rod of Aaron, and the tables of the Law. With much greater reason should we honour this living Ark of the new Covenant. Indeed, what does the manna prefigure but the Divinity of the Son of God, come down from heaven to unite Himself with our humanity? He is, also, the Miraculous Rod and the Living Stone upon which the commandments of the Law of Grace were written, being engraved upon His Sacred Body by the scourges, the thorns, the nails, and the lance. The immaculate bosom of Our Lady is then incomparably more worthy of honour than the ancient ark which prefigured it.

O Most Holy and Most Happy Lady, raised in Paradise to the highest degree of beatitude and happiness ! we beg you to have compassion on us who groan in the desert of this world. You are in the abundance of delights, and we in the abyss of miseries ; obtain for us strength to endure our tribulations virtuously, always leaning on your Beloved Son, the only pledge of our hopes and remedy of our evils. O Glorious Virgin, pray for the Church, assist the Holy Father, the Prelates, Bishops, and all Superiors; and assist England especially, which by your devoted servant St. Edward, was consecrated to you as your dowry: *Dota Mariæ.* (Translator.)

You are the Mother of Jesus, Who has deigned to become our Brother, and hence you are our Mother; why, then, shall we not cast ourselves into your arms with perfect confidence, invoking your maternal love and imitating your virtues? O God, what a blessing for us to be sons of such a Mother! If we love and serve her with a truly filial love, she will enrich us with her favours. And, meanwhile, let us present her with the flowers of every virtue: but, above all, with the lily of purity, the rose of ardent charity, and the violets of holy humility and simplicity. She loves nothing so much as hearts deepened by humility, opened by simplicity, and enlarged by charity; and she prefers to be in the company of souls near the manger and at the foot of the Cross; that is, with the poor and the afflicted, in order to succour and console. them.

SPIRITUAL FLOWERS.

Mary is like a lily amidst thorns: she loves and suffers at the same time. When the thorns are blown about by the wind, they tear the lily on all sides; but it revenges itself by causing to exhale, through the apertures of its wounds, a sweet fragrance, which perfumes the thorns that have so cruelly wounded it. In imitation of Mary, figured by the lily amidst thorns, let your only revenge for your afflictions be to increase your love for those who are the cause of your pains.—*Père Avrillion.*

Mary is compared to the white lily, on account of her innocence and exemption from all sin; and as the lily is beautiful amongst the thorns where it has sprung up, so was Mary distinguished amidst the women of Judea. The lily loses nothing of its whiteness, although amongst thorns, and the august Virgin, tortured in the Person of her Son, by the Jewish Deicides, preserved the innocency of her soul and the purity of her heart, rendering good for evil.—*St. Francis of Sales.*

Mary is that most beautiful and lofty cedar, from which God detached the finest branch, to transplant it on Calvary.—*The same.*

Lose not sight of eternity, and the adversities of this life will not trouble you.—*The same.*

EXAMPLE.

The 'Regina Cœli.'

Baronius and St. Gregory of Nyssa relate that in the year 690 the city of Rome was in danger of becoming a desert, on account of the number of persons who became victims to a terrible pestilence. St. Gregory, surnamed the Great, successor to Pope Gelasius II., who had fallen a victim to this disease, saw that all human precautions and resources were of no avail, and he resolved to have recourse to the Mother of God.   He gave orders that the picture of the Most Holy Virgin—which is believed to have been painted by St. Luke—should be carried in a general procession of all the Clergy and laity, as far as Santa Maria Maggiore.   The violence of the plague was such that eighty persons perished during the procession; but before its termination an Angel was seen in human form above Adrian's Tower (called afterwards the Castle of St. Angelo, in memory of this event), sheathing a sword tinged with blood, as in the time of David; and from that moment the pestilence completely ceased.   At the same time many voices were heard in the air, singing: *Regina cœli, lætare, alleluia; quia quem meruisti portare, alleluia; resurrexit sicut dixit, alleluia*—'Rejoice, O Queen of Heaven, for He Whom you deserved to bear has risen, as He said, from the grave; God be praised.   The Holy Pontiff immediately added: *Ora pro nobis Deum, alleluia*—'Pray to God for us, God be praised.'

This having occurred at Easter, the Church from that time ordered all the Clergy and faithful to recite this Antiphon during Paschal season.

Prayer.—Oh! most desolate of Mothers! what a sword has pierced your Heart!   All the blows

which wounded your Son Jesus fell upon you. By
His pains you were tortured, by His wounds
you were torn. His last adieu renewed all your
sorrows; but when He breathed His last sigh
with what anguish was your heart oppressed, O
Mother of love and of sorrow! Obtain, I beg of
you, that I may follow your example in loving and
suffering! Yes, Queen of Martyrs, let me share
your martyrdom. Love gave you the Cross, let
the Cross fill my heart with love ; and if, to enable
me to love, it be necessary that I suffer and die,
obtain for me this grace, that I may love all that
comes to me from God, whether it be sorrows,
afflictions, or death. Amen.

Ejaculation.—Pray for me, O Queen of Martyrs !

Practice.—When you are tempted to complain,
or to be impatient under opposition, reflect upon
Mary at the foot of the Cross.

TWENTY-SIXTH DAY.

MARY AFTER THE ASCENSION OF CHRIST.

GOD placed two beautiful luminaries in the heavens
on the fourth day of the Creation ; one called the
greater, the other the *lesser light;* the former to
rule over the day, the latter, over the night.
Although God decreed that darkness should
succeed the day, He, the increated Light, would
not allow the night to be entirely deprived of light.

When, in His Providence, He wished to create the spiritual world in His Church, He placed in it, as in a Divine firmament, two great luminaries. The greatest is Jesus Christ, Our Saviour and Master—an abyss of light, and the source of splendour, the true Sun of Justice; the lesser luminary is the Most Holy Mother of this Divine Saviour; a most glorious Mother, resplendent and beautiful as the moon.

The Son of God came down upon earth, like the sun upon our atmosphere, to clothe Himself with our humanity, and formed our light and day; a most longed-for day, which lasted about thirty-three years, during which time He illumined the Church with the splendour of His miracles, His example and His doctrine. But the hour having at last arrived when this precious Sun was to set and cast Its rays over the other hemisphere—that is, heaven—what else could remain on earth but darkness and obscurity? And, in fact, night quickly spread around—the night of the many persecutions raised against the Apostles. But that its darkness might be more tolerable, it also had its luminary in the person of the Most Holy Virgin, who remained with the disciples and the faithful, after the Ascension of her Divine Son. This we learn from St. Luke: the Most Holy Mary was with the disciples in the upper room on the day of Pentecost, and persevered with them in communion and prayer.

Jesus Christ would leave her still in the world: firstly, that as a luminary she might be the comfort of the faithful immersed in the night of tribulations; secondly, that by surviving her Divine Son she might acquire greater merit, so that it might be truly said of her—many daughters have gathered riches, you have surpassed them all; thirdly, that her presence might be a convincing proof against the heresy that arose after the Ascension of Our Lord, which held that He had not taken a natural Body but one merely in appearance. Thus, even in her lifetime, were verified in her regard the words of Holy Church, 'You, august Virgin, have destroyed all heresies.'

The Most Holy Virgin lived after the Ascension of her Divine Son until she reached the age of sixty-three; and thus this mystic Ark of the new Covenant dwelt under tents in the desert of this world.

Our Divine Lord, wished that His Most Holy Mother should, after having been an example to virgins and to mothers, become the model of widows by her modesty and her love for the hidden life. Widows may be compared to the little lowly violet, which has no brilliancy in its colour but has a scent which, without being too strong, is marvellously sweet. Oh, what a beautiful flower in the Church is the Christian widow ! Lowly, through humility, and without splendour in the eyes of the world, since sl e flies from it ; she is unable to meet the gaze of men when her heart no longer desires their love.

The Apostle St. Paul orders his disciple St. Timothy, to honour those *who are widows indeed ;* that is, those who are so in heart and mind. ' Blessed,' says Our Lord, ' are the pure of heart ' and ' poor in spirit.'

Widows in spirit and in desire are deserving of the highest esteem ; for what means the word ' widow ' but need and destitution. Honour, then, be rendered to those who are such in mind and heart, for they are humble and their Protector is the Lord !

SPIRITUAL FLOWERS.

Let it be your desire to see God, your fear to lose Him, your sorrow not yet to possess Him, and your joy to do everything that can lead you to Him; you will then live in the abundance of peace. —*St. Teresa.*

Remember that you have but one soul; that you will die but once ; that you have but one life, and that a very short one ; but one glory, and that eternal; your heart will then detach itself from everything.—*The same.*

The soul that loves God lives more in the next world than in this ; because the soul lives more in the object of its love than in the subject which it animates.—*St. John of the Cross,*

The true widow of the Church is a little March violet. By her devotion she spreads a sweet perfume. She usually keeps herself hidden under the leaves of her abjection, and her mortification is seen by her quiet, modest demeanour.—*St. Francis of Sales.*

EXAMPLE.

A Courageous Son of Mary.

The Saints are accustomed to say 'My Mother' when speaking of the Blessed Virgin Mary; and some time ago, under the influence of this idea, a touching scene took place. A countryman was at Leipsic, a town which may be called the heart of Protestantism, where he entered by mistake the hall of a university, in which some Lutheran Doctors were disputing upon religion. He was recognised as a fervent Catholic, by a medal attached to his rosary hanging from his pocket; and he soon became the object of the bitter derision of the Lutherans.

The good man, without being disconcerted, took a dollar from his old purse, and, throwing it on the table where the Doctors were seated, exclaimed, 'Well, then, who will bet with me which of us is the most learned in matters of religion?'

The president laid down his piece of money; and then casting a glance of contempt upon the peasant's rosary, said to him, 'What is the name

of the Mother of God?' The pious peasant replied, in a most respectful tone of voice, 'Her
name is Mary.' Then, quickly turning to the
Doctor, he said, 'Tell me the name of *my
Mother.*'

This question contained a mystery; a Catholic
would have penetrated it. and would have replied,
'She is called Mary.' However, the Protestant
Doctor was not sufficiently instructed to understand it. He remained silent, filled with spite at
the ingenious and pious trick of the countryman,
who, judging that he had come off victor, took up
the two pieces of money, and said, with admirable
calmness, 'Gentlemen, when you dispute again
upon religion, I beg of you to let me know.' He
then retired; and the lesson was as perfect as it
was well merited.

Prayer.—O Mary, my Sovereign! O Mother of
my Saviour! You are blessed amongst all women,
pure amongst all virgins, the Queen of all creatures.
All nations call you Blessed. Let me exalt your
greatness as much as it is possible for me to exalt
it, and love you, as much as I can love you. May
I call upon you continually and contribute to make
you honoured, as far as I am able. I should wish
to see the whole universe prostrate at your feet,
and all hearts burning with your love, that they
may all love your Divine Son, as you loved Him
in this world, and will love Him for all eternity.
I earnestly entreat this grace, O my Mother,

although I acknowledge and confess myself un-worthy to obtain it.

Ejaculation.—O Holy Virgin, enable me to speak of your greatness.

Practice.—Examine if the virtues of Mary are to you as that lèsser luminary in whose light you walk on in the way that leads to Paradise.

TWENTY-SEVENTH DAY.

MARY IN THE UPPER ROOM AT JERUSALEM.

THE Eternal Father bestowed an incomparable gift upon the world when He gave it His Only Son. Jesus Christ Himself said: 'God hath so loved the world as to give it His Only Son ;' and St. Paul exclaims: 'How has He not with Him given us all things ?'—*Quomodo non etiam omnia cum illo nobis donavit ?*

Almighty God, in the ancient Law, had bestowed an infinity of blessings upon His chosen people; but they were given according to measure. In the Law of Grace, however, He had no sooner seen His Beloved Son ascended into heaven than He opened His Hands to pour forth His graces and gifts upon all the faithful, according to the pro-phecy of Joel, that *supra omnem carnem*—' over all men' would He diffuse His Holy Spirit.

If we desire to receive this Divine Spirit, let us beg Our Lord to bestow Him upon us through the

merits of his Most Holy Mother, the glorious
Virgin Mary, and through the love He bore to
her ; and we shall thus, like the Apostles, be with
Mary the Mother of Jesus. We shall never understand how necessary is this condition. St. Elizabeth had no sooner spoken to the Most Holy
Virgin than she was immediately, says St. Luke,
' filled with the Holy Ghost.' Nor is this a subject of wonder, because Mary is the Spouse of the
Holy Ghost, the Daughter of the Eternal Father,
and the Mother of the Eternal Son.

The Evangelist St. Luke, by observing that
men and women were assembled in the room,
admonishes us that we must all hope to receive
the Holy Ghost ; but he mentions in particular
the presence of *Mary the Mother of Jesus,* to insinuate that she was there as the Queen of the
Apostles. How mistaken, then, are those who say
that we honour the Most Holy Virgin too much !
This august Virgin, it is true, had already received
the Holy Spirit and the fulness of grace in the
Annunciation, but in the upper room she received
a great superabundance of grace.

Whoever, then, desires to receive the Holy Ghost,
let him unite himself to Mary ; because he who
separates himself from her, does not gather but
scatters. Let us serve her, honour her, that He
Who comes into our hearts, by her mediation, may
also receive us by the same mediation.

To conclude, we may learn a very useful lesson

from the words of St. Luke about the Disciples when they had received the Holy Ghost: 'All spoke in divers tongues according as the Holy Ghost gave them to speak'—*Prout Spiritus Sanctus dabat eloqui illis;* that is, that though all spoke, yet they did not speak in the same manner. The Apostles preached the new Law; and those who did not preach publicly, animated one another to praise and magnify the Lord. Let us, however, understand that there is an efficacious method of speaking without even uttering a word, and it is by the good example which we give to our neighbour.

David says: 'The heavens declare the glory of God. Day unto day uttereth speech, and night unto night showeth knowledge.' These words signify that the beauty of the heavens invites men to admire the magnificence of the Creator. Indeed, when on a clear night we contemplate the beauty of the heavens, we do not feel less animated to admire and adore the Omnipotence and Wisdom of God, Who has studded it with such beautiful stars, than when we observe the inaccessible light of the sun in its full meridian splendour. What conclusion are we to draw from all this but that we, who are something more than all the rest of creation (since all things were made for us, and not we for them), should, by our good example, announce the glory of God more perfectly than the heavens and the stars. Good example is a silent but a most efficacious influence. In this manner we can all preach, although we have not all received the gift of tongues. Is it a less wonder to see a soul adorned with many sublime virtues than to see the heavens decorated with magnificent stars? How much, my God, do I need the Spirit of strength when I feel myself so weak and infirm! However, I glory in my infirmity *that the Power of my God may dwell in me.* Let us glory in our weakness, which makes us fitting receptacles of the Power of God. May He grant that this sacred fire, which can entirely change us into Him, may transform our hearts into His pure Love, that we may be all love and not lovers only. May He grant me also to receive and make good use of the gift of understanding, that my mind may be more enlightened to penetrate clearly the sacred mysteries of our holy Faith; for this understanding has a wonderful power to subjugate the will to the service of Him Whom it recognises to be so good and so worthy of love. Yet, as true love is active, we need counsel, that we may be able to discern how to exercise this love; and then our soul is excellently endowed with the sacred gifts of Heaven.

May the Holy Spirit, Who favours us with His gifts, form our whole consolation, and be eternally adored by my mind and by my heart! May He be always our wisdom and our understanding, our counsel and our fortitude, our knowledge and our piety, and fill us with the spirit of the fear of the Lord.

SPIRITUAL FLOWERS.

Mary is the root of Jesse, upon whom the Holy
Spirit rested.   The Son of the Virgin is the flower
thereof ; a red and white flower, chosen amongst
thousands—the flower upon which the Angels gaze
with continuous desire ; a flower whose fragrance
renews life ; a flower of everlasting bloom, whose
beauty is incorruptible, and whose glory will never
fade.—*St. Bernard.*

Mary is the root of that beautiful flower upon
which the Holy Spirit rests with the fulness of His
gifts.   Whoever then desires to obtain the seven
gifts of the Holy Ghost, must seek the flower upon
the stem ; because we reach the flower through the
stem, and through the flower we find the Holy
Spirit, Who thereon reposes.   Let us go to Jesus,
through Mary; and by means of Jesus, we find the
grace of the Holy Spirit.—*St. Bonaventure.*

Give your soul to God a thousand times in the
day ; fix your interior eyes upon His sweetness, in
imitation of Mary; place Him upon your breast as
a delicious nosegay, and make every possible effort
to excite within you an impassioned love for this
Divine Spouse.—*St. Francis of Sales.*

There is no doubt that he who perfumes the
world by the odour of his good example, thus
teaching others the way of justice, will one day
shine in eternity as a most splendid star in the
firmament.—*The same.*

EXAMPLE.

The Prayer 'Memorare.'

St. Francis of Sales had received, in his youth, a miraculous proof of the protection of Mary. Being assaulted by a violent temptation to believe himself reprobated by God, he experienced such anguish that he compared it to the sorrows of death and the torments of hell. After a month passed in these desolating trials, earnestly desiring to be delivered from them, he humbly prostrated himself before a statue of the Blessed Virgin, and with great confidence recited. the *Memorare*, beseeching Our Lady to obtain from her Divine Son that, if he should ever have the misfortune of being eternally separated from his God, he might at least love Him during the present lifetime with all his powers.

The Most Holy Virgin could not be deaf to such a petition, and Francis quickly recovered the peace of heart he had lost. From that time he had the greatest confidence in this prayer, and recited it in every difficult undertaking, and recommended it warmly to all whom he directed.

'I remember,' says the Bishop of Belley, 'to have learnt this prayer from him, and in order to impress it more deeply in my heart, and to make use of it in all my afflictions, I wrote it down at the beginning of my breviary. I know, moreover, that

15

he commended it much to the Nuns of the Visitation. He wished it to be repeated above all in times of great temptations, because the Mother of God is as terrible to the enemy as an army in battle array; the blessed fruit of her womb having. crushed the head of the infernal serpent.'

It is generally believed that St. Bernard was the author of this prayer.

Prayer to ask for the Seven Gifts of the Holy Ghost.—August Spouse of the Holy Ghost, Most Holy Virgin Mary, the inexhaustible source of grace, deign to obtain for me from your Divine Spouse the gift of Wisdom, which may detach me from the goods of the world, and make me love those of heaven; the gift of Understanding, which may teach me my duties; the gift of Counsel, which may enlighten me in the way of salvation; the gift of Fortitude, which may sustain my weakness; the gift of Knowledge, which may teach me the eternal truths; the gift of Piety, which may render the service of God sweet to me; and the gift of Fear, which may inspire me with a holy respect and tender love towards the God of infinite mercy. Ah! my continued resistance to the inspirations of the Holy Spirit have rendered me unworthy of such a benefit, but, aided by your prayers, I confidently hope to obtain from the author of *every perfect gift* the graces that are necessary to live holily in this life, and thus one day attain to the eternal beatitude of heaven. Amen.

Ejaculation.—Pray for me, O Spouse of the Holy Ghost.

Practice.—Accustom yourself in every difficulty to say at once: *O Mother of Good Counsel, inspire me!*

TWENTY-EIGHTH DAY.

HOW PRECIOUS IN THE SIGHT OF GOD WAS THE DEATH OF MARY.

ACCORDING to the common opinion of the Doctors of the Church, when the Blessed Virgin Mary had attained the age of sixty-three she died, or rather, she slept the sleep of death. But how is it, some will say, that Our Lord, Who loved His Holy Mother so tenderly, did not grant her the privilege of exemption from death, since death is the wages of sin, and she had never sinned? How contrary are such thoughts to those of God, and how far removed are such judgments from His! We know that death became precious when Our Lord permitted that its blow should fall upon Him, on the Tree of the Cross. Certainly, the Most Holy Virgin thought it no advantage or privilege not to die, but she always desired death, for she saw it lovingly embraced by her Divine Son. He had rendered it so sweet and desirable that the Angels would consider themselves most fortunate to be able to die, and the Saints looked upon it as a happiness, and therefore experienced great consolation in it.   Our adorable Saviour, who is Life Itself, gave life to death by His own death, so that to those who die in the grace of God, it is the beginning of eternal life.

Consider this Queen, dying of a fever, that was sweeter to her than health, because it was the fever of Divine love, which, by burning up her heart, consumed it so completely as to open to her soul the way by which it flew into the arms of her Divine Son.

All the Saints die in the habit of holy Love ; but some amongst them die in the exercise of this Divine love; others, on account of it, as the Martyrs ; and others, by its power.   But the most sublime degree of holy love is to die of love itself; and this occurs when the soul is so inflamed by charity that it can no longer be detained by the bonds of the flesh.

If it be true that such as is *the life of a man such will be his death,* what else can have been the death of the Most Holy Virgin but the death of love ? This is certain ; because she who is called in the language of Sacred Scripture, the *Mother of fair Love* could only die the death of love.   We read not of ecstasies and raptures in the life of Our Lady, and for this reason, that they were continual. She loved God with so tender, so strong, and so ardent a love, at the same time so tranquilly, and with so much peace, that although her love went on increasing, the increase was not impetuous, but she continually, and almost imperceptibly, hastened towards this so greatly desired union of her soul with God, like a river that calmly flows to the ocean.

The hour having then arrived when the Most Holy Virgin was to leave the earth, Divine Love separated her soul from her body, and incomparably pure as it was, it flew directly to heaven. Ah! what obstacle could detain her whom the Celestial Spouse calls 'His beloved, all fair and without spot'? Our imperfections and the stains of our sins are the only obstacle to our entrance into heaven at the moment of our death; and it is these that are the origin of the flames of Purgatory.

The Saints are ever burning with the fire of Divine love; and by their exemplary lives spread a continual odour of sanctity in the presence of men and of God. This odour is incomparably increased at their death; hence the Prophet says: 'Precious in the sight of the Lord is the death of the Saints.'

If, then, the Saints are odoriferous and burning lamps, what shall we say of the Most Holy Virgin, whose perfection immeasurably surpassed that of all the Saints united together? If in life she was a Burning Lamp, fed with the perfumed oil of every virtue, what a fragrance must she have exhaled at the hour of her death! So great was this

fragrance that young virgins, as we read in the
Canticles, were attracted by it : ' We will run after
thee to the odour of thy perfumes,' ' the young
maidens have loved thee.'

SPIRITUAL FLOWERS.

The soul of Mary was released from her body as
naturally as fragrance sent from a flower and as the
ripe fruit falls from the tree.—*St. Francis of Sales.*

As the palm conceals its flower until the heat of
the sun causes it to expand, so the just soul conceals the flowers of its virtue by humility, until Our
Lord, by calling her to Paradise, gives the highest
degree of perfection to her love.—*The same.*

The thought of death is not sad for a soul who
loves God, because it is the beginning of her
eternal happiness.—*St. John of the Cross.*

O Death, most beautiful Death! wherefore shall
we fear thee, if in thee is found life? He alone
should fear thee who has persevered in sin until
his last breath.—*St. Teresa.*

EXAMPLE.

Letters addressed to the Most Holy Virgin.

Persons filled with lively faith often write letters
to the Blessed Virgin Mary, placing them at the
feet of her image, or upon their heart, on some
solemn occasion; and this practice is very dear
to her.

It is no new practice : for we see, from the Sacred Books and the history of the Church, that the most remarkable men made use of it to obtain some special grace. King Ezechias carried into the Temple the insulting letter addressed to him by Zennacherib, and laid it on the Altar as if to invite Almighty God to read it, and his prayer was heard, as we read in the Fourth Book of Kings.

The Emperor Theodosius, about to fight against Eugenius, wrote to St. Ambrose, to beg him to recommend the expedition to the God of armies. The Saint, during Mass, took the letter into his hands, and presented it to God. The result of the battle is well known.

When the Angelic Doctor, St. Thomas, met with some difficult passage in Holy Scripture, he wrote down the difficulty and placed it on his heart when he went to celebrate Mass, and the difficulties vanished.

Our Lord looks upon prayers addressed to the Blessed Virgin and to the Saints as though they were made to Himself. If we wish to obtain some grace, let us write a letter to Mary, and place it upon our heart before we approach Holy Communion. St. Stanislaus Kostka, desired to die on the Eve of the Assumption, that he might assist at its celebration in heaven. He wrote a letter to Our Blessed Lady for this purpose, and, on the feast of St. Lawrence, placed it on the Altar, asking the Saint to present it to the Queen of Heaven. The same day he was attacked by a most burning fever, and after four days went to celebrate the feast of his dear Mother Mary in heaven.

Prayer (of St. Alphonsus Liguori to obtain a happy death).—O Mary! what will be my death? When I think of the moment which is to decide my eternal destiny, I fear and tremble at the sight of my sins. O Mother, full of goodness, the Blood of Jesus Christ and your patronage are alone my hope. Ah, console me in that terrible moment, O Consoler of the afflicted! If I am now tormented by remorse for my offences, through the uncertainty of pardon, the danger of falling again, and the judgments of God, what will it be at that moment? I am lost if you do not fly to my relief. O my sovereign Lady, obtain for me, before my death, lively sorrow for sin, true amendment, and entire fidelity to God; and may I at that moment invoke you more frequently, that I may not despair at the sight of my sins. Pardon me my rashness, O my Queen; but I beg you also to come yourself to console me by your presence. You have granted this favour to so many of your servants, and why should not I also hope for it? It is true I do not merit it; but I love you, O Mary, and confide in you. I expect then your presence and assistance, that I may go forth from this world loving God, and you also, my Holy Mother, and never cease to love you through all eternity. Amen.

Ejaculation.—Do not abandon me at the hour of my death, O my Most Holy Mother !

Practice.—Spend this day as if it were the last of your life.

TWENTY-NINTH DAY.

MARY, LIKE JESUS, DIES OF DIVINE LOVE.

OUR Lady died of Divine love, like her adorable Son. The foundation of this belief is, that having but one life with her Divine Son, she could have but one and the same death. In reality, they were two distinct persons ; but they had one heart, one soul, one mind, one life !

If this was said of the first Christians ; if Jesus Christ lived in St. Paul, because his spirit was dead in the Heart of his Saviour, with much greater truth could it be said that Jesus Christ and His Most Holy Mother had but one heart and one soul, and, consequently, one life ; for there never was a Mother so loving or so much loved ; and the quality of Mother and only Son gives us the idea of all that is most perfect and most excellent in love.

If the Apostle St. Paul could say that he had no other life than that of his Divine Master, with greater reason could Mary, the Mother of this amiable Master, say : ' I have no other life than that of my Divine Son : He lives in me and I in

Him.' And having lived the life of her Son, she must have died the death of her Son. This death was prophesied to her, by holy Simeon, in these words : 'Thy own soul a sword shall pierce.'

Three kinds of swords can pierce the soul : the first, the sword of the Word of God, which, in the saying of the Apostle, 'is more, penetrating than a two-edged sword'; the second, the sword of suffering and sorrow, according to the prophecy of Simeon ; and the third, the sword of Divine Love, of which Jesus Christ speaks : 'I came not to bring peace, but the sword.' Now, the soul of Our Lady was pierced by all these three kinds of swords in the death of her Son.

When a heavy blow falls upon an object, everything near it feels its effects. Thus, although the body of the Most Holy Virgin was not united to that of her Divine Son in His Passion, yet, her soul being inseparably united to Him, it follows that all the blows with which His Blessed Body was bruised wounded her soul.

Love causes us to feel the afflictions of those we love, as we see in St. Paul, who was weak with the weak, afflicted with those in tribulation ; and yet the soul of this Apostle certainly was not so closely united to the faithful as the soul of Our Lady to the soul and body of Jesus. No wonder, then, that the thorns, the nails and lance, which pierced the head, hands, feet and side of Our Lord, pierced also through and through the soul of His Mother.

Truly may we exclaim : O Most Holy Virgin ! how deeply was your soul pierced by the love, the suffering, and the words of your Son ! And, oh, how deep a wound love gave you, when you saw the Son, Who loved you so much, and Who possessed all the affections of your heart, expiring through love ! How bitterly did sorrow, too, wound your soul, when you saw the sufferings that led your only Son to death ! And, as for His words, like a strong wind they inflamed your love, excited your sorrow, and almost engulfed the vessel of your heart in an ocean of grief.

Love caused Mary to be penetrated with sorrow ; and the sufferings of her Son were expressed in words that pierced her heart like darts. And, as a stag wounded by the hunter, flees with the arrow fixed in the wound, to die afar off, and sometimes, long after it has received the blow; so Our Lady, wounded by the sword of sorrow in the Passion of her Son upon Calvary, survived the wound she had received many years, but at last it caused her death. Oh, loving wound ! Oh, sword of charity ! how dear and beloved wast thou to the tender heart which thou didst pierce !

The philosopher Aristotle narrates that when the wild goats of Candia are wounded by a dart, they have recourse to the herb dittany, and by means of this plant the dart comes out of the wound. Ah ! who is there that does not feel his heart wounded by the thought of the Passion of Jesus Christ, contemplating Him scourged, crowned with thorns and crucified? But, alas! I scarcely dare to say it: the greater number who are pierced by this dart run quickly, like those goats, to the dittany of worldly consolations in order to remove from their heart the wound of Divine love. The Blessed Virgin, on the contrary, zealously preserved this dart, and it formed all her glory and her triumph.

Spiritual Flowers.

Thorns are the flowers of Calvary, and sufferings the flowers of the Cross; and this is the support sought for by the languishing love of Mary.—*Bossuet.*

Oh how sweet will death be to the Christian who has done penance for his sins during life! He will pass instantly to the ineffable joys of Paradise. —*St. Teresa.*

Mystical death is accompanied by a sweetness and a satisfaction a thousand times greater than the full life of the senses.—*P. Milley.*

The more a soul knows the perfections of God, the more does the desire to see Him increase within itself.—*St. John of the Cross.*

The happiness of dying without regret well repays us for living without pleasures.—*The same.*

Example.

The Fourteen Joys of the Most Holy Virgin.

St. Thomas of Canterbury had the pious custom of reciting seven *Ave Marias* every day in honour of the Seven Joys of Our Lady upon earth : the Annunciation, the Visitation, the Birth of Our Lord, the Epiphany, the Finding in the Temple, the Resurrection, and the Ascension. One day the Blessed Virgin appeared to him, and said : 'Thy devotion, Thomas, is very pleasing to me ; but why dost thou commemorate only the joys I experienced whilst on earth ? Henceforth, be mindful also of those that I enjoy in heaven ; I assure thee that I will console and present to my Son, at the hour of their death, all those who during life shall have honoured the latter, as well as the former joys.' The holy Archbishop, filled with consolation at these words, exclaimed : 'But how can I do so, Most Holy Virgin, when I know not these joys ?' The august Mother of God then taught the Saint to recite seven *Ave Marias* in honour of the following joys : the honour that the Most Holy Trinity conferred upon her above all creatures ; the excellence of her Virginity, which raised her above the Angels and the Saints ; the splendour of her glory, which illuminates heaven ; the veneration paid to her by the Blessed, on account of her dignity of Mother of God ; her power with her

Divine Son in our behalf ; the graces with which she was enriched when on earth, and the reward reserved in heaven for those who are devout to her during life ; finally, her accidental glory, which will continually increase until the Day of Judgment.

Many Saints have practised this devotion with fruit, and a great number of the devoted servants of Mary have made use of it to honour their august Mother.

Prayer of St. Alfonso Maria di Liguori.— O Mary! I acknowledge that you are the most beautiful, the most holy, and most amiable of all creatures. Ah ! would that all knew you, O Holy Virgin, and loved you as you deserve. I rejoice that you are so revered by all the Blessed in heaven, and by so many faithful souls on earth, but especially that you are so much loved by God. Most amiable Queen ! I also love you, miserable sinner that I am, and I desire to love you more ; obtain for me, then, this love, O my dear Mother, because it is a sign of predestination. I know that you will help me, and by your help I shall conquer, if I cease not to recommend myself to you. But I fear that I may not always invoke you in occasions of danger ; succour me then always, O Mary, my good Mother, and never permit me to offend my God. Amen.

Ejaculation.—In your love do I wish to live and die, my Blessed Mother !

Practice.—Offer an act of mortification to God,

through the Blessed Virgin, for those who are to die this day.

THIRTIETH DAY.

THE DEATH OF MARY WAS SWEET AND TRANQUIL.

As the peaceful morning dawns, not by fits and starts, but steadily and gradually, so that its progress is scarcely perceptible, so did Divine love increase in the heart of Our Lady, the glorious Virgin Mary. Her progress in charity was tranquil, uniform and uninterrupted, so that she continually pursued her course towards the Divinity Whom she loved.

Consider that love is, in its nature, calm, tranquil, and full of sweetness, and becomes violent only when it meets with some opposition. But if its dominion in a soul be undisputed, and if nothing oppose its progress, then it works steadily and gains its victories with ease. We may understand, then, how the heart of the Mother of pure Love experienced all its power, without any impetuous movement, for in her there was no resistance to overcome.

Observe the course of great rivers : when the bed is not level and the current is encumbered with masses of rock, the waters splash and foam, and roll back again with a great noise ; but when the bed is smooth the waters flow on placidly and without effort. Such is the case with holy love, when it meets with obstacles,—and where does it not find them? It is constrained to struggle with a kind of violence against the human inclinations that oppose it; to use force, and make great efforts in order to bend the will, to remove impediments, and to open a passage for itself to the heart it seeks to possess. In the Blessed Virgin, however, everything favoured and seconded the attractions of grace and of Divine love, and although her love was incomparably greater than that of any other creature, it continually went on increasing with the greatest calm and sweetness.

If iron were not held down by its weight it would find no obstacle to the continued attraction of the magnet, and its strong and even motion would continually increase in proportion as the iron and magnet drew nearer to each other. Thus it was with the Most Holy Virgin at her death. As there was nothing in her that could impede the action of Divine love, she became more and more closely united to her adorable Son through sweet ecstasies, until she became, so to speak, immersed in the bosom of His goodness; and thus, without even knowing it, she quitted her body and was reunited to her Divine Son in heaven.

It was fitting that as love had produced the sorrows of death in this Divine Mother at the foot of the Cross, so death should in its turn, produce the sovereign delights of love. Ah! may this

Most Holy Virgin obtain for us, by her prayers, grace to live in holy love, and may it alone be the object of all our desires, and of all the affections of our hearts !

SPIRITUAL FLOWERS.

St. Gregory says that the pomegranate, by its bright red colour, its beautiful corona, and numerous seeds so well arranged, sweetly represents charity. Charity is red, by the ardour with which it burns for God, is adorned with the variety of every virtue, and obtains and wears for ever the crown of eternal rewards.—*St. Francis of Sales.*

Bees never sting so sharply as when they are themselves mortally wounded. How can we fail to be wounded with love for our adorable Saviour, when we contemplate Him wounded for us, even unto death and the death of the Cross; to be wounded, I say, with a wound the more painfully loving, as His was more lovingly painful; nor can we ever love Him as much as His death and His love merit.—*The same.*

EXAMPLE.

Novenas in Honour of the Blessed Virgin.

In the various tribulations of life, in great afflictions, dangers and temptations, when we require special assistance from God, an almost certain means to obtain it is to make a Novena in honour

16

of the Most Blessed Virgin Mary. How many souls have been heard by God, by having had recourse to the Most Holy Virgin through a Novena !

The Children of Mary apply themselves with special devotion and fervent piety to the celebration of her festivals, and, in return, the Blessed Virgin obtains for them an abundance of heavenly blessings. St. Gertrude saw one day a great number of souls under the mantle of Mary, guarded by her with warm affection, and she understood that they had prepared themselves, by devout exercises of piety, for celebrating the Feast of the Assumption of Our Lady.

Prayer.—O Queen of Paradise ! raised above all the heavenly choirs, seated at the right hand of your Divine Son, I prostrate myself at your feet, miserable sinner that I am, and conjure you to cast upon me those eyes of mercy which bring grace and the friendship of Almighty God wherever they are turned. Observe, O Most Holy Mary, in how many dangers I am of losing my soul, and shall always be as long as I am on earth ; but I place all my hopes in you. I love you, my Mother, with all my heart, and wish to love you for ever. Ah ! pray to your Divine Son for me ; tell Him to protect me, and He will assuredly have compassion on my poor soul. O my sweetest and most compassionate Mother, in this hope do I rest, and wish also to live and die Amen.

Ejaculation.—O Mary ! love gave you the Cross !
May the Cross give us love !

Practice.—Examine what would give you most
fear if you were going to die now, and begin
earnestly to amend.

THIRTY-FIRST DAY.

THE RESURRECTION AND ASSUMPTION OF THE BLESSED VIRGIN.

THERE can be no doubt whatever that Our Lord
fulfilled towards Mary the precept which He gave
in general to all children to honour their parents.
Indeed, where is the son who would not raise his
mother from the grave to lead her to Paradise, if he
had it in his power ? The great triumph of the
Assumption of the Blessed Virgin is celebrated by
all the Saints, and by the whole Church Militant.

After the Ark of the Covenant had dwelt for a
long period under tents and pavilions, King Solomon ordered it to be placed in the marvellous
Temple he had prepared for it. The joy of the
Hebrews on that occasion was so great that the
blood of the sacrifices flowed through the streets
of Jerusalem ; the air was filled with clouds of
incense, and the houses and public squares re-
sounded with harmonious music.

But, O God ! if the solemnity of the reception

16— 2

of the Ark was so great, what must have been that
of the Most Glorious Virgin, Mother of the Son of
God, the true Ark of the New Covenant, upon the
day of her Assumption !   O incomprehensible joy !
—festival of wonders !—which makes all devout
souls who are the true daughters of Jerusalem, exclaim : ' Who is she that goeth up from the desert
leaning upon her Beloved ?'   The entrance of the
Most Blessed Virgin into heaven was the most
magnificent that ever could or can be witnessed
after that of Jesus Christ.   She ascends from the
desert of this lower world, so perfumed with spiritual
gifts that, except in the Person of her Divine Son,
she has no equal in heaven.   The Queen of Saba,
coming to Jerusalem to have a proof of the wisdom
of Solomon, brought with her a great quantity of
perfumes, gold, and precious stones.   But, when
the Most Holy Virgin entered heaven, she carried
with her such an amount of the pure gold of charity,
so much perfume of devotion and of virtue, and so
many precious gems of patience and of suffering,
that we can safely say no one ever had so great an
accumulation of merits to offer her Divine Son !
Yes, indeed, she abounded in delights, because
during her life on earth she had abounded in good
works and in sufferings.

We may say that, in one sense, the Assumption
of Our Lady was even more glorious than the
Ascension of Jesus Christ; because the Angels
only were present at the Ascension, whilst at the

Assumption of Our Lady the King of Angels Himself attended her.

What a triumph was it for Heaven, and what a consolation for earth! Ah, let us in spirit dwell and live in heaven, because *there* is our treasure and our life. O my God! how beautiful is heaven now that its sun is Our Blessed Saviour, and His bosom is the Source of Love, where the Blessed drink and quench their thirst! If we look up there, we shall see our names written in characters of Love, which can be read only by Love, and engraved only by Love. O God! and will my name also be there? Let me trust so; because although my heart burns not with ardent Charity, it has, however, its desire and its principle, and bears written upon it the Sacred Name of Jesus, which I hope nothing will be able to cancel. O what a joy for us when we shall see those characters denoting our eternal happiness! As for me, although those eternal blessings occupy all my desires and affections, yet all Paradise would be nothing to me if I did not find there the never-ending Love of the Eternal God, Who lives and reigns for ever and ever.

Let us bear in mind that Jesus Christ looks upon us from heaven, and sweetly invites us to come and enjoy the delights of His goodness and the abundance of His love. The Most Holy Virgin also invites us as a Mother, saying to each of us: 'Courage, my child; despise not the ardent desires

of my Son, and my sighs and petitions for thy
salvation. And yet, how often have we not preferred the miserable vanities and bitter pleasures
of earth to those incomparable joys! Ah, faithful
souls; let us henceforth accept the favours which
the Most Holy Virgin and the Saints offer us.
Let us promise them to walk quickly on towards
heaven; and let us take hold of the hand of our
good Angel-guardian, that we may never again
stumble, but happily reach the gates of a blessed
eternity.

SPIRITUAL FLOWERS.

The qualities of the material rose vividly represent the attributes of Mary, the Mystical Rose.
The perfume of the rose signifies the joys of the
Most Blessed Virgin; its thorns represent to us
her sorrows; and the beauty of its colour her glory
in heaven.

Mary is the beautiful Lily who looks down from
her high throne upon all other flowers, and sees
them inferior to herself.—*St. John Damascen.*

The difference between material and spiritual
rose-trees is this, that in the former, the roses fade
and the thorns remain; whilst, in the latter, the
thorns pass away and the roses remain.—*St. Francis
of Sales.*

EXAMPLE.

The Novena of St. Gertrude to the Blessed Virgin.

St. Gertrude, a Benedictine nun, cherished a great devotion to the Most Blessed Virgin. On the eve of the Annunciation she had a vision, in which she seemed to see her religious Sisters offering nosegays of sweet flowers to Our Lady. These were collected by Our Lady and placed on her bosom, and she then adorned them with precious stones, and offered them to her Divine Son. The Saint understood that those flowers were the afflictions which these Daughters of Mary and Spouses of Jesus had endured with Christian resignation, during the course of the Novena, preceding the festival.

Another time, whilst St. Gertrude was reciting the *Ave Maria* in choir with her religious Sisters, she saw three streams come forth from the Most Holy Trinity and meet together in the heart of the Blessed Virgin, descending from her and flowing over those who during these days recited this angelical salutation. It was on this occasion that she was taught to salute Our Lady, at least once a day, in these words : *Illos tuos misericordes oculos ad nos converte*, and was promised that, if she persevered in this practice during her whole life, she would receive the greatest consolations at the hour of her death.

Prayer.—O Mary, sovereign of the universe !

our joy, our support and our defence! interest
yourself in my favour before God, and obtain that
I may be one day called to enjoy the happiness
of heaven! I beseech you, O ever immaculate
Virgin; I know you to be omnipotent with your
Divine Son, for the salvation of sinners, and for
the consolation of the afflicted, and I also know
that you have need of no other recommendation
than that of our miseries, for you are by excellence
the Mother of Mercy. Amen.

Ejaculation.—O my tender Mother! help me to
live always united to your Divine Son Jesus.

Practice.—Consecrate yourself generously to
Mary, and renew this consecration every Saturday.

ACT OF CONSECRATION OF ST. FRANCIS OF SALES
TO THE MOST HOLY VIRGIN.

*In concluding these pious exercises of the Month of
Mary let us, in the spirit of St. Francis of Sales,
recite the following Act of Consecration, which he
often repeated to the Queen of Heaven, and in which
the beauty of his soul and the purity of his heart are
well depicted.*

I salute you, most sweet Virgin Mary, Mother of
God; you are my Mother and my Mistress; and
therefore, I entreat you to accept me as your son
and your servant; I wish to have no other Mother
than you. I beg you, then, my good, and gracious,
and most sweet Mother, to deign to console me in

all my troubles and tribulations, both spiritual and corporal. Remember, most sweet Virgin Mary, that you are my Mother, and that I am your son. You all powerful, and I poor, weak and vile. Nevertheless, I beseech you, O sweetest Mother, to keep me and defend me in all my ways and in all my actions, for, alas! I am poor and wretched, and in need of your most holy protection. Do, then, my beloved Mother, preserve and deliver my soul and body from all dangers and evils, and make me share in your blessings, your virtues, and, in particular, in your holy humility, your surpassing purity and your ardent charity.

Tell me not, gracious Virgin, that you cannot do so, because your Son gave you all power in heaven and on earth. Neither tell me that you ought not to hear me, for you are the common Mother of all poor mortals, and of me in particular. If you could not grant my prayer, then I should excuse you, saying: It is true that she is my Mother, and that I am her son, but she is not able to help me. If you were not my Mother, then, indeed, I should have patience, saying: She is rich enough to be able to assist me, but, alas! not being my Mother, she does not love me. But since, most sweet Virgin, you are not only my Mother, but are also powerful, how can you be excused if you do not console me, and come to my relief and assistance? You see, my Mother, that it is difficult for you to reject any request that I may make you.

Be, then, exalted in heaven and on earth, glorious Virgin and dear Mother Mary, and, for the honour and glory of your Divine Son Jesus, accept me for your son, without regard to my miseries and sins. Deliver me from all evil of soul and body, obtain for me every virtue, and first of all humility ; and bestow upon me all the benefits and graces necessary to make me pleasing to the Most Holy Trinity, Father, Son, and Holy Ghost. Amen.

THE END.

J. WASHLOURNE, PRIN.x   1o PATERN INNER ROW, LONDON.

Miraculous Prayer.

AUGUST Queen of Heaven! Sovereign Mistress of the Angels! Thou, who from the beginning hast received from God the power and mission to crush the head of Satan; we humbly beseech thee to send thy holy legions that, under thy command and by thy power, they may pursue the evil spirits; encounter them on every side: resist their bold attacks, and drive them hence into the abyss of everlasting woe. Amen.

'Who is like unto God!'

An Indulgence of 40 days is attached to the devout recital of this prayer.

✠ ETIENNE, *Bishop of Lausanne.*

All ye holy Angels and Archangels keep us and defend us. Amen.

O good and tender Mother! Thou shalt ever be our love and our hope.

A Prayer in time of Temptation.

O Divine Mother! Send thy Angels to defend me, and drive the cruel enemy from me.

These prayers were approved by the Archbishop of Tours, and the Bishops of Bayonne and Nantes in the year 1863.

ORIGIN OF THE MIRACULOUS PRAYER.

A pious priest of the Diocese of Bayonne, the Abbé Cestac, is the founder of two Religious Congregations in the aforesaid city, viz., the Servants of Mary, who devote themselves to the work

of the Sisters of the Good Shepherd, though not
cloistered : and the Bernardines, who are contem-
platives. To one of these devout Religious the
Blessed Virgin deigned to make the following
communication, which is contained in a letter from
the Abbé Cestac to M. Dupont of Tours.

'Anglet, near Bayonne.

'SIR,

'It is not exactly correct to say that the
Blessed Virgin appeared to a good, simple saint of
the Community, but rather, I should say, that this
soul received a supernatural communication from
this Divine Mother, or at any rate conceived
she had received such communication from on
high. She was at prayer, when a ray of divine
light illumined her soul. She saw in spirit the
vast desolation caused by the devil throughout the
world, and at the same time she heard the Divine
Mother telling her that it was true that hell had
been let loose upon the earth ; but that the time
had come when we were to pray to her as Queen
of Angels, and when we were to ask of her the
assistance of the heavenly legions to fight against
these deadly foes of God and of men.

'"But, my Good Mother," answered this soul,
"you who are so kind, could you not send them
without our asking you ?"

'"No," she answered ; "because prayer is one
of the conditions required by God Himself for
obtaining favours."

'And the soul believed she heard the prayer I
send you. Naturally, I was made the depositary
of this prayer, and my first duty was to submit
it to my Lord Bishop, who has benignly deigned
to approve of it. It was then that Our Lady made

known to me that I should get it printed at the
expense of her Work, and distribute it gratis.
Since that time, this prayer has received the approbation of their Lordships the Archbishops and
Bishops of Tours, of Toulouse, of Besançon, of
Tarbes. It is being reprinted at Lille, it is being
translated into Spanish, and spread far and wide.

(Signed) 'CESTAC,
'Priest of the Diocese of Bayonne.'

It would appear that the devil was terribly
enraged at the publication of this prayer, for the
Abbé Cestac in a recent letter to M. Dupont tells
him that the very day on which he sent to Tours
20,000 copies with an offering of 300 francs for the
tomb of St. Martin (sent to him for that purpose),
a large building three storeys high, was cast to the
ground : while a similar misfortune befell the same
Community at another of their establishments,
some distance off. In neither case, however, was
anyone hurt ! This occurred on the 11th of
November, 1863, Feast of St. Martin of Tours.
The Abbé Cestac adds that Providence came to
the aid of the good Religious, and enabled them
to restore their injured property. It is likewise
affirmed that seven printing presses were broken
while in the act of printing the prayer, and that
the only place at which it could be printed was at
Le Puy, where there is a celebrated Shrine of Our
Blessed Lady, to which crowds of devout pilgrims
flock.

Copies of this "Miraculous Prayer" at 1s. *the* 100 *can be had of*

R. WASHBOURNE, 18 PATERNOSTER ROW,

LONDON.

Concise Portrait of the Blessed Virgin.

She was :—

1. A true admirer of God.
2. A real lover of her Son.
3. A Virgin, both in body and mind.
4. Humble of heart.
5. Grave in speech.
6. Prudent in counsel.
7. Given to labour.
8. Reserved in discourse.
9. Fond of reading.

She excelled :—

10. In Faith.
11. In Modesty.
12. In Piety.
13. In Silence.

Never did She :—

14. Offend her parents.
15. Despise little ones.
16. Deride the weak.
17. Slight the poor.

It was a principle with Her :—

18. To serve God above all.
19. To live in retirement.
20. To cause nobody trouble.
21. To do good to all.
22. To honour the aged.
23. Not to envy her equals.
24. To shun vainglory.
25. To love virtue.
26. To follow right reason in all things.

There never appeared anything light or frivolous :

27. In her gait.
28. In her air.
29. In her discourse.
30. In her behaviour.
31. In her looks.
32. In her actions.

Copies of this " Concise Portrait" at 1s. *the* 100 *can be had of*

R. WASHBOURNE, 18 PATERNOSTER ROW,

LONDON.

BOOKS FOR THE MONTH OF MAY.

Our Lady's Month;

Or, Short Lessons for the Month of Mary, and the Feasts of Our Lady. By Very Rev. A. P. Canon BETHELL. 18mo., cloth, 1s.

Our Lady's Month;

Extracts from the Writings of Cardinal Manning, Cardinal Newman, the Saints, and others. By J. S. FLETCHER. 32mo., cloth, 6d.; better bound, 1s.

Corona Beatæ Mariæ Virginis.

Thoughts about the Blessed Virgin, for every day in the year, taken from the Writings of the Saints. 32mo., cloth, 1s.

Regina Sæculorum;

Or, Mary Venerated in All Ages. Devotions to the Blessed Virgin from Ancient Sources. Fcap. 8vo., cloth, 2s.

Mary Foreshadowed;

Or, Considerations on the Types and Figures of Our Blessed Lady in the Old Testament. By the Very Rev. Father THADDEUS, O.S.F. Fcap. 8vo., cloth, 3s.

LONDON:

R. WASHBOURNE, 18 PATERNOSTER ROW.

The Child of Mary's Manual.

Compiled from the French. With Ordinary of the Mass. 32mo., cloth, 9d.

Rules of the Children of Mary in the World. 1d.

Children of Mary Card of Enrolment.

Beautifully designed, exquisitely coloured. With Inscription. Folio, 1s.

Little Office of the Immaculate Conception.

In Latin and English. The Latin Text has the approval of the Congregation of Sacred Rites (17th May, 1876), and to which the Indulgence is attached. The English version is by Provost Husenbeth. With Imprimatur of the Cardinal Archbishop of Westminster. 32mo., cloth, 6d.

Chats about the Rosary.

By MARGARET PLUES. Fcap. 8vo., prettily bound, 2s. 6d.

The Lord's Prayer and the Hail Mary.

Tales for the Young. By EDWARD COX. Fcap. 8vo., prettily bound, 1s.

LONDON:

R. WASHBOURNE, 18 PATERNOSTER ROW.

ROBERT WASHBOURNE'S
CATALOGUE OF BOOKS,

18 PATERNOSTER ROW, LONDON.

PRAYER BOOKS (290) **SEE PAGE 30.**

By Sister Rose Gertrude ; Little Dick's Christmas Carols and other Tales. By Amy Fowler. Cloth 1s. 6d.

Principles of Religious Life. By Very Rev. F. C. Doyle, O.S.B. New Edition, revised and corrected. 8vo, 10s. 6d. [*In the Press.*

St. Bonaventure's Life of St. Francis of Assisi. New Cheaper Edition, 2s. 6d.

The Works of St. Francis of Assisi. New Cheaper Edition, 3s.

Divine Favours Granted to St. Joseph. By Fathers Binet and Jennesseaux, S.J. With Prefatory Note by Rev. Fr. de Hummelauer, S.J. 2s. 6d.

The Month of Mary, according to the Spirit of St. Francis of Sales ; or, Thirty-one Considerations, with Examples, Prayers, etc. By Don Gaspar Gilli. Translated and abridged from the Italian by a Sister of the Institute of Charity. 3s. [*In the Press.*

St. Thomas Aquinas, Patron of Youth, Protector of Learning and Study, Patron of Vocations to the Priesthood and the Religious State. A Short Sketch of his Life and Virtues. By Francis Hays. Cloth extra, 1s.

Papal Rights and Privileges in their True Light. An Exposition of the Roman Question. Specially addressed to Non-Catholics. By Francis Hays. 2d., 100 for 12s. 6d.

Our Christian Heritage. By Cardinal Gibbons, Archbishop of Baltimore, author of "The Faith of our Fathers." Cloth 6s.

The Roman Missal, in Latin and English, for the Laity, with the latest English Masses. 860 pages. Cloth 6s. ; soft morocco 7s. 6d. ; calf or morocco 10s. ; russia 12s.

An Edition without the Lenten Week-day Masses, in any of the above styles of binding, 1s. less.

Dramas will be found on page 11.

*** *All other Books not mentioned in this Catalogue supplied.*

Catalogue of Catholic American Books supplied.

Catalogues of Dusseldorf Pictures, Medals, Crucifixes, Scapulars, Rosaries, Incense, Candlesticks, Vases, &c., &c., supplied.

Altar Missals, Breviaries, Diurnals, &c., kept in stock.

Special Agent for Duffy's Books.

R. Washbourne, Paternoster Row, London.

Christmas Legends. From the German by O S. B. 1s. 6d.

1890. Catholic Home Almanac. Containing a variety of tales. Beautifully illustrated. 4to. 1s. 2d. post free.

The Catholic Child's History of England. By E. M.

Convent Life; or, the Duties of Sisters Dedicated in Religion to the Service of God. Intended chiefly for Superiors and Confessors. By Father Devine, Passionist. 5s. net.

The Lord's Prayer and the Hail Mary; or, Tales for the Young. By Edward Cox. 1s.

The Strange Adventures of Little Snowdrop, the Tale of a Green Coat, a Bunch of Violets, and Lazy Nancy. By Clara Mulholland. Illustrated. 3s. 6d.

Digby's Mores Catholici; or Ages of Faith. 4 vols., 4to, subscription, 60s. net, vols. 1 and 2 now ready, 20s. each net.

The Credentials of the Catholic Church. By Very Rev. Canon Bagshawe, D.D. *Cheap Edition.* 1s. nett; postage 3d.

Angeli Dei; or, Stories of Guardian Angels. Selected and adapted from the German of the Very Rev. Dr. Joseph A. Keller. 2s.

St. Joseph's Help; or, Stories of the Power and Efficacy of St. Joseph's Intercession. From the German of the Very Rev. J. A. Keller, D.D., Author of "Angeli Dei." 3s.

Faber Birthday Book. Selections for every day, from the Writings of the late Rev. Fr. Faber. Compiled by H. Beatson Laurie. 2s. 6d.

One of His Little Ones, and other Tales. In prose and verse. By J. S. Fletcher. 1s. 6d.

The Story of Little Tina, and other Tales. By Mrs. Shapcote. 1s.

Our Lady's Month. A Manual of Devotion for the month of May. Extracts from the Writings of Cardinal Manning, Cardinal Newman, the Saints, and others. Compiled by J. S. Fletcher, author of "One of His Little Ones." Cloth, 6d.; silver, 1s.

Corona Beatæ Mariæ Virginis. Thoughts about the Blessed Virgin, for every day in the year, taken from the Writings of the Saints. 32 mo., very prettily bound, 1s.

At the Gates of the Sanctuary; or, The Postulant and the Novice. From the Latin of Dom Presinger, O.S.B., by Very Rev. F. C. Doyle, O.S.B. 7s. 6d.

Eucharistic Hours. Devotion towards the Blessed Sacrament of the Wise and of the Simple in all Times. Gems from the Treasury of the Church's Doctrine, and the deep mines of her history, offered to them that hold and to them that seek the Gospel Pearl of great price. By Mrs. Shapcote. Crown 8vo., 4s.

Catechism of Christian Doctrine. The *revised* edition. 1d.

The Office of Holy Week, according to the Roman Rite. Cloth, 1s. Soft morocco, 2s.

Washbourne's Edition, arranged by the Editor of his Missal. (See page 21.)

A Rule of Christian Life. Written and Practised by the noble young lady, Maria Franchi de' Cavalieri, Child of Mary, and preceded by some particulars respecting her life, by the Rev. Francis Xavier Rondina, S. J. Translated from the Italian (with the editor's permission), by Richard J. Webb, M.A. Cloth 1s.

The Catechism and Holy Scripture. By Rev. J. B. Bagshawe, D.D., author of "The Threshold of the Catholic Church," "Credentials of the Catholic Church." 1s. 6d. ; better bound, 2s.

Catholic Premium Book Library. In handsome bindings, 1s., 1s 6d., 2s., 2s. 6d., 3s., and 3s. 6d. each. *Detailed List on application.*

Thoughts of Many Hearts. By a Member of the Ursuline Community, Thurles, translator of Bellecius "Solid Virtue." 32mo., 2s.

Jesus Calls Thee. Thoughts for one in indecision. By J. S. Fletcher. 6d. A very useful little book for those in doubt.

Faith of our Fathers. A Magazine. 1d.

The Little Treasury of Leaflets. 1st and 2nd series, each, cloth, 1s. and 2s. ; roan, 1s. 6d. and 2s. 6d. ; common morocco, 3s. ; best calf or morocco, 5s. ; Russia, 6s.

A Friendly Voice ; or, The Daily Monitor, and Visits to the Blessed Sacrament. By author of "Golden Sands." 6d.

The Child of Mary's Manual. Compiled from the French. Third Edition, with Imprimatur. 9d.

Little Office of the Immaculate Conception. Latin and English : with Imprimatur of the Cardinal-Archbishop of Westminster. Cloth 6d. Soft morocco, 1s.

This edition has the great advantage over most English and other prayerbooks, of reproducing the only Latin text which has the approval of the Congregation of Sacred Rites (17 *May,* 1876), *and to which the Indulgence is attached. Provost Husenbeth's English Version has, where necessary, been revised to agree with this text.*

Catholic Hymn Book. By Rev. Langton George Vere. 192 pages, price 2d. ; in cloth, 4d. ; soft morocco, 1s This is the best and cheapest Hymn book printed. *An Abridged Editon, in* 64 *pages, is now ready.* Price 1d, or in cloth, 2d.

Lily of St. Joseph. A tiny manual of Prayer, with Singing, Mass, Litanies. and the Confraternity of St Joseph. Compiled by Rev. R. Richardson. New edition, with additions, 2d., cloth, 3d. 4d. and 6d. ; soft morocco, 1s. Larger edition, without Hymns, 1d., with Fr. Vere's Hymns, 6d.

OREMUS, A Liturgical Prayer Book : with the Imprimatur of the Cardinal Archbishop of Westminster. 32mo., 452 pages, cloth, 2s. ; French morocco, 3s. ; calf or morocco, 5s.; extra gilt, 6s. 6d. ; Russia, 7s. 6d. Also in more expensive bindings.

A Smaller Oremus ; an abridgment of the above. Cloth, 6d. ; Japanese, 1s. ; French morocco, 1s. 6d.; calf or morocco, 2s. 6d.; extra gilt, 4s.; russia, 5s. Also in superior and more expensive bindings.

Child's Picture Prayer Book. Mass, Benediction, &c. Sixteen coloured Illustrations, cloth, 9d. ; stronger bound, 1s. ; prettier bound, 1s. 6d. ; full gilt, 2s. ; soft morocco, full gilt, 3s.

ADELSTAN'S (Countess) Life and Letters. From the French of the Rev. Père Marquigny, S.J., 1s. 6d.

Adolphus ; or, the Good Son. Gilt, 6d.

Adrian and Emily : a Tale of Two Conversions ; or, the Brides of Kensington. By Miss Bridges. 1s. With Sir Thomas Maxwell and his Ward. 2s.

Adventures of a Protestant in Search of a Religion. By Iota. 3s. 6d.

Adventures of Little Snowdrop, and other Tales. By Clara Mulholland. With 4 Illustrations. 3s. 6d.

Agnes Wilmott's History, and the Lessons it Taught. By the author of " Bertram Eldon," " Nellie Gordon," &c. 1s. 6d. ; with three other Tales. 2s.

A'KEMPIS—Following of Christ. Dr. Challoner's Edition, 48mo. (or miniature edition, with red border round pages), morocco, 1s. 6d., 2s. 6d., 4s., 4s. 6d. ; calf, 2s., 2s. 6d., 4s., 4s. 6d. ; Russian, 5s. 32mo., 6d. ; red edges, 1s.; French morocco, 2s.; calf or morocco, 4s.; gilt, 5s. ; russia, 7s. 6d., 9s. and 12s. ; ivory, with rims and clasp, 15s., 16s., 18s.; mor. antique, with corners and clasps, 17s. 6d.; russia, ditto, ditto, 16s. 20s. With Reflections, 1s. ; soft morocco, 3s. 6d. ; with red borders round pages, cloth, 3s. 6d. ; soft morocco, 7s. 6d. ; calf, 10s. 6d. ; antique morocco, 15s.

Albertus Magnus, Life of. By Rev. Fr. Dixon. 8vo. 6s.

Allah Akbar—God is Great. An Arab Legend of the Siege and Conquest of Granada. From the Spanish. By Mariana Monteiro. 2s. 6d.

ALLISON (M. Sinclair), Snowflakes and other Tales. 1s.

All Souls' Forget-me-Not. Prayers and Meditations for the Holy Souls. Edited by Canon Moser. 2s. 6d.

AMHERST (Rt. Rev. Dr.), Lenten Thoughts. 1s. ; stronger bound, 1s. 6d.

ANDERDON (Rev. W. H., S.J.), To Rome and Back. Fly-Leaves from a Flying Tour. 12mo., 2s.

ANDERSEN (Carl), Three Sketches of Life in Iceland. Translated by Myfanwy Fenton. 1s. 6d.

Angeli Dei ; or, Stories of Guardian Angels. From the German of the Rev. Dr. Keller. 2s.

Angels (The) and the Sacraments. 1s. With Snowflakes and other Tales. 1s. 6d.

———— Month of the Holy Angels. By Abbé Ricard. 1s.

Anglicanism, Harmony of. (Church Defence). By T. W. M. Marshall. 1s.

Annie's First Prayer and Only a Picture. 1s. ; with Bessy or the Fatal Consequences of Telling Lies. 1s. 6d.

ARNOLD (Miss M. J.), Personal Recollections of Car-
dinal Wiseman, with other Memories. 12mo., 2s.

ARRAS. (Madame d') The Two Friends; or Marie's Self-
Denial. 12mo., 1s.

Art of Christian Warfare with Wrong. By Rev. F. H.
Laing, D.D. 1s.

Aunt Margaret's Little Neighbours; or, Chats about the
Rosary. By Miss Plues. 12mo., 2s. 6d.

Ave Maria; or Catesby's Story. By Rev. F. Drew. 1s.

BAGSHAWE (Rev. J. B. Canon, D.D.), The Credentials
of the Catholic Church. 1s. nett. (postage 3d.).

——— Threshold of the Catholic Church. A Course of
Plain Instructions for those entering her Communion. 1s. *nett*
(postage 3d.).

——— The Catechism and Holy Scripture. 1s. 6d., or
better bound, 2s.

Baker's Boy; or, Life of General Drouot. Gilt, 6d.

BALDESCHI. Ceremonial according to the Roman
Rite. Translated by Rev. J. D. Hilarius Dale. 12mo., 6s. 6d.

Bambozzi (Fr. Benvenuto, O.M.C.), of the Conventual Friars
Minor, Life of, from the Italian (2nd edition) of Fr. Nicholas
Treggiari, D.D. 3s. 6d.

BAMPFIELD (Rev. G.), Sir Ælfric and other Tales.
18mo., 6d.; cloth, 1s.

Battista Varani (B.), *see* Veronica (S.). 12mo., 5s.

Battle of Connemara. By Kathleen O'Meara. 2s, 6d.

BELLECIUS (Fr.), Solid Virtue. New edition. 12mo., 7s. 6d.

Bellevue and its Owners. A Tale for Boys. By C. Pilley.
1s. 6d.

BELLINGHAM (Lady Constance) The Duties of Chris-
tian Parents. Conferences by Père Matignon. Translated. 3s.6d.

Benedict's (S.) Manual. 3s.

——— Life and Miracles. By S. Gregory the Great. From
an old English version. By P. W. (Paris, 1608). Edited by
Bishop Luck, O.S.B. 1s.; or in stronger binding, 2s.

——— Explanation of the Medal. 1d.

Bernardine (St.) of Siena, Life of. 5s.

Bertie. An Old Man's Story. By Ernest I. Stuart. 1s. 6d.

Bertram Eldon, and how he found a Home. By M. A.
Pennell, author of "Nellie Gordon" (6d), "Agnes Wilmott's
History" (1s. 6d.). 1s.; with three other Tales. 2s. 6d.

Bessy; or, the Fatal Consequence of Telling Lies. By Miss K. M.
Weld. 1s.; with two other Tales. 1s. 6d.

BETHELL (Rev. A.), Our Lady's Month ; or, Short Lessons for the Month of May, and the Feasts of Our Lady. 18mo., 1s.

Bible. Douay Version. 12mo., 3s. ; Persian calf or soft morocco, 7s. 6d. ; morocco, 9s. 18mo., 2s. 6d. ; Persian, 5s.; calf or morocco, 7s. ; gilt, 8s. 6d. 8vo., 6s., cloth. 4to., Illustrated, 25s. **New Testament.** 18mo., good type, 1s.

Bible History. By Rev. R. Gilmour. Illustrated. 2s.

Bible Stories. *See* Ram, p. 24 ; Walker, p. 29

Blessed Sacrament, Meditations on. 1s. 6d. Visits to. 6d.

———— *See* **Eucharistic Hours,** page 11. 4s.

Blessed Virgin, Devotions to. From Ancient Sources. 2s.

———— History of. By Orsini. Translated by Dr. Husenbeth. 3s.6d.

———— Thoughts about, for every Day in the Year. 1s.

———— Life of. Proposed as a model to Christian women. 12mo., 1s.

———— *See* Our Lady, p. 23 ; Leaflets, p. 17 ; May, p. 19.

BLOSIUS, Spiritual Works of :—The Rule of the Spiritual Life ; The Spiritual Mirror ; String of Spiritual Jewels. Edited by Rev. Fr. John Bowden. 3s. 6d.

Bluebeard ; or, the Key of the Cellar. A Drama in 3 Acts. 6d.

Blue Scapular, Origin of. 18mo., 1d.

BLYTH (Rev. Fr.), Devout Paraphrase on the Seven Penitential Psalms. To which is added "Necessity of Purifying the Soul," by S. Francis de Sales. 18mo., 6d.

Bobbie and Birdie ; or, Our Lady's Picture. A Story for the very little ones. By Frances J. M. Kershaw. 2s.; with **The Gamekeeper's Little Son,** and other Tales. 3s. 6d.

BOLTON (Rev. T. F.), Reunion of Christendom with Rome. The Necessity of Union. 6d.

BONA (Cardinal), Easy Way to God. By Father Collins. 3s.

BONAVENTURE (S.), Life of St. Francis of Assisi. From the Italian by the author of "The Life of St. Teresa." 2s. 6d.

Boniface (S.), Life of. By Mrs. Hope. 12mo., 6s. nett

BOWDEN (Rev. Fr. John), Spiritual Works of Louis of Blois. 12mo., 3s. 6d.

———— Oratorian Lives of the Saints. (Page 22). 5s. each.

BOWDEN (Mrs.), Lives of the First Religious of the Visitation of Holy Mary. 2 vols., 12mo., 10s.

BOWLES (Emily), Eagle and Dove. Translated from the French of Mdlle. Zénaide Fleuriot. 5s.

BRADBURY (Rev. Fr.), Sophia and Eulalie. (The Catholic Pilgrim's Progress). 2s. 6d.

BRAYE (Lord), A Selection from the Poems of. 1s.

BRIDGES (Miss), Adrian and Emily, a Tale of Two Conversions ; or, The Brides of Kensington. 1s.

BRIDGES, Sir Thomas Maxwell and his Ward. 1s. 6d.

Bridget (S.), Life of, and other Saints of Ireland. 12mo., 1s.

Broken Chain. A Tale. Gilt, 6d.

BROWNLOW (Rev. Canon), "Vitis Mystica"; or, the True Vine : a Treatise on the Passion of our Lord. 2s. 6d.

———— St. Marychurch, in Saxon and Norman Times. 1s. ; cloth, 1s. 6d.

———— Christmas with Bishop Grandisson ; or, the Services in Exeter Cathedral, A.D. 1368. 6d.

Bruno. A Tale imitated from the Swedish. 1s.

Buddhism, Esoteric. The new Gospel of Atheism. By E. H. Dering. 6d. ; cloth, 1s.

BURDER (Abbot), Confidence in the Mercy of God. By Mgr. Languet. 12mo., 3s.

———— The Consoler ; or, Pious Readings addressed to the Sick and all who are afflicted. By Père Lambilotte. 3s. 6d.

———— Novena in favour of the Souls in Purgatory. 2d.

———— Souls in Purgatory. Spiritual Bouquets. 32mo., 2d.

Burial of the Dead. For Children and Adults. (Latin and English.) Clear type edition, 32mo., 6d.; roan, 1s.

BUTLER (Alban), Lives of the Saints. 4 vols., 8vo., 36s. nett. 12 vols., small 8vo., 30s.

CALIXTE—Life of the Ven. Anna Maria Taigi. Translated by A. V. Smith Sligo. 3s. 6d.

Callista. Dramatised by Dr. Husenbeth. 1s.

CAMERON (Marie), The Golden Thought, and other Stories. 1s. ; or in 2 vols., 6d. each.

    1. The Golden Thought, and The Brother's Grave.

    2. The Rod that bore Blossoms, and Patience and Impatience.

CARAHER (Hugh), A Month at Lourdes and its Neighbourhood. Two Illustrations. 12mo., 2s.

CARR (Monsignor). A Lamp of the Word and Instructor's Guide ; being a Series of Charts of the whole Course of Christian Doctrine in the Catechism. 2s. 6d. nett ; or post free on receipt of 2s. 9d.

Catechisms — The Catechism of Christian Doctrine. *Revised edition*, 1d.

———— Cardinal Wiseman's edition *offered at Half Price*, ½d.

———— Canon Bagshawe's edition. 1s. 6d.

———— Bishop Challoner's Grounds of Catholic Doctrine. Paper, 2d. · cloth, 4d.

———— Frassinetti's Dogmatic. 2s.

———— Keenan's Controversial. 2s.

———— of Confirmation. To which is added The Ceremony of Confirmation, etc. 3d.

R. Washbourne, Paternoster Row, London

Catherine Hamilton. By M. F. S. 1s. 6d.; }
Catherine Grown Older. By M. F. S. 1s. 6d.; } in 1 vol., 2s. 6d.

Catherine's Promise, and Norah's Temptation. By Mrs. Seamer. 1s.; with three other Tales. 1s. 6d.

Catholic Controversial Letters. By Rev. P. Sweeny, DD. 3s.

Catholic Directory for Scotland. 1s.

Catholic Mother's Lullaby. By Mrs. Shapcote. 2d.

Catholic Piety. Small 32mo., 6d.; large 32mo., 1s. and upwards.

Catholic Pilgrim's Progress—The Journey of Sophia and Eulalie to the Palace of True Happiness. 2s. 6d.

Catholic Premium Book Library. In very elegant bindings from 1s. to 3s. 6d. a vol. (Detailed List on application.)

CHALLONER (Dr.), Grounds of Catholic Doctrine. Paper, 2d.; cloth, 4d.

——— Memoirs of Missionary Priests. 8vo., illustrated, 8s.

Chats about the Commandments. By Miss Plues. 2s. 6d.

Chats about the Rosary. By Miss Plues. 2s. 6d.

CHAUGY (Mother Frances Magdalen de), Lives of the First Religious of the Visitation. 2 vols., 12mo., 10s.

Child (The) of Mary's Manual. Third edition, 32mo. 9d.

Child's Picture Prayer Book, with Mass, Benediction, &c. With 16 Illustrations. Cloth, 9d.; stronger, 1s.; prettier, 1s. 6d.; gilt, 2s.; leather, 3s.

Children of Mary Card of Enrolment. Folio, 1s., post free.
Children of Mary in the World, Rules of. 32mo., 1d.

Christmas Legends. Seven Legends, translated from the German by O. S. B. 1s. 6d.

Christmas Revels; or, the Puritan's Discomfiture. A Burlesque. 6d.

CHRISTOPHER (S.) The Rose of Venice. A Tale. 3s.6d.
Church Defence. By T. W. M. Marshall. 1s.
Cistercian Legends of the XIII. Century. 3s.
Clare's Sacrifice. By C. M. O'Hara. A Tale for First Communicants. 6d.
COLLINS (Rev. Fr.), Legends of the XIII. Century. 3s.
——— Easy Way to God. From the Latin of Cardinal Bona. 3s.
——— Spiritual Conferences on the Mysteries of Faith and the Interior Life. 12mo., 5s.

COLOMBIERE (Father Claude de la), The Sufferings of Our Lord. Sermons preached in the Chapel Royal, St. James's in the year 1677. Preface by Fr. Doyotte, S.J. 18mo., 1s.

Colombini (B. Giovanni), Life of. By Belcari. Translated from the editions of 1541 and 1832. 3s. 6d.

Comedy of Convocation in the English Church. Edited by Archdeacon Chasuble. 8vo., 2s. 6d. nett.

Comfort for the Sick. Selections from Crasset's Meditations. Translated by the Right Rev. T. B. Snow, O.S B. 2d.

Communion (Holy), practised according to the intentions of Our Saviour. 1s.

Communion, Prayers for, for Children. Preparation, Mass before Communion, Thanksgiving. 32mo. 1d.

Conferences. *See* Collins, Lacordaire, Matignon, Ravignan.

Confession and Holy Communion : Young Catholic's Guide. By Dr. Kenny. 32mo , 4d.

Confidence in the Mercy of God. By Mgr. Languet. Translated by Abbot Burder. 12mo., 3s.

Confirmation, Instructions for the Sacrament of. A very complete book. To which is added The Ceremony of Confirmation. 72 pages, 3d.

Consoler (The) ; or, Pious Readings addressed to the Sick and all who are afflicted. By Père Lambillotte. 3s. 6d.

Contemplations and Meditations on the Public Life of Our Lord, according to the Method of St. Ignatius. Translated from the French by a Sister of Mercy. Revised by the Rev. W. T. Amherst, S.J. 6s.

Contemplations on the Most Holy Sacrament of the Altar ; or Devout Meditations to serve as Preparations for, and Thanksgiving after, Communion. 1s. 6d.

Contemporary Prophecies. By Bishop Dupanloup. 6d.

Continental Fish Cook ; or, a Few Hints on Maigre Dinners. By M. J. N. de Frederic. Third edition, with additions, 6d. and 1s.

Contrast (A), and Herbert Montague, Walter Ferrers' School-days, and Bertram Eldon. 2s. 6d.

Convert Martyr ; or, "Callista," by the Rev. Dr. Newman. Dramatised by the Rev. Dr. Husenbeth. 1s.

Corona Beatæ Mariæ Virginis. Thoughts about the Blessed Virgin, for every Day in the Year, taken from the Writings of the Saints. 1s.

COTTON (Amelia L.), A Sketch of the Life of S. Francis of Assisi. 1s.

——— Eucharist (The), and the Christian Life. From the French of La Bouillerie. 3s. 6d.

COX (Edward), The Lord's Prayer and the Hail Mary. Tales for the Young. 1s.

CRASSET'S Meditations. Edited by the Right Rev. T. B. Snow, O.S.B. 2 vols., 8s.

Credentials of the Catholic Church. By Rev. Canon Bagshawe, D.D., author of "The Threshold of the Catholic Church." Cheap edition, 1s. nett (postage 3d.).

Credo ; or Justin's Martyrdom. By Rev. F. Drew. 1s.

CUSACK (M. F.)—Life of Most Rev. Dr. Dixon. 7s. 6d.
    Meditations for Advent and Easter. 3s. 6d.
    Nun's Advice to her Girls. 12mo., 2s. 6d.
    Retreat for the Three Last Days of the Year. 1s.

Dark Shadow (The). A Tale. 12mo., 2s. 6d.

Daughter (A) of S. Dominick : (Bells of the Sanctuary). By Grace Ramsay. 2s. 6d. net.

DAVIS (Rev. R. G.) Garden of the Soul. Small 32mo., 6d. ; Illustrated, 1s. ; large 32mo , 1s. and upwards. See pages 30 & 32.

DEHAM (Rev. F.) Sacred Heart of Jesus, offered to the Piety of the Young engaged in Study. 1s.

DERING (Edward Heneage), Esoteric Buddhism : the New Gospel of Atheism. 6d. ; cloth, 1s.

Diary of a Confessor of the Faith. 12mo., 1s.

Directorium Asceticum ; or, Guide to the Spiritual Life. By Scaramelli. 4 vols., 12mo., 24s.

DIXON (Fr., O.P.) Albertus Magnus: his Life and Scholastic Labours. From original documents, by Dr. Sighart. 8vo. 6s.
——— Life of St. Vincent Ferrer. From the French of Rev. Fr. Piadel. 12mo., 5s.

Dominus Vobiscum ; or, the Sailor Boy. By Rev. F. Drew. 1s.

DOYLE (Canon, O.S.B.), Life of Gregory Lopez, the Hermit. 12mo., 3s. 6d.
———Principles of Religious Life. New Edition, revised and corrected. 8vo., 10s. 6d.
——— Lectures for Boys. The Sundays of the Year, 3s. 6d. ; Our Lady's Festivals, etc., 2s. 6d. ; The Passion of Our Lord, 3s. ; and The Sacred Heart, 3s.
——— At the Gates of the Sanctuary ; or, the Postulant and the Novice. 7s. 6d.

DOYOTTE (Fr., S.J.), Elevations to the Heart of Jesus. 2s.

DRANE (Augusta Theodosia), Inner Life of Pere Lacordaire. Translated from the French of Père Chocarne. 6s. 6d.

DREW (Rev. F.), Little Books of St. Nicholas. 1s each. 1 to 8 now ready. 1. Oremus ; 2. Dominus Vobiscum ; 3. Pater Noster. 4. Per Jesum Christum; 5. Veni Creator; 6. Credo; 7. Ave Maria ; 8. Ora pro nobis ; or, in 2 vols., 6s.

DRAMAS. Bluebeard. A Drama in 3 Acts. Mixed. 6d.
———— Christmas Revels. Burlesque. 6d.
———— Convert Martyr; or, "Callista" dramatised. 1s.
———— The Duchess Transformed (Girls, 1 Act). Comedy. 6d.
———— The Enchanted Violin (Boys, 2 Acts). Comedy. 6d.
———— Ernscliff Hall (Girls, 3 Acts). Drama. 6d.
———— Filiola (Girls, 4 Acts). Drama. 6d.
———— He would be a Lord. Molière's Le Bourgeois Gentil-homme. (Male.) Comedy in 3 Acts. 6d.
———— Mary Queen of Scots. (Mixed, 3 Acts) Tragedy, 6d.
———— Reverse of the Medal (Girls, 4 Acts). Drama. 6d.
———— The Secret (Girls, 1 Act). Drama. 6d.
———— Shandy Maguire (Boys, 2 Acts), a Farce. 6d.
———— St. Eustace (Boys, 5 Acts). Drama. 6d.
———— St. William of York (Boys, 2 Acts). Drama. 6d.
———— The Violet Sellers (3 Acts). Drama for Children. 6d.
———— The Wanderers; or, Faith's Welcome (Boys, 1 Act). 6d.
———— Whittington and his Cat. Drama for Children. 9 Scenes. By Henrietta Fairfield. 6d.
———— *See* R. Washbourne's American List.
Duchess (The), Transformed. By W. H. A. A Comedy. 6d.
DUPANLOUP (Bishop) Contemporary Prophecies. 6d.
Dusseldorf Society for the Distribution of Good Religious Pictures. 2 vols., folio, half-morocco, £15.
    Subscription 9s. a year, allots over 100 pictures.
Duties of Christian Parents. Conferences by Père Matignon. Translated from the French by Lady Constance Bellingham. 3s. 6d.
Eagle and Dove. Translated by Emily Bowles. 5s.
Easy Way to God. By Cardinal Bona. 12mo., 3s.
Emily and Nancy, and other Tales. By Lady Herbert. 1s.; with Rose Fortescue. 1s. 6d.
Emmanuel ; or, the Deserted Child. Gilt, 6d.
Enchanted Violin, The. A Comedy in 2 Acts (Boys), 6d.
English Martyrs, of Yorkshire. By a Religious of St. Mary's Convent, York. 1s. 6d.
Epistles and Gospels. Good clear type edition, 4d.; roan, 1s. This edition is more complete than any other one.
Ernscliff Hall. A Drama in Three Acts, for Girls. 12mo., 6d.
Eucharist (The) and the Christian Life. 3s. 6d.
Eucharistic Hours. Devotions towards the Blessed Sacrament. Gems from the Treasury of the Church's Doctrine. By Mrs. Shapcote. 4s.

Eustace (St.). A Drama in 5 Acts for Boys. 6d.

FABER Birthday Book. Selections for every day, from the Writings of the late Rev. Fr. Faber. 2s. 6d.

FAIRFIELD (Henrietta), Whittington and his Cat. A Drama, in 9 Scenes, for Children. 12mo., 6d.

Fairy Ching (The); or, the Chinese Fairies' Visit to England. By Henrica Frederic. 1s. ; with six other Tales. 2s. 6d.

Faith of our Fathers. By Most Rev. Abp. Gibbons, 1s. 6d. & 3s. nett.

Fardel (Sister Claude Simplicienne), Life of. With the Lives of others of the First Religious of the Visitation. 6s.

Father Pacificus the Capuchin. Episode in his life. By Lady Herbert. 6d.

Father Placid ; or, the Custodian of the Blessed Sacrament. 1s. ; with Paul Seigneret the Seminarist of Saint Sulpice. 2s.

FAVRE (Abbe), Heaven Opened by the Practice of Frequent Confession and Communion. 2s. 6d.

Favre (Mother Marie Jacqueline), Life of. With the Lives of others of the First Religious of the Visitation. 6s.

Feasts (The) of Camelot, with the Tales that were told there. By Mrs. E. L. Hervey. 2s. 6d.

Filiola. A Drama in Four Acts, for Girls. 12mo., 6d.

First Communion and Confirmation Memorial. Beautifully printed in gold and colours, folio. New edition, 6d.

First Communion ; or, Clare's Sacrifice. By Miss O'Hara. 6d.

First Communion, Emily, Nancy, etc. By Lady Herbert. 1s.

First Religious of the Visitation of Holy Mary, Lives of. Translated, with a Preface, by Mrs. Bowden. 2 vols., 10s.

FLETCHER (J. S.) Our Lady's Month. Extracts from the Writings of Cardinal Manning, Cardinal Newman, the Saints, and others. Cloth, 6d.; better bound, 1s.

———— Jesus calls thee. Thoughts for one in indecision. 6d

———— One of His Little Ones, and other Stories. 1s. d.

FLEURIOT (Mlle. Zenaide), Eagle and Dove. Translated by Emily Bowles. 5s.

Flowers of Christian Wisdom. By Henry Lucien. 1s. 6d.

Fluffy. A Tale for Boys. By M. F. S. 2s. ; with Little Dick and other Tales. 3s.

Following of Christ. *See* A'Kempis.

For Better. not for Worse. By Rev. Langton George Vere. 2s. 6d.

Foreign Books, obtained from America, France, Germany, Italy, etc., without delay.

FOWLER (Amy—Sister Rose Gertrude)—Little Dick's Christmas Carols, and five other Tales. 1s. 6d.

Francis of Assisi (St.) Works of. Translated by a Religious of the Order. New Edition, corrected, 3s.

———— **Life of.** By S. Bonaventure. Translated by Miss Lockhart. 2s. 6d.

" It speaks to the heart with a vital power which no work of merely natural genius can command."—CARDINAL MANNING.

—————— **A Sketch of the Life of.** By Amelia Lucy Cotton. 1s.

FRANCIS OF SALES (S.), Consoling Thoughts. 18mo., 2s.

———— **Necessity of Purifying the Soul.** 6d.

———— **Sweetness of Holy Living.** 1s.

FRASSINETTI—Dogmatic Catechism. 2s.

FREDERIC (Henrica), The Fairy Ching ; or, the Chinese Fairies' Visit to England. 1s.

———— **Story of a Paper Knife.** 1s.

FREDERIC (M. J. N. de) Continental Fish Cook : or, a Few Hints on Maigre Dinners. 3rd edition, 6d. and 1s.

Friendly Voice ; or, the Daily Monitor. Red border, cloth, 6d.

Gamekeeper's Little Son, and other Tales for Children. By F. I. M. Kershaw. 2s.

Garden of the Soul. Small 32mo., 6d. ; Illustrated, 1s. ; large 32mo., 1s. and upwards. See pages 30 and 32.

Gathered Gems from Spanish Authors. By M. Monteiro. 3s.

GAUME (Abbe), Catechism of Perseverance. 4 vols., 20s. Abridged in 1 vol., 2s.

George Lawson ; or, the Dark Shadow. A Tale. 2s. 6d.

GEUDENS (V. Rev. Fr.), Life of S. Norbert. 3s. 6d. net.

GIBBONS (His Eminence Cardinal), The Faith of our Fathers; Being a Plain Exposition and Vindication of the Church Founded by our Lord Jesus Christ. 3s. ; paper covers, 1s. 6d. *nett.*

———— **Our Christian Heritage.** 6s.

GILLI (Don Gaspar), The Month of Mary, according to the Spirit of St. Francis de Sales ; or, Thirty-one Considerations, with Examples, Prayers, etc. From the Italian by a Sister of the Institute of Charity. 2s. 6d. and 3s.

GILMOUR (Rev. R.), Bible History. Illustrated. 2s.

Glittering Stars on Our Lady's Mantle. By Rev. F. Thaddeus, O.S.F., 2s.

Golden Thought of Queen Beryl, and other Stories. By Marie Cameron. 1s. ; or in 2 vols. 6d. each ; with three other Tales. 2s. 6d.

Good for Evil, and Joe Ryan's Repentance. By Mrs. Seamer. 1s. ; with The Old Prayer Book, and Charlie Pearson's Medal. 1s. 6d.

GRANT (Bishop), Pastoral on St. Joseph. 32mo., 3d. & 4d.

Gregory Lopez, the Hermit, Life of. By Canon Doyle, O.S.B. 3s. 6d.

Grounds of the Catholic Doctrine. By Bishop Challoner. Large type edition, 18mo., paper, 2d. ; cloth, 4d.

Harmony of Anglicanism. Church Defence. By T. W. Marshall. 1s.

HAY (Bishop), Devout Christian. 12mo., 2s. 6d.
———— Sincere Christian. 12mo., 2s. 6d.

HAYS (Francis), Life of St. Thomas Aquinas. 1s.

Heaven Opened by the Practice of frequent Confession and Holy Communion. By the Abbé Favre. 2s. 6d.

HEIGHAM (John), A Devout Exposition of the Holy Mass. Edited by Austin John Rowley, Priest. 3s.

HENRY (Lucien), Flowers of Christian Wisdom. 1s. 6d.

HERBERT (Lady), True Wayside Tales. 3s. ; or in 5 vols., cheap edition, 6d. each.
   1. The Brigand Chief, and other Tales. 2. Now is the Accepted Time, and other Tales. 3. What a Child can do, and other Tales. 4. Sowing Wild Oats, and other Tales. 5. The Two Hosts, and other Tales.

———— Second Series of True Wayside Tales. 3s., or separately
———— Moothoosawmy, & other Indian Tales. 1s. Emily, &c. 1s.
   The Two Cousins, &c. 1s.

———— Third Series of True Wayside Tales. 3s.

HERBERT (Wallace), My Dream and other Verses. 1s.
———— The Angels and the Sacraments. 1s.

HERVEY (E. L.), Stories from many Lands. 12mo., 3s. 6d.
———— Rest, on the Cross. 12mo., 3s.
———— The Feasts of Camelot, with the Tales that were told there. 2s. 6d.

He would be a Lord (Molière's Le Bourgeois Gentilhmome), comedy in 3 Acts. 6d.

HOFFMAN (Franz), Industry and Laziness. 2s. 6d.

Holy Family Card of Membership. A beautiful design. Folio. Price 6d., or 8d., post free, on a roller ; 4s. 6d. a dozen, or post free 5s.

Holy Isle ; or, Lives of some Saints of Ireland. 1s.

Holy Places : their Sanctity and Authenticity. 3s. 6d.

Holy Readings. By J. R. Digby Beste, Esq. 2s.

Horace. Literally translated by Smart, 1s. 6d. Latin and English, 2s. 6d.

Holy Week Book according to the Roman Rite. In addition to the Offices usually included, this Edition gives the Vespers and Compline for each day; the Blessing of the Holy Oils on Maundy Thursday; and the Matins, Lauds, Mass, Vespers, and Compline for Easter Sunday. 252 pages; cloth 1s.; soft morocco 2s.

"The compiler has done his work carefully and well, and the publisher has done his part well, in bringing out the book so neatly, and considering the amount of matter, at so low a price."—The Very Rev. W. A. CANON JOHNSON, D.D.

The Roman Missal. By the same Editor. $5\frac{1}{2}$ inches by $3\frac{3}{4}$, $1\frac{1}{2}$ inch thick. Printed from new type on specially made paper. Price, in cloth, red edges, 6s.; soft morocco, 7s. 6d.; calf or morocco, 10s. 6d.; russia, 12s.

Also an edition without the Lenten Week-day Masses, in all the above bindings, 1s. less. An abridged edition is nearly ready.

"All the new Masses granted of late are contained in this edition, therefore a number of Masses are here which have not hitherto appeared in any English Missal. . . . The book is carefully edited. We trust it will become very popular."—*Dublin Review.*

HUSENBETH (Rev. Dr.), Convert Martyr. 1s

———— **Little Office of the Immaculate Conception.** In Latin and English. 32mo., cloth, 6d.; soft morocco, 1s. *Please refer to page 3 for particulars of this edition.*

———— **Our Blessed Lady of Lourdes.** Paper cover, 6d., with the Novena, cloth, 1s; Novena, separately, 3d.; Litany, 1d.

Hymn Book (The Catholic). Edited by Rev. L. G. Vere. 1d., cloth 2d.; larger edition, 192 pages, 2d., cloth, 4d., soft morocco, 1s.

Iceland (Three Sketches of Life in). By Carl Andersen. 1s. 6d.; with three other Tales. 2s. 6d.

Imitation of Christ. *See* A'Kempis.

Indian Tales. Edited by Lady Herbert. 1s.

Industry and Laziness. From the German of Hoffman. 2s. 6d.

IOTA. The Adventures of a Protestant in Search of a Religion. 3s. 6d.

Italian Revolution (The History of). The History of the Barricades. By Keyes O'Clery, M.P. 8vo., 4s.

Jack's Boy. By M. F. S, author of "Fluffy." 2s. 6d.

John of God (S.), Life of. 5s.

Joseph (S.). Novena to, with a Pastoral by the late Bishop Grant. 32mo., 3d.; cloth, 4d.

Joseph (S.) Divine Favours granted to St. Joseph. By F. Binet and F. Jennesseaux, S.J. With Prefatory Note by Rev. Fr. de Hummelauer, S.J. 2s. 6d.

Joseph's (S.) Help; or, Stories of the Power and Efficacy of St. Joseph's Intercession. By Rev. Dr. Keller. 3s,

———— *See* Leaflets, page 17.

Journey of Sophia and Eulalie to the Palace of True Happiness. (The Catholic Pilgrim's Progress.) From the French by Rev. Fr. Bradbury. 2s. 6d.

Kainer ; or, the Usurer's Doom. By James King. 1s. ; with five other Tales. 2s. 6d.

KEENAN (Rev. S.), Controversial Catechism. 12mo., 2s.

KELLER (Rev. Dr. J. A.) Angeli Dei ; or, Stories of Guardian Angels. Translated by a Benedictine Nun at East Bergholt. 2s.

——————— **St. Joseph's Help ; or, Stories of the Power and Efficacy of St. Joseph's Intercession.** Translated by a Benedictine Nun at East Bergholt. 3s.

KENNY (Dr.), Young Catholic's Guide to Confession and Holy Communion. 32mo., 4d.

KERSHAW (Frances I. M.), Bobbie and Birdie ; or, Our Lady's Picture. A Story for the very little ones. 2s.

——————Gamekeeper's Little Son, and other Tales for Children. 2s.

Key of Heaven. Small 32mo., 6d. ; large 32mo., 1s. and upwards.

Killed at Sedan. By Samuel Richardson, A.B , B.L. 5s.

KING (James). Industry and Laziness. 2s. 6d.

——————— **Kainer ; or, the Usurer's Doom.** 1s.

LA BOUILLERIE (Mgr. de), The Eucharist and the Christian Life. Translated by L. C. 12mo., 3s. 6d.

Lacordaire. The Inner Life of Pere Lacordaire. From the French of Père Chocarne. By Augusta Theodosia Drane. 6s. 6d.

LAING (Rev. Dr.), Knight of the Faith.
    Absurd Protestant Opinions concerning *Intention*. 4d.
    Catholic, not Roman Catholic. 4d.
    Challenge to the Churches. 1d.
    Descriptive Guide to the Mass. 1s.
    Favourite Fallacy about Private Judgment and Inquiry. 1d.
    Protestantism against the Natural Moral Law. 1d.
    What is Christianity ? 6d.
    Whence does the Monarch get his right to Rule ? 2s. 6d.

——————— **The Art of Christian Warfare with Wrong.** 1s.

——————— **What sort of Intollerance is Righteous ?** 1s.

LAMBILOTTE (Pere), The Consoler. Translated by Abbot Burder. 3s. 6d.

R. Washbourne, Paternoster Row, London

LANE-CLARKE (T. M. L.) The Violet Sellers. A Drama for Children in 3 Acts. 6d.

LANGUET (Mgr.), Confidence in the Mercy of God. Translated by Abbot Burder. 12mo., 3s.

Leaflets. ½d. each ; 3d. dozen ; 50 for 7d. ; or 1s. per 100.

Act of Reparation to the Sacred Heart.
Archconfraternity of Our Lady of Angels.   Ditto, Rules.
Christmas Offering (or 7s. 6d. per 1000).
A Devotion to S. Joseph.
New Indulgenced Prayer to St. Joseph.
Divine Praises.
Gospel according to S. John, *in Latin.*   6d. per 100.
Indulgenced Prayers for Souls in Purgatory.
Indulgences attached to Medals, Crosses, Statues, &c.
Intentions for Indulgences.
Litany of Our Lady of Angels.
Miraculous Prayer—August Queen of Angels.
Prayer for England : O Lord ! behold the suppliant band.
    Hymn by Rev. Father Bridgett, C.SS.R.
Prayer for one's Confessor.
Prayers for the Holy Souls in Purgatory.   By St. Liguori.
Prayers after Mass, ordered by Pope Leo XIII.
Union of our Life with the Passion of our Lord.
Visits to the Blessed Sacrament.

Leaflets. 1d. each ; 9d. dozen ; 50 for 2s. 6d. ; or 4s. per 100.

Act of Consecration to the Holy Angels.

Act of Consecration to the Sacred Heart.

Concise Portrait of the Blessed Virgin.

Consoling Thoughts.

Explanation of the Medal or Cross of St. Benedict.   6s. per 100.

Indulgenced Prayers for the Rosary of the Holy Souls. 2s. 6d. per 100.

Indulgenced Prayer before a Crucifix.   6s. per 100.

Litany of Our Lady of Lourdes.   6s. per 100.

Litany of the Blessed Virgin.   English metre.

Litany of the Sacred Heart.   English metre.

Litany of the Seven Dolours.

Office of the Sacred Heart.   6s. per 100.

Prayer to S. Philip Neri.

Prayer to the Wounded Shoulder of Our Lord

Prayers for Three Days before and after Holy Communion.

Legend of Sir Ælfric, and other Tales.   By Father Bampfield.   1s.

Legends (Seven), of Christmas.   From the German by O. S. B. 1s. 6d.

Legends of the Saints.   By M. F. S.   3s.

Legends of the Thirteenth Century.   By Rev. H. Collins.   3s.

Lenten Thoughts. By Bishop Amherst. 1s.; better bound, 1s. 6d.

Lily of S. Joseph: A tiny Manual of Prayers and Hymns for Mass. 2d.; cloth, 3d., 4d, 6d.; soft morocco, 1s. Another edition, 1d., with Fr. Vere's Hymns. 6d.

LINGARD (Dr.), Anglo–Saxon Church. 2 vols., 12mo., 10s.

Links with the Absent; or, Chapters on Correspondence. By a Member of the Ursuline Community, Thurles, author of "Thoughts of Many Hearts." 1s. 6d.

Little Books of St. Nicholas. By Rev. F. Drew.

    Ora Pro Nobis; or, Tristram's Friends. 1s.

    Ave Maria; or, Catesby's Story. 1s.

    Credo; or, Justin's Martyrdom. 1s.

    Veni Creator; or, Ulrich's Money. 1s.

    Per Jesum Christum; or, Two Good Fridays. 1s.

    Pater Noster; or, an Orphan Boy. 1s.

    Dominus Vobiscum; or, The Sailor Boy. 1s.

    Oremus; or, Little Mildred. 1s.

Or in 2 vols, 6s.

Little Dick's Christmas Carols, and five other Tales. By Amy Fowler (Sister Rose Gertrude). 1s. 6d.

Little Mildred, or Oremus. By Rev. F. B. Bickerstaffe Drew. 1s.

Little Office of the Immaculate Conception. Latin, with English by Dr. Husenbeth. 6d.; soft morocco, 1s. See page 3.

Little Prayer Book for ordinary Catholic Devotions. 3d.

Little Snowdrop, and other Tales. By Clara Mulholland. With 4 full-page original Illustrations. 3s. 6d.

Little Tina's Story, and other Tales. By Mrs. Shapcote. 1s.

' Little Virtues and Little Defects of a Young Girl at School and at Home. 1s.

Lives of the First Religious of the Visitation of Holy Mary. By Mother Frances Magdalen de Chaugy. 2 vols., 10s.

Lord's Prayer and Hail Mary. Tales for Youth. By E. Cox. 1s.

Lost Children of Mount St. Bernard. Gilt, 6d.

Lourdes, Our Blessed Lady of. By Rev. Dr. Husenbeth. 18mo., 6d.; with the Novena, cloth, 1s.; better bound, 1s. 6d.

———— Novena to, for the use of the Sick. 3d.

———— Litany of. 1d.

———— Month at Lourdes. By H. Caraher. 2s.

LUCK (Bishop, O.S.B.), Short Meditations for every Day in the Year. For the Regular Clergy. From the Italian. 6s. Edition for the Secular Clergy and others, 2 vols, 9s.

———— S. Gregory's Life and Miracles of St. Benedict. 1s.; stronger bound, 2s.

MACDANIEL (M. A.), Novena to S. Joseph. 3d.; cloth, 4d,

Maid of Limerick, and other Tales. Catholic Progress. 2s. 6d.

Man at Twelve: the Story of a Boy. 1s.

Margarethe Verflassen. Translated from the German by Mrs. Smith Sligo. 2s. 6d.

Marie, the little Sister of Charity, Agnes Wilmott, The Nameless Grave, and Jane Murphy. 2s.

Marie's Self-Denial. By Madame d'Arras. 1s.

MARQUIGNY (Pere), Life and Letters of the Countess Adelstan. 1s. 6d.

MARSHALL (Rev. Dr.), Doctrine of Purgatory. 1s. *nett.*

MARSHALL (T. W. M), Harmony of Anglicanism—Church Defence. 8vo., 1s.

MARSHALL (Arthur), Oxford Undergraduate. 1s.

Mary Foreshadowed ; or, Considerations on the Types and Figures of Our Blessed Lady in the Old Testament. By Rev. Fr. Thaddeus, O.S.F. 3s.

Mary Magdalene (St.) Life and Meditations. 2s.

Mary Queen of Scots. A Tragedy in 3 Acts (mixed). 6d.

Mary Venerated in all Ages—Regina Sæculorum. 2s.

Mass, A Devout Exposition of. By Rev. A. J. Rowley. 3s.

Mass, Ordinary of. 2d.; bound with Fr. Vere's Hymn Book. 1s.

MATIGNON (Pere)The Duties of Christian Parents. 3s.6d.

MATTHEW (St.) Gospel of. 1d.

May Readings or Considerations, with examples, for every day, from the Italian of Don Gaspar Gilli, by a Sister of the Institute of Charity. 2s 6d. and 3s.

May Readings for every day, from the Writings of Cardinal Manning, Cardinal Newman, the Saints, and others. By J. S. Fletcher. Cloth, 6d. ; silver, 1s.

May Readings for the Feasts of Our Lady. By Rev. A. P. Canon Bethell. 18mo., 1s.

Meditations for Every Day. By Crasset. Edited by Rev. T. B. Snow, O.S.B. 2 vols., 8s.

Meditations on the Blessed Sacrament 1s. 6d.

Meditations on the Life of Our Lord. By Mrs. Abel Ram. 3s.

Meditations for every Day in the Year. By Bishop Luck. Secular, 2 vols., 9s. Regular, 2 vols. in one, 6s.

MEYRICK (Rev T.), Life of St. Wenefred. 12mo., 2s.

——— The Early Popes. St. Peter to Charlemagne. 6s.

——— St.Eustace. A Drama (5 Acts) for Boys. 6d.

M. F. S., Catherine Hamilton. 1s. 6d. ; }
——— Catherine Grown Older. 1s. 6d. ; } in one vol., 2s. 6d.

M. F. S., Fluffy. A Tale for Boys. 2s.

———— Jack's Boy. 2s. 6d.

———— Legends of the Saints. 3s.

———— My Golden Days. 2s.; or in 3 vols., 1s. each.

        Yellow Holly, and other Tales. 1s.

        Tableaux Vivants, and other Tales. 1s.

        Wet Days, and other Tales. 1s.

———— Our Esther. 2s. 6d.

———— Out in the Cold World. 2s. 6d.

———— Stories of Holy Lives. 3s.

———— Stories of Martyr Priests. 3s.

———— Stories of the Saints. Five Series, 3s. each.

———— Story of the Life of S. Paul. 1s. 6d.

———— The Three Wishes. A Tale. 1s. 6d.

———— Tom's Crucifix, and other Tales. 3s. 6d., or in 5 vols. 1s. each.

    Tom's Crucifix, and Pat's Rosary.

    Good for Evil, and Joe Ryan's Repentance.

    The Old Prayer Book, and Charlie Pearson's Medal.

    Catherine's Promise, and Norah's Temptation.

    Annie's First Prayer, and Only a Picture.

Missal. New edition, with the New Masses. *See* next page.

Mission Cross. By Mrs. Bartle Teeling. 1s. 6d.

Monk of the Monastery of Yuste. By Mariana Monteiro. 1s. 6d.

MONTEIRO (Mariana), Allah Akbar—God is Great. An Arab Legend of the Siege and Conquest of Granada. 2s. 6d.

———— Monk of the Monastery of Yuste ; or, The Last Days of the Emperor Charles V. An Historical Legend of the 16th Century. 1s. 6d.

———— Gathered Gems from Spanish Authors. 12mo., 3s.

Moothoosawmy, and other Indian Tales. By Lady Herbert. 1s.

Mora (Ven. Elizabeth Canori), Life of. Translated from the Italian, with Preface by Lady Herbert. 3s. 6d.

Most Beautiful among the Children of Men. Meditations on the Life of Our Lord. By Mrs. Abel Ram. 3s.

MULHOLLAND (Clara). The Strange Adventures of Little Snowdrop, and other Tales. With 4 full-page original Illustrations. 3s. 6d.

R. WASHBOURNE'S
ENTIRELY NEW EDITION OF
𝕿𝖍𝖊 𝕸𝖎𝖘𝖘𝖆𝖑.

5½ inches by 3¾, 1½ inch thick. Printed from new type on specially made paper. Price, in cloth, red edges, 6s. ; soft morocco, 7s. 6d. ; calf or morocco, 10s. ; russia, 12s., etc.

Also an edition without the Lenten Week-day Masses, in all the above styles of binding, 1s. less. An abridged edition is nearly ready.

'His Eminence is well pleased with the appearance of the book.' —Extract from a letter from the Very Rev. Canon Johnson, D.D.

Dublin Review, January, 1888.—'This is a new, well edited, well printed edition of the Missal in English, of convenient size and neatly bound. Completeness and convenience of use have been aimed at, and with considerable success. There are several introductory pages of "Notes and Directions," explaining the division, etc., of the ecclesiastical year, and how the precedence of feasts is arranged, with other explanatory and rubrical matter. It is also a happy thought to have prefixed to the Ordinary of the Mass some Morning Prayers, Litanies, Communion Devotions, etc., thus relieving one of the need of taking with us a Prayer-book as well as the Missal to Mass. The Introits, Graduals, Offertories, and Communion Verses are given in both Latin and English, because at High Masses sung by the choirs ; the Epistles and Gospels are in English only. The copy before us has an appendix for England, another of Benedictine, and a third of Jesuit "Propers," and an appendix for Ireland is at press. All the new Masses granted of late are contained either in the body of the book or in one of the appendices; a number of Masses are therefore here which have not hitherto appeared in any English Missal. The book is carefully edited, and has, it is stated, had the advantage of an official examination by the Rev. W. Hill, of St Bede's College, Manchester. It also bears the imprimatur of the Cardinal Archbishop of Westminster, and, as far as we have been able to examine it, is an excellent edition of the Missal. We trust it will become very popular.'

My Conversion and Vocation. By Rev. Father Schouvaloff, 5s.

My Dream, and other Verses. By the Author of "The Angels and the Sacraments." 1s.

My Golden Days. By M. F. S. 2s., or in 3 vols., 1s. each.

My Lady, at Last. A Tale, by M. Taunton. 3s. 6d.

Nellie Blane, A Conversion and a Deathbed, The Dying Gipsy, Catherine's Promise, and Norah's Temptation. 1s. 6d.

Nellie Gordon, the Factory Girl; or, Lost and Saved. By M. A. Pennell. 18mo., 6d.

Never Despair, but dare to be wise. 2s. net.

Newman's (Cardinal) Grammar of Assent, a Study on. 6d.

New Testament. 18mo., 1s.; large type, 1s. 6d. Persian calf, 7s. 6d., morocco, 10s.

Nicholas ; or, the Reward of a Good Action. Gilt, 6d.

Nina and Pippo, the Lost Children of Mt. St. Bernard. 6d.

NOBLE (Miss E.), and others, Story of Marie, and other Tales, 2s. ; Nellie Blaine, and other Tales, 1s. 6d. ; The Nameless Grave, and other Tales, 2s. ; A Contrast, and other Tales, 2s. 6d. ; Pat and his Friend, and other Tales, 2s. 6d.

Norbert (S.), Life of, with The Nature and Mission of the Pre-monstratensian Order. By V. Rev. Fr. Geudens. 3s. 6d. nett.

Novena for the Holy Souls in Purgatory. By Abbot Burder. 2d.

Novena to Our Blessed Lady of Lourdes for the use of the Sick. 18mo., 3d.

Novena to St. Joseph, with a Pastoral by Bishop Grant. 3d. ; cloth, 4d.

O'CLERY (Keyes, K.S.G.), The History of the Italian Revolution. The Revolution of the Barricades (1796-1849). 4s.

O'HARA (C. M.), Clare's Sacrifice. An impressive little Tale for First Communicants. 6d.

Old Prayer-Book (The), and Charlie Pearson's Medal, 1s. ; with Good for Evil, and Joe Ryan's Repentance, 1s. 6d.

Old Testament Stories. 1s. 6d. cloth ; 2s. better bound.

OLIVER (Lætitia), Father Placid ; or, the Custodian of the Blessed Sacrament. 1s.

———— Rose Fortescue ; or, the Devout Client of Our Lady of Dolours. 1s.

O'MEARA (Kathleen), The Battle of Connemara. 2s. 6d.

One of His Little Ones, and other Stories. In Prose and Verse. By J. S. Fletcher. 1s. 6d. ; with The Mission Cross. 2s. 6d.

Ora Pro Nobis; or, Tristram's Friends. By Rev. F. Drew. 1s.

Oratorian Lives of the Saints. 5s. a vol.

    I. S. Bernardine of Siena, Minor Observatine.
    II. S. Philip Benizi, Fifth General of the Servites.
    III. S. Veronica Giuliani, and B. Battista Varani.
    IV. S. John of God. By Canon Cianfogni.

Ordinary of the Mass. 2d. Bound with Fr. Vere's Hymn-Book. Soft morocco, 1s.

Oremus ; or, Little Mildred. By Rev. F. Drew. 1s. ; with Three other of Fr. Drew's Tales, 3s.

Oremus, A Liturgical Prayer Book. Small edition, 6d., large edition, 2s., and upwards. See page 32.

Our Christian Heritage. By Cardinal Gibbons. 6s.

Our Esther. By M.F.S., Author of "Out in the Cold World." 2s. 6d.

Our Lady's Month, according to the Spirit of St. Francis of Sales. By Don Gaspar Gilli. 2s. 6d. and 3s.

Our Lady's Month. By Rev. A. P. Canon Bethell. 1s. and 1s. 6d.

Our Lady's Month. By J. S. Fletcher. Cloth, 6d. ; silver, 1s.

Our Lady's Festivals : Lectures for Boys. By Very Rev. Canon Doyle, O.S.B. 2s. 6d.

Our Lord's Life, Passion, Death, and Resurrection. 1s.

Out in the Cold World. By M. F. S., Author of "Fluffy." 2s. 6d.

Oxford Undergraduate of Twenty Years Ago. By Arthur Marshall. 8vo., 1s.

Panegyrics of Fr. Segneri, S.J. Translated from the original Italian. With a Preface, by Rev. W. Humphrey, S.J, 12mo., 6s.

Passion of Our Lord, Harmony of. By Gayrard, 1s. 6d.

—— — Lectures for Boys. By Very Rev. Canon Doyle, O.S.B. 3s.

Pat and his Friend, The Beggars, Kainer, or the Usurer's Doom, and Life in Iceland, 2s. 6d.

Pater Noster ; or, an Orphan Boy. By Rev. F. Drew, 1s.

Patrick's (St.) Prayer Book : Garden of the Soul, with all the Sacraments in full, Epistles and Gospels, and Fr. Vere's Hymns. 2s.

Patrick (S.), Life of. 1s.

Penitential Psalms Paraphrased. By Rev. F. Blyth. 6d.

PENNELL (M. A.), Agnes Wilmott. 1s. 6d.

—— Bertram Eldon. 12mo., 1s.

—— Nellie Gordon, the Factory Girl. 18mo., 6d.

Pens, Washbourne's Free and Easy. Fine, or Middle, or Broad Points, 1s. per gross.

Per Jesum Christum ; or, Two Good Fridays. By Rev. F. Drew. 1s.

Philip Benizi (S.), Life of. 5s.

PHILPIN (Rev. F.), Holy Places; their sanctity and authenticity. With three Maps. 3s. 6d. ; cheap edition, 2s. 6d.

PILLEY (C.), Walter Ferrers' School Days ; or, Bellevue and its Owners. 1s. 6d.

PIUS IV. Profession of Faith. Grounds of Catholic Doctrine. Paper, 2d. ; cloth, 4d.

PLAYS. *See* Dramas, page 8.

PLUES (Margaret), Chats about the Rosary. 2s. 6d.

—— Chats about the Commandments. 2s. 6d.

Popes, Early, Lives of. By Rev. T. Meyrick. 6s.

Portiuncula, Indulgence of. 1d. ; 100 for 6s.

R. Washbourne, Paternoster Row, London.

PRADEL (Fr., O. P.), Life of St. Vincent Ferrer. Translated by Rev. Fr. Dixon. 5s.

PRAYER BOOKS. A large variety, 2d. and upwards. See p. 31.

PRICE (Rev. E.), Sick Calls. 12mo., 3s. 6d.

PRINS (Chevalier Leopold de), Hymnal. Music. 2s.

————————, Vespers and Benediction. Music. 3s. 6d.

Purgatory, Doctrine of. By Rev. W. Marshall, D.D. 1s. *nett.*

Purgatory, Indulgenced Prayers for Souls in. 1s. per 100.

Purgatory, Month of the Souls in Purgatory. By Ricard, 1s.

Purgatory, Novena for the Holy Souls. By Abbot Burder, from the French of Abbé Serré. 2d

Purgatory, Prayers for Holy Souls in. By St. Liguori. 1s. per 100.

Purgatory, Spiritual Bouquets to the Souls in Purgatory. By Abbot Burder. 2d.

PYE (Henry John, M.A.), Revelation. Being the substance of several conversations on First Principles. 6d.

——— The Religion of Common Sense. 1s.

QUINN (Mary), Mary Queen of Scots. A Tragedy in 3 Acts (Mixed) 6d.

RAM (Mrs. Abel), Meditations on the Life of Our Lord. With a Preface by the Cardinal Archbishop of Westminster. 3s.

RAVIGNAN (Pere), The Spiritual Life, Conferences. Translated by Mrs. Abel Ram. 12mo., 5s.

RAYMOND-BARKER (Mrs. F.) Life and Letters of the Countess Adelstan. 1s. 6d.

——— Paul Seigneret (Seminarist and Martyr). 1s. 6d.

——— Regina Sæculorum. 2s.

——— Rosalie ; or, Memoir of a French Child. 1s. 6d.

——— Science and Faith upon the Sacred Heart. 2s.

Regina Sæculorum ; or, Mary Venerated in all Ages. Devotions to the Blessed Virgin from Ancient Sources. 2s.

Religion of Common Sense. By H. J. Pye, M.A. 12mo., 1s.

Rest, on the Cross. By Eleanora Louisa Hervey. 12mo., 3s.

Revelation. By Henry John Pye, Esq. 6d.

Reverse of the Medal. A Drama for Girls. 12mo., 6d.

RIBADENEIRA—Life of Our Lord. 12mo., 1s.

RICARD (Abbe), Month of the Holy Angels. 18mo., 1s.

——— Month of the Souls in Purgatory. 18mo., 1s.

R. Washbourne, Paternoster Row, London

RICHARDSON (Rev. Fr.), Lily of St. Joseph. A little Manual of Prayers and Hymns for Mass. 64mo., 2d., cloth, 3d. 4d., and 6d. ; soft morocco, 1s. 32mo., 1d., with Fr. Vere's Hymns, cloth, 6d.

RICHARDSON (Samuel, A.B., B.L., of the Middle Temple), Killed at Sedan. A Novel. Crown 8vo., 5s.

RICHE (Abbé A.), Agreement of Science and Faith upon the Sacred Heart of Jesus. 2s.

Road to Heaven. A game. 1s., with the Rules bound, 2s.

Rome (To) and Back. Fly-Leaves from a Flying Tour. Edited by Rev. W. H. Anderdon, S.J., 12mo., 2s.

Rosalie ; or, the Memoir of a French Child, told by herself. By Mrs. F. Raymond-Barker. 1s. 6d.

Rosary in Sixteen Pictures with Meditations. 9d.

Rosary for the Souls in Purgatory, with Indulgenced Prayer. 4d., 6d. and 1s. Medals separately, 1d. each, or 9d. a dozen. Prayers separately, ½d. each, 4d. a dozen, or 2s. 6d. for 100.

Rosary, Chats about the; Aunt Margaret's Little Neighbours. 2s. 6d.

Rose Fortescue ; or, the Devout Client of Our Lady of Dolours. By Lætitia Oliver. 1s. ; with **Emily and Nancy,** and other Tales, 1s. 6d.

Rose of Venice. A Tale. By S. Christopher. Crown 8vo., 3s. 6d.

ROWLEY (Rev. Austin John), A Devout Exposition of the Holy Mass. Composed by John Heigham. 3s.

Rule of Christian Life. By Maria Franchi de' Cavalieri, with sketch of her life, by Rev. Father Rondina, S.J. Translated by Richard Webb, M.A. 1s.

RUSSELL (Rev. M.), Emmanuel : Eucharistic Verses. 2s

———— **Erin :** Verses Irish and Catholic 2s. } in one vol., 5s.

———— **Madonna.** Verses on Our Lady and the Saints, 2s.

RYAN (Bishop). What Catholics do not Believe. 12mo., 1s.

Sacred Heart. Act of Consecration to. 1d.; or 4s. per 100.

————————, **Act of Reparation to.** 1s. per 100.

————————, **Elevations to the.** By Rev. Fr. Doyotte, S.J. 2s.

————————, **Lectures for Boys.** By Canon Doyle, O.S.B. 3s.

————————, **Month of,** from St. Omer. By G. M. Ward. 2s

·———————— **offered to the Piety of the Young engaged in Study.** By Rev. F. Deham. 32mo., 1s.

————————, **Office.** 1d.

————————, **Treasury of.** 32mo., 1s. 6d.; French morocco, 2s.; calf or morocco, 5s. 18mo., 2s. 6d.; roan, 3s. ; soft morocco, 5s.

Saints, Lives of, from Alban Butler. Selected and edited by the Rt. Rev. Mgr. Goddard. 3s. 6d.

Sacristan's Manual. By Rev. J. D. H. Dale. 2s. 6d.

SCARAMELLI—Directorium Asceticum ; or, Guide to the Spiritual Life. 4 vols. 12mo., 24s.

School of Jesus Crucified. By Fr. Ignatius, Cong. Pass. 2s. 6d.

SCHOUVALOFF (Rev. Father, Barnabite), My Conversion and Vocation. Translated from the French, with an Appendix, by Fr. C. Tondini. 12mo., 5s.

SCHULTHES (Wilhelm), Mass of the Holy Child Jesus. The vocal part only, 4d.

SEAMER (Mrs.), *See* M. F. S., pages 19 and 20.

SEBASTIAN (Fr.), Manual of the Infant Jesus. 2s. 6d.

——————————————————————————- **Cross and Passion.** 2s.6d.

————————————————————————- **Seven Dolours.** 2s. 6d.

————————————————————————- **a Happy Eternity.** 2s. 6d

Secret, The. A Drama for Girls in 1 Act. By Mrs. Sadlier. 6d.

SEGNERI (Fr., S.J.), Panegyrics. Translated from the original Italian. With Preface by Rev. W. Humphrey, S.J. 6s.

SEGUR (Mgr.), Books for Little Children. Translated. 32mo., 3d. each. Confession, Holy Communion, Child Jesus, Piety, Prayer, Temptation and Sin. In one volume, cloth, 1s. 6d.

Seigneret (Paul), Seminarist and Martyr, Life of. 1s. 6d. ; with **Father Placid.** 2s.

Sermons. *See* Doyle, 2 vols., 10s. 6d. ; Scaramelli, 4 vols., 24s. ; Segneri, 6s. ; Gahan, 8s. ; Perry, 2 vols., 7s.

Shandy Maguire. A Farce for Boys. 2 Acts. 6d.

SHAPCOTE (Mrs.), Eucharistic Hours. Devotion towards the Blessed Sacrament. Gems from the treasury of the Church's Doctrine. 4s.

—————— **The Catholic Mother's Lullaby.** Music and Words, 2d.

—————— **The Story of Little Tina, and other Tales.** 1s.

—————— **Leaflets from the Model Life.** [*In the press.*

SIGHART (Dr.), Life of Bl. Albertus Magnus. 6s.

Sir Ælfric and other Tales. By Rev. G. Bampfield. 1s.

Sir Thomas Maxwell and his Ward. By Miss Bridges. 1s. 6d.; with **Adrian and Emily.** 2s.

SMITH-SLIGO (A. V., Esq.), Life of the Ven. Anna Maria Taigi. Translated from French of Calixte. 3s. 6d.

SMITH-SLIGO (Mrs.) Margarethe Verflassen. 2s. 6d.

SNOW (Right Rev. T. B., O.S.B.) Crasset's Meditations for Every Day. 2 vols., 8s.

——— Comfort for the Sick. Selections from Crasset's Meditations for Every Day in the Year. 2d.

——— Prayers for Communion for Children. 1d.

Snowflakes and other Tales. By M. Sinclair Allison. 1s. with Angels and the Sacraments. 1s. 6d.

Solid Virtue. By Father Bellécius, S.J. With a Preface by the Most Rev. Dr. Croke, Archbishop of Cashel and Emly. New edition, revised and corrected. Crown 8vo., 7s. 6d.

Sophia and Eulalie. (The Catholic Pilgrim's Progress.) From the French by Rev. Fr. Bradbury. 12mo., 2s. 6d.

Spiritual Conferences on the Mysteries of Faith and the Interior Life. By Father Collins. 12mo., 5s.

Spiritual Life. Conferences by Père Ravignan. Translated by Mrs. Abel Ram. 12mo., 5s.

Spiritual Life of Rev. Fr. Schouvaloff. 12mo., 5s.

Spiritual Works of Louis of Blois. Edited by Rev. F. John Bowden. 12mo., 3s. 6d.

Stations of the Cross, Chromos, with Prayers. By St. Alphonsus. 6d., larger, 9d.

Stories from the Holy Scriptures. Illustrated. 2s. net.

Stories for my Children. Angels and the Sacraments. 1s.

Stories of Holy Lives. By M. F. S. 12mo., 3s.

Stories of Martyr Priests. By M. F. S. 12mo., 3s.

Stories of the Saints. By M. F. S. Five Series, each 3s.

Stories from many Lands. Compiled by E. L. Hervey. 3s. 6d.

Story of a Paper Knife. 1s. ; with The Golden Thought, and other Tales, and Fairy Ching's Visit to England, 2s. 6d.

Story of Little Tina, and other Tales. By Mrs. Shapcote. 1s.

Story of Marie, True and False Riches, The Two Friends, and The Village Lily, 2s.

Story of the Life of St. Paul. By M. F. S., author of "Stories of the Saints." 1s. 6d. ; with Tales of the Jewish Church. 3s.

Strange Adventures of Little Snowdrop, a Tale of a Green Coat, a Bunch of Violets, and Lazy Nancy. By Clara Mulholland. With 4 full-page Illustrations 3s. 6d.

STUART (E. I.) Bertie. An Old Man's Story. 1s. 6d.

Sufferings of Our Lord. Sermons preached by Father Claude de la Colombière, S.J., in the Chapel Royal, St. James's, in the year 1677. 18mo., 1s.

R. Washbourne, Paternoster Row, London.

Sure Way to Heaven. A Little Manual for Confession and Holy Communion. 32mo., 6d.; persian, 2s. 6d.; calf or morocco, 3s. 6d.

SWEENY (Rev. P., D.D.) Catholic Controversial Letters.   3s.

Sweetness of Holy Living. By St. Francis de Sales.   1s.

Taigi (Ven Anna Maria), Life of. By Calixte ; translated by A. V. Smith-Sligo, Esq., 3s. 6d.

Tales of the Jewish Church. By Charles Walker.   1s. 6d., 2s. ; with Story of the Life of St. Paul, 3s.

TAUNTON (M.), My Lady, at Last. A Tale.   3s. 6d.

TEELING (Mrs. Bartle), The Mission Cross, Saturday Night in Rose Court, etc.   1s. 6d.

———— **The Violet Letters (Drama in 3 Acts),** 6d.

TERESA (S.), Book of the Foundations.   3s. 6d.

———— **Letters of.**   Translated by Canon Dalton.   12mo., 3s. 6d.

———— **Way of Perfection.**   12mo., 3s. 6d.

———— **The Interior Castle.**   12mo., 3s. 6d.

THADDEUS (Rev. Father, O.S.F.), Mary Foreshadowed; or Considerations on the Types and Figures of Our Blessed Lady in the Old Testament.   3s.

———— **Glittering Stars on Our Lady's Mantle.**   2s.

Thomas Aquinas (St.), his Life and Virtues.   By Francis Hays.   1s.

Three Wishes. A Tale.   By M. F. S.   1s. 6d. ; with Little Tina and other Tales.   2s.

Threshold of the Catholic Church. By Dr. Bagshawe.   1s. *nett* (postage 3d.), 12 copies for 10s. (postage 1s. 2d.).

Tom's Crucifix, and other Tales. By M. F. S.   12mo., 3s. 6d., or in 5 vols., 1s. each.

TONDINI (Fr. C), Change in Faith ; or, Development. A critical Exposition of St. Vincent of Lerins.   Addressed to Anglicans.   6d.

True Wayside Tales. By Lady Herbert.   First Series, 3s., or in 5 vols., 6d. each.   Second Series, 3s., or separately in 3 vols., 1s. each.   **Third Series.**   3s.

Two Cousins, and other Tales. By Lady Herbert.   1s.

Two Friends ; or Marie's Self-Denial. By Madame d'Arras.   1s. ; with three other Tales.   2s.

Ursuline Manual ; soft morocco 2s. 6d., calf or morocco 4s.

Veni Creator; or, Ulrich's Money. By Rev. F. Drew.   1s.; with Three other of F. Drew's Tales, 3s.

VERE (Rev. G. L.), The Catholic Hymn Book.   32mo., 2d.; cloth, 4d.; soft morocco, 1s.; abridged edition, 1d., cloth, 2d.

———— **For Better, not for Worse.** A Tale.   2s. 6d.

Veronica Giuliani (S.), Life of, and B. Battista Varani, 5s.

Village Lily. A Tale of First Communion. 1s. ; with three other Tales, 2s.

Vincent Ferrer (S.), of the Order of Friar Preachers ; his Life, Spiritual Teaching, and Practical Devotion. By Rev. Fr. Andrew Pradel, O.P. Translated from the French by the Rev. Fr. T. A. Dixon, O. P. 5s.

Violet Sellers, The ; a Drama in 3 Acts, for Children. 6d.

VIRGIL. Literally translated by Davidson. 12mo., 1s. 6d.

"Vitis Mystica"; or, the True Vine. By Canon Brownlow. 2s. 6d.

WALKER (Charles), Tales of the Jewish Church. 1s. 6d., 2s.

Walter Ferrers' School Days; or, Bellevue and its Owners. By C. Pilley. 1s. 6d. ; with three other Tales. 2s. 6d.

Wanderers (The) ; or, Faith's Welcome. A Play for Boys. One Act. 6d.

WEBB (Richard, M.A.), Rule of Christian Life. Written and Practised by Maria Franchi de' Cavalieri. 1s.

WELD (Miss K. M.), Bessy ; or, the Fatal Consequences of Telling Lies. 1s.

Wenefred (St.), Life of. By Rev. T. Meyrick. 12mo., 2s.

What Catholics do not Believe. By Bishop Ryan. 12mo., 1s.

William (St.), of York. A Drama in Two Acts. (Boys.) 12mo., 6d.

WILSON (John), The Rural Postman—Poems, author of "Pomfret Cakes." 32mo., 1s.

WISEMAN (Cardinal), Doctrines and Practices of the Catholic Church. 12mo., 3s. 6d.
———— Science and Religion. 12mo., 5s.

Wiseman (Cardinal), Recollections of. By M. J. Arnold. 2s.

WOOD (Alexander), The Vatican and the Quirinal. 1s. 6d.

Young Catholic's Guide to Confession and Holy Communion. By Dr. Kenny. 4d.

Zuma. A Peruvian Tale. Gilt, 6d.

R. WASHBOURNE'S
Catalogue of
CATHOLIC BOOKS
IMPORTED FROM
AMERICA,
SENT POST FREE ON APPLICATION.

Garden, Little, of the Soul. Edited by the Rev. R. G. Davis. *With Imprimatur of the Cardinal Archbishop of Westminster.* This book, as its name imports, contains a selection from the "Garden of the Soul" of the Prayers and Devotions of most general use. Whilst it will serve as a *Pocket Prayer Book* for all, it is, by its low price, *par excellence,* the Prayer Book for children and for the very poor. In it are to be found the old familiar Devotions of the "Garden of the Soul," as well as many important additions, such as the Devotions to the Sacred Heart, to Saint Joseph, to the Guardian Angels, and others. The omissions are mainly the Forms of administering the Sacraments, and Devotions that are not of very general use. It is printed in a clear type, on a good paper, both especially selected, for the purpose of obviating the disagreeableness of small type and inferior paper. Thirty-Third Thousand.

32mo., price, cloth, 6d.; with Epistles and Gospels, 6d.; stronger bound, 8d., with clasp, 1s.; blue cloth, 1s.; with clasp, 1s. 6d. Soft morocco, 1s.; with E. and G. 1s. 6d.; with clasp, 1s. 6d. and 2s. French morocco extra gilt, 2s.; with E. and G., 2s. 6d.; with clasp, 2s. 6d. and 3s. Calf or morocco, 2s. 6d.; with E. and G., 3s.; with clasp, 3s. 6d. and 4s. Calf or morocco, extra gilt, 4s.; with E. and G., 4s, 6d.; with clasp, 5s. and 5s. 6d. German calf or morocco, red and gold edges, 3s. 6d., or with soft padded sides, 4s.; with Epistles and Gospels, 6d. extra. Russia, 5s., 5s. 6d., 6s., 6s. 6d., 7s. 6d, 8s. Russia antique, 17s. 6d. Ivory, with rims and clasp, 10s. 6d., 13s., 15s., 17s. 6d. Imitation ivory, with rims and clasp, 2s. 6d. Calf or morocco tuck (as a pocket-book), 5s. 6d.

Illustrated edition, cloth, 1s.; soft morocco, 1s. 6d.; extra gilt, 2s. 6d.; calf or morocco, 3s.; extra gilt, 4s., with Epistles and Gospels, 6d. extra.

Catholic Piety; or, Key of Heaven, with Epistles and Gospels. Large 32mo., roan, 1s. 6d.; soft morocco, 2s.; with clasp, 2s. 6d.; Persian, 4s.; with clasp, 5s.

Catholic Piety; or, Key of Heaven. 32mo., 6d.; rims and clasp, 1s.; French morocco, 1s. With Epistles and Gospels, roan, 1s.; French morocco, 1s. 6d.; with clasp, 2s.; morocco, 3s.; with clasp, 4s.

Key of Heaven; or, Garden of the Soul. Very large Type. 18mo., cloth, 1s.; with Epistles and Gospels, 1s. 6d.; French morocco, 2s. 6d.; extra gilt, 3s.

Little Prayer Book for ordinary Catholic Devotions. 3d.

Manual of Catholic Devotions. 4d.; with Epistles and Gospels, cloth, 6d., with rims, 1s.; roan, 1s.; calf or morocco, 2s. 6d.

Path to Paradise. 32 full-page Illustrations. 32mo., cloth, 3d. With 50 Illustrations, cloth, 4d. Superior edition, 6d. and 1s.

Treasury of the Sacred Heart. 18mo., 2s. 6d.; roan, 3s.; Soft morocco, 5s. 32mo., 1s. 6d.; leather, 2s.; calf or mor., 5s.

Garden of the Soul. (WASHBOURNE'S EDITION.) Edited by the Rev R. G. Davis. *With Imprimatur of the Cardinal Abp. of Westminster.* Thirty-fourth Thousand. This Edition retains all the Devotions that have made the GARDEN OF THE SOUL, now for many generations, the well-known Prayer-book for English Catholics. During many years various Devotions have been introduced, and, in the form of appendices, have been added to other editions. These have now been incorporated into the body of the work, and, together with the Devotions to the Sacred Heart, to Saint Joseph, to the Guardian Angels, the Itinerarium, and other important additions, render this edition pre-eminently the Manual of Prayer, for both public and private use. The version of the Psalms has been carefully revised, and strictly conformed to the Douay translation of the Bible, published with the approbation of the LATE CARDINAL WISEMAN. The Forms of administering the Sacraments have been carefully translated, *as also the rubrical directions,* from the Ordo Administrandi Sacramenta. To enable all present, either at baptisms or other public administrations of the Sacraments, to pay due attention to the sacred rites, the Forms are inserted without any curtailment, both in Latin and English. The Devotions at Mass have been carefully revised, and enriched by copious adaptations from the prayers of the Missal. The preparation for the Sacraments of Penance and the Holy Eucharist have been the objects of especial care, to adapt them to the wants of those whose religious instruction may be deficient. Great attention has been paid to the quality of the paper and to the size of type used in the printing, to obviate that weariness so distressing to the eyes, caused by the use of books printed in small close type and on inferior paper.

32mo. Embossed, 1s. ; with rims and clasp, 1s. 6d. ; with Epistles and Gospels, 1s. 6d.; with rims and clasp, 2s. French morocco, 1s. 6d. ; with rims and clasp, 2s. ; with E. and G., 2s. ; with rims and clasp, 2s. 6d. French morocco extra gilt, 2s. 6d.; with rims and clasp, 3s.; with E. and G., 3s.; with rims and clasp, 3s. 6d. Calf or morocco, 3s. 6d.; with best gilt clasp, 5s.; with E. and G., 4s., with best gilt clasp, 5s. 6d. Calf or morocco extra gilt, 5s.; with best gilt clasp, 6s. 6d.; with E. and G., 5s. 6d.; with best gilt clasp, 7s. German calf or morocco, red and gold edges, 4s. 6d. ; with E. and G., 5s. ; ditto soft padded sides, 5s. 6d. ; with E. and G. 6s, Russia, 6s. 6d. ; with E. and G., 7s., Ivory, 14s., 16s., 18s., and 20s.; with E. and G., 14s. 6d., 16s. 6d., 18s. 6d., and 20s. 6d.

This GARDEN OF THE SOUL, with Epistles and Gospels, can also be had, with Fr. Vere's Hymn Book, bound in cloth, 2s.

The Epistles and Gospels. *Complete,* cloth, 4d.; roan, 1s.

"This is one of the best editions we have seen of one of the best of all our Prayer Books. It is well printed in clear, large type, on good paper."—*Catholic Opinion.*
"A very complete arrangement of this which is emphatically the Prayer Book of every Catholic household. It is as cheap as it is good, and we heartily recommend it."—*Universe.* "Two striking features are the admirable order displayed throughout the book, and the insertion of the Indulgences in small type above Indulgenced Prayers In the Devotions for Mass, the editor has, with great discrimination, drawn largely on the Church's Prayers, as given us in the Missal."—*Weekly Register.*

The Roman Missal adapted to the use of the Laity.
From the Missale Romanum, as corrected under a decree of the
Tridentine Council, issued by command of Pope St. Pius V., and
revised by authority of Popes Clement VIII., Urban VIII., and
Leo XIII., containing all the New Masses, and thirty which have
not appeared in English Missals, with English and other
Appendices in Latin and English, and a collection of Prayers.
860 pages, cloth, 6s. ; soft morocco, 7s. 6d.; calf or morocco, 10s.;
Russia, 12s.; *or without the Lenten Week-Day Masses,* in all the
above bindings, 1s. each less. *This edition contains the New
Masses of BB. Fisher, More, Campion, and others, and the New
Mass for Rosary-Sunday.* An Abridged edition is nearly ready.
Also the special Masses for Ireland.

The Office of Holy Week according to the Roman Rite.
In addition to the Offices usually included, this Edition gives the
Vespers and Compline for each day ; the Blessing of the Holy
Oils on Maundy Thursday ; and the Matins, Lauds, Mass, Vespers,
and Compline for Easter Sunday. 18mo., 252 pages ; cloth, 1s. ;
soft morocco, 2s.

All Souls' Forget-me-Not. Edited by Canon Moser. 3s.

Child's Picture Prayer Book, with Mass, Benediction,
&c. 16 coloured Illustrations. Cloth, 9d. ; stronger, 1s. ; prettier,
1s. 6d. ; gilt, 2s. ; leather, 3s.

Ordinary of the Mass. 2d. Bound with Fr. Vere's Hymn Book.
Soft morocco, 1s.

Oremus : A Liturgical Prayer Book. With the Imprimatur
of the Cardinal Archbishop of Westminster. An adaptation of the
Church Offices : containing Morning and Evening Devotions ;
Devotions for Mass, Confession, and Communion, and various
other Devotions ; Hymns, Lessons, Collects, Epistles and Gospels
arranged for Sundays, Feasts, and Week Days ; and short notices
of over 200 Saints' Feast Days. 32mo., 452 pages, cloth, 2s. ;
French morocco, 3s. ; German calf or morocco, red and gold
edges, 5s. ; or with soft padded sides, 6s.

A Smaller Oremus. An abridgment of the above. Cloth, 6d.,
Japanese, 1s. ; soft morocco, 1s. 6d. ; calf or morocco, 2s. 6d. ;
extra gilt, 4s., Russia, 6s.

A Short Form of Prayers. Adapted for sailors. 1d.

Sure Way to Heaven. Cloth, 6d.: Persian, 2s. 6d.; morocco, 3s. 6d.

Lily of St. Joseph, The ; a little Manual of Prayers and Hymns
for Mass. 64mo., 2d.; cloth, 3d. ; better bound, 4d. and 6d. ; soft
morocco, 1s. 32mo., 1d., with Fr. Vere's Hymns, cloth, 6d.

Ursuline Manual. Soft morocco, 2s. 6d.; calf or morocco, 4s.
with clasp, 5s. 6d.

CPSIA information can be obtained
at www.ICGtesting.com
Printed in the USA
LVHW081923200319
611264LV00014B/577/P

9 781376 012347